The
Concrete
House

BUILDING SOLID, SAFE, and EFFICIENT with INSULATING CONCRETE FORMS

Pieter A. VanderWerf

STERLING

New York / London

Library of Congress Cataloging-in-Publication Data

VanderWerf, Pieter A.
The concrete house : building solid, safe & efficient with insulating
concrete forms / Pieter A. VanderWerf.
        p. cm.
  Includes bibliographical references and index.
  ISBN-13: 978-1-4027-3629-2 (alk. paper)
  ISBN-10: 1-4027-3629-0 (alk. paper)
1. Concrete houses–Design and construction 2. Insulating concrete
forms. I Title.

TH4818.R4V36 2007
690'.837--dc22

                                            2007012959

10 9 8 7 6 5 4 3 2 1

Published by Sterling Publishing Co., Inc.
387 Park Avenue South, New York, NY 10016
© 2007 by Pieter A. VanderWerf
Distributed in Canada by Sterling Publishing
c/o Canadian Manda Group, 165 Dufferin Street
Toronto, Ontario, Canada M6K 3H6
Distributed in the United Kingdom by GMC Distribution Services
Castle Place, 166 High Street, Lewes, East Sussex, England BN7 1XU
Distributed in Australia by Capricorn Link (Australia) Pty. Ltd.
P.O. Box 704, Windsor, NSW 2756, Australia

Book design and layout by Cecile Kaufman
Illustrations by Shari VanderWerf

Printed in China
All rights reserved

Sterling ISBN-13: 978-1-4027-3629-2
        ISBN-10: 1-4027-3629-0

For information about custom editions, special sales, premium and
corporate purchases, please contact Sterling Special Sales
Department at 800-805-5489 or specialsales@sterlingpub.com.

Contents

Preface

I WROTE THIS BOOK to help homebuyers who are interested in having a house built with insulating concrete forms. Insulating concrete forms are also known as ICFs. They are a new building product used to make the walls of a house or another building. ICFs create a "sandwich" wall, with a layer of construction-grade foam on each face and steel-reinforced concrete in the middle. In my opinion, the finished ICF house is superior to conventional construction in several key ways. However, it is important to look at all the facts and then decide if this type of house is right for you. If it is, there are many things you should learn so you can get the most house for your money. Since this is a new way to build, there are also several new things you should check on before and during construction to make sure that all goes well.

When I was younger I worked on crews that built conventional wood houses. Since 1993 I've worked a lot with ICFs. I was a general contractor in the construction of my own house, which was built out of ICFs in 1994 and 1995. I was at the job site supervising contractors almost every day, and did some of the work myself. Since then I've moved to another town where I bought a conventional, existing home. This has given me a chance to compare the two types of houses.

Nowadays I make my living studying new construction technologies for manufacturing companies and trade associations. Much of the work I perform involves studying ICFs. I have taken training courses from the ICF manufacturers, advised other ICF homebuyers, done multiple research projects on ICFs, and interviewed hundreds and hundreds of people. Those I have interviewed include all sorts of people involved with both ICF and conventional homes:

people buying ICF homes, people buying regular wood-frame homes, people who have lived in ICF homes, people who have lived in wood homes, people building their own homes, contractors building homes with ICFs, contractors building regular wood homes, building inspectors, subcontractors, people at ICF product companies, and so on.

I have formed strong opinions about what a homebuyer should be doing to get the best house. Sometimes the impulse to tell people what to do burns inside me—for example, when I see a buyer making the same mistakes that have plagued so many others. With this book I'm saying exactly what's on my mind—telling you what I think you should do and how to decide if ICFs are right for you. Personally, I love them. However, I also know that not everyone wants and needs what I want and need. If you do decide you want a house built from ICFs, I'll tell you how to make sure you get a good one and how to get the most out of it.

Of course, I get a lot of the information in this book from other publications and Web sites. When I think you might benefit from going back to these other sources, I mention them in the text so you can look them up. In fact, there are three particular sites that are important enough for me to mention right now. These are the Web sites with the best information about ICFs. They have directories and news pages that are kept up-to-date, making them a good source for a lot of timely information. They are: **www.forms.org** (the Web site of the Insulating Concrete Form Association), **www.ICFWeb.com** (an independent, for-profit Web site), and **www.concretehomes.com** (a site about all types of concrete homes from the Portland Cement Association). I describe these sites further in Chapter 1, and refer to them later in the book.

ACKNOWLEDGMENTS

TO MAKE SURE the material in this book is as complete as possible, I got help and advice from a lot of people. *Please note:* All the opinions and judgments in this book are strictly my own. I did not seek clearance or approval from anyone else for anything I wrote. In fact, I tried to stay independent so I could say what I think. But a lot of the basic information and many ideas originally came from others, so I do want to give thanks to all of them. I truly couldn't have done it without them.

Special thanks goes to those who helped produce the book. Dan Kokonowski did a great deal of research and editing and also a great set of drawings. Mark Nicholson did research and some of the drawing work as well, and Ivan Panushev did additional research. My wife Shari did final detail and coloring on all the drawings, as well as a ton of formatting and reformatting and organizing. Shari also did a lot of the tolerating, forbearing, and everything else you have to do for an obsessed spouse. Also thanks to my sons Kyle, Cameron, and Noah, because they're the coolest and most fun kids anybody could have, and also because I know they'll get a charge out of seeing their names in print.

I talked with a lot of homeowners to gather information, but I really need to thank Scott Delmonico and Aaron Morrone especially. They showed tremendous patience in providing me with information, answering extensive questions, and generally giving me the details of the construction of their houses and what life has been like living in them.

Although I did not seek anyone's approval for what I wrote, I got wonderful photos and diagrams from many organizations. To their credit, they gave these illustrations to me without asking to see the manuscript, no questions asked. They are: American Polysteel, LLC ▪ Arxx Building Products ▪ Concrete Home Building Council ▪ ConForm Pacific, Inc. ▪ Distinctive Concrete Boston, Inc. ▪ ECO-Block, LLC ▪ Energy Conservatory ▪ Formtek, Inc. ▪ Institute for Business and Home Safety ▪ Insulating Concrete Form Association ▪ INSUL-DECK, LLC ▪ Kaw Valley Chapter, Habitat for Humanity ▪ Logix Insulated Concrete Forms, Ltd. ▪ New Holland Construction ▪ Nudura Corporation ▪ Perform Wall, LLC ▪ Phil-Insul Corp. ▪ Polyguard Products, Inc. ▪ Portland Cement Association ▪ Quad-Lock Building Systems, LLC ▪ ReddiForm, Inc. ▪ Reward Wall Systems, Inc. ▪ Simpson Strong-Tie Co., Inc. ▪ Wind-Lock Corporation.

I hope you learn a lot from this book and I hope the information is as useful to you as it has been to me.

CHAPTER 1

What Is an ICF and Why Should I Care?

ICF STANDS FOR "insulating concrete form." It's a new product for constructing the exterior walls of a house or another building. ICFs create a "sandwich" wall, with one layer of construction-grade foam on each face and reinforced concrete in the middle. A house built with ICFs has many

ICF houses come in all styles and look like conventionally built houses.

advantages that I consider important, and apparently a lot of other people agree with me. The Portland Cement Association estimates that in 2006 there were over 90,000 houses built at least partly with ICFs in the United States and Canada, and that number is growing at a rate of about 20% each year.

What's so great about ICFs?

Houses built with ICFs are more energy efficient, stronger, and more resistant to high winds and other natural disasters than typical wood-frame houses. They are more comfortable in hot and cold weather, and quieter. They're also very durable—the concrete doesn't rot, rust, warp, or get eaten by termites.

To my mind, these advantages are major. The money saved on heating and cooling bills can be upwards of a thousand dollars a year. The comfort difference is clearly noticeable. There are fewer drafts, the temperature stays much more even, and there are virtually no "cold spots" along the walls. ICF houses have proven to be much more resistant to wind damage in hurricanes and tornadoes, and their strength against wind is also borne out in lab tests. They block out the sound from traffic and storms and lawn mowers much better than wood-frame houses do, and that has been verified in the lab, too. In situations where wood walls may rot or be eaten by pests, concrete walls stay intact. I will go into more detail on all of these things in later chapters.

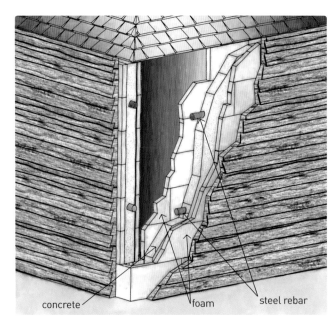

concrete   foam   steel rebar

1-2. Cutaway view of an ICF wall in a house.

So with ICFs they build the house out of concrete?

Yes, the construction crews use ICFs to build the *outside walls* of a house out of concrete (Figs. 1-1 and 1-2). But it's not just plain concrete. There is also a layer of construction-grade foam insulation on each face. Usually, the remainder of the house is built of the same materials used in a conventional house.

THE BASICS OF CONSTRUCTION

For those of you who aren't very familiar with construction, perhaps it's worth going over the basics of how conventional houses are built and how ICFs are different.

OK, what materials are used to build a conventional house?

About 85% of all houses in the United States and Canada are built of wood frame. If there's a basement or crawl space foundation, that part is built of concrete. That's because concrete is so durable, even in wet ground. But for the walls that are entirely above the ground (often called the **above-grade walls**), the

1-1. Wall under construction. (Quad-Lock Building Systems, Ltd.)

material is wood. These walls are built by nailing together hundreds of long pieces of "two-by" lumber. Some workers call these pieces "sticks" or **studs** for short (Fig. 1-3). You often see the wooden skeletons in the shape of a house along the road when you drive past a new development. The inside walls are built of the same wood, and floors and roofs are usually built by nailing together similar but larger pieces of wood. When this skeleton is done, the workers nail sheets of plywood or foam or another sheet material over the outside to form a sort of skin on the building. This is called **sheathing**. After the sheathing is on, building paper and windows and doors are installed. Building paper is a water-resistant felt or paper that covers the wooden walls to help protect them from any water that might get through from outside. At this point the inside of the house is somewhat protected from the weather so crews can work more easily on the interior. Some contractors say that at this point the house is "tight to the weather."

Then the electrical crew comes in to run wires through the walls and attach outlet and switch boxes to the studs. A different crew puts fiberglass insulation into the spaces between the studs to make the house more energy efficient. Outside another crew applies the exterior finish. This may be vinyl siding, wood siding, stucco, brick, or another type of finish over the walls to cover them. This will protect the walls from the elements and make them look nice (Fig. 1-4). On the interior of the house, another crew puts sheets of a paper-faced gypsum board over the inside of the walls to cover the insulation, wiring, and skeletal frame of the house. This gypsum board is commonly called **wallboard** or **drywall**.

top plate

studs

floor

bottom plate

exterior sheathing

1-3. Cutaway view of an exterior stud wall in a wood-frame house.

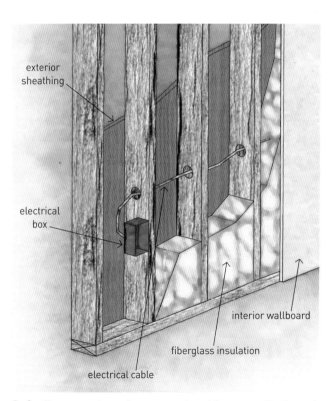

exterior sheathing

electrical box

interior wallboard

fiberglass insulation

electrical cable

1-4. Cutaway view of a conventional frame wall, viewed from inside.

I skipped over the plumbers and the heating/cooling crew. They do their work around the same time that the electrician does, but nowadays pipes and ducts are not run in the outside walls very much. These things are generally routed through the floors and interior walls. So these contractors don't work much with the parts of the house that are built of ICFs.

Incidentally, the contractors that install the heating and cooling system have a special name. You will hear it over and over again, so you may as well learn it now. They are called **heating, ventilation, and air-conditioning** contractors, or just **HVAC** contractors for short. They install the **HVAC equipment**—the furnaces, air conditioners, fans, ductwork, and the like.

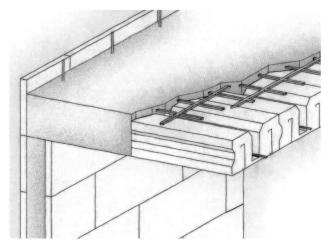

1-5. Cutaway view of an ICF deck on ICF walls.

BUILDING WITH ICFS

Exactly what parts of the building are different with ICFs?

The outside walls, for one. Those are built out of ICFs. In addition, the other parts of the building that connect to the outside walls may be a little different. A few other items (like the HVAC equipment) are affected by ICFs, even though they don't actually come in contact with them.

Other parts of the building besides the outside walls may be built of ICFs, but this is less common. Sometimes it makes sense to build an interior wall out of ICFs. And there are new "deck" systems that are a variation on insulating concrete forms that allow you to build floors and roofs with concrete. These deck systems consist of a layer of foam and a layer of concrete that's poured on top of the foam. This way you get a floor or roof deck that combines the same two materials found in an ICF wall (Fig. 1-5). We'll talk about all these possibilities later.

OK, but what does the ICF itself consist of?

Most ICF systems consist of big, hollow blocks. The most common blocks are 16 inches high, 48 inches long, and about 10 inches thick. They are made of foam. Usually the foam is the same variety of foam

used to make disposable coffee cups, except that in this case it's higher-density construction-grade material.

Instead of nailing a lot of pieces of wood together, the wall crew stacks up the blocks which have teeth or slots that line them up and hold them together much like children's building blocks. When you look down on this wall from the top, you see that the wall is hollow inside. When the workers get to the top of the first story, they fill the hollow center with concrete. Technically it's **reinforced concrete** because they also put steel bars in it for strength. The concrete hardens, and in a few days the walls become very rigid and strong. If it's a two-story house, there is a bit more to the sequence of work. The crew builds the first story out of ICFs. Then it builds the floor for the second story. After that they stack up the ICFs for the second-story walls. When the crew is at the top, the roof goes on. After that, the construction of the rest of the house is pretty much the same as in a conventional wood-frame house.

What exactly does "concrete form" mean?

A concrete form is anything you pour concrete into to give the concrete a particular shape. It functions like a mold for gelatin does. You pour the concrete in, and it hardens in the shape of the form. Most forms are what we call **removable** or **reusable forms**. Like the gelatin mold, you take the form off after the concrete is hard enough to hold its own shape. That's how most basements are built. Workers use forms made of wood, steel, or aluminum that come in sections 2 to 3 feet wide and 8 to 9 feet tall. They hook them together to put them in the shape of the basement walls, pour the concrete into them, then remove the forms a few days later. This produces the hard, gray concrete walls extending out of the ground that we see on most houses.

Don't they remove ICFs after the concrete is hard?
No. Except for a few unusual jobs, the crew always leaves the foam in place permanently. This makes the wall a sort of sandwich, with a layer of foam on each side, and a layer of concrete in the middle. Different brands of ICFs have different dimensions, but usually each foam layer is about 2 inches thick. The thickness of the concrete layer depends mostly on how much strength you need for a particular wall. For a basement it's usually 8 inches thick, and for the walls of a house above the ground it's usually about 6 inches thick. So the total wall thickness, including foam layers, is usually about 12 inches for basement walls and 10 inches for above-grade walls.

Why not remove the foam?
The foam is really where a lot of the value of the ICF comes from. It serves several purposes. First of all, it's a great insulator. Your house ends up being more energy efficient and comfortable with all that foam than the usual wood-frame wall does with fiberglass insulation. Second, by cutting slots in the foam you can make convenient places to run electrical wires and other things that go in the wall.

So do all the advantages of ICFs come from the foam?
No, the concrete provides a lot of pluses, too. Reinforced concrete is a stronger, more massive, and more durable material than the wood that goes into a standard house wall. This contributes a lot to almost all of the major benefits of ICF houses. It's really the combination

of the two materials—foam and reinforced concrete—that make the ICF wall perform so well.

ABOUT CONCRETE

Exactly what is in concrete?
This is a good question. The answer is complicated, and even contractors often get it wrong. Most people confuse concrete with cement. The word *cement* really means any glue. But in construction, when we say cement we usually mean a gray powder made of minerals that has an almost magical property. When you mix it with a little water, it makes a paste that gradually gets harder and harder. In a few days it's as hard as the average rock. It even looks like a rock.

There are actually a couple of different combinations of minerals that will harden like this when mixed with water. Several are used in construction, and they all are technically called *cement*. However, nowadays 99% of all construction cement is of a particular variety that was invented by an Englishman named Joseph Aspdin over 150 years ago. Its full name is **portland cement** (Fig. 1-6). He named it after the part of England that inspired his work. Today it's made all over the world by many different companies. It's so common that we usually just call it *cement* and drop the "portland" part.

Technically, the word *concrete* means just about any mixture of things bound together with a glue to make a solid. But in construction it almost always means a mixture of portland cement with different rocks and sand (Fig. 1-7). When you add water to it, the cement hardens and transforms the whole mass into a hard solid, a lot like plain cement does. But concrete is a lot less

1-6. Portland cement. (Portland Cement Association)

1-7. The ingredients of concrete. (Portland Cement Association)

expensive. Portland cement by itself is fairly expensive. If you add rocks and sand in the right way, the whole mix ends up being just about as hard and strong as cement alone, and you replace a lot of the expensive part (cement) with things that are pretty cheap (rocks and sand). So concrete, not plain cement, is what our basements are built of. In warmer parts of the country without basements, the foundation may be shorter "stem" walls or a floor slab, but they're still made of concrete. Other things commonly built with concrete include sidewalks, bridges, and high-rise buildings.

CONCRETE HOUSES

Why haven't houses been built out of concrete before?

They have, for over a hundred years. In fact, in most of the world concrete is the main material for house construction. Just about the only places where wood houses are widely built are areas with lots of cheap lumber: the United States, Canada, Scandinavia, Siberia, etc. Everywhere else, concrete and steel are the construction materials of choice. There are also a lot of houses built of wood in Japan because it's a highly regarded traditional form of construction. But even in Japan wood house construction is declining and many people are shifting to concrete and steel. In South

America, where there is an abundant supply of wood, people tend to build with other materials because of the high population of insects that attack wood. That's also why contractors in North America are building more and more houses out of concrete now. Even though we have access to cheap lumber, there are advantages to concrete homes that make people want them.

However, not until recently have there been many practical ways to build houses out of poured concrete in North America. Only a few poured concrete houses were built from time to time in the United States. One famous case is a small housing development built by Thomas Edison in New Jersey around the turn of the century (Fig. 1-8). He came up with a system for making houses out of concrete using removable forms. Unfortunately, the formwork technology in that day was not very flexible. The methods he used were fine for making simple boxes, one after the other. But if you wanted more variety from house to house, using his standard forms became difficult.

Improvements in the industry in recent years have resolved these issues. ICFs in particular are easy to cut, bend, and paste into whatever shape and details you want. When you pour the concrete, it takes whatever shape the foam is in. Attaching things to the ICFs is

1-8. Concrete homes built with Thomas Edison's form system. (Portland Cement Association)

also easy. This makes it practical to put on any finishes that are used on wood frame—stucco, vinyl, clapboard, brick—you name it.

What's this "reinforced concrete" you mentioned before?

Reinforced concrete is concrete that has steel bars embedded in it for strength. The bars are called **steel reinforcing bars**, but a lot of people call them **rebar** for short. Practically all ICF walls have rebar in the concrete. The contractors position the rebar in key locations throughout the wall (Fig. 1-9). When the concrete is poured, it surrounds and "locks on" to the rebar. The combination of the concrete and rebar is what makes the wall so strong.

I can't believe that the same foam that's used to make coffee cups can hold concrete.

You and half the rest of the world. But it can and it does, hundreds of times every day. First, remember that this is only the same *variety* of foam used in coffee cups, not exactly the same foam. Saying they are both foam is about like saying a soup can and an armored tank are both steel. Both the coffee cup and most ICFs are made of what is technically called **expanded polystyrene**, or **EPS** for short. But the EPS in insulating concrete forms

1-10. A house built with ICFs. (ECO-Block, LLC)

is about 2 inches thick and it's specially formulated and manufactured to be dense and strong.

Many people think that the forms will break when the heavy concrete hits them. But with the forms used today and the trained crews, that's rare. It does happen on some occasions, but when it does, a good ICF crew fixes the break in about ten minutes.

Will an ICF house look different from a normal house?

ICF houses almost always look just like the other houses on the block (Fig. 1-10). If they don't, it's because the owner wanted his house to look different, not because the ICFs couldn't do the same things that wood can. ICF houses have the same shapes and floor plans, the same kinds of windows and doors, the same siding or stucco or bricks on the outside, and the same wallboard and paint on the inside. Just about the only way you can tell that the walls are ICFs by looking is that they're thicker than wood-frame walls. If you look closely at the windows, you can see that there is a deeper windowsill. But that's about it.

But how do you attach anything to the wall if it's just foam?

There are a number of ways. You have a range of options that are basically the same as the ways you attach things to the walls in a wood-frame house: to the wallboard, to special plates behind the wallboard, and to the studs. See Chapter 11 for details of how to fasten things to ICF walls.

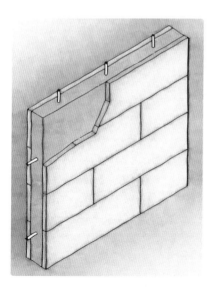

1-9. Cutaway view of reinforced concrete, showing embedded steel bars.

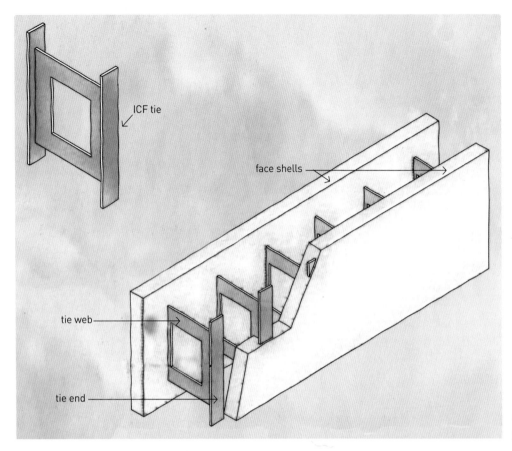

ICF tie

face shells

tie web

tie end

1-11. Cutaway view of an ICF block.

I thought ICF houses didn't have studs. How can you "attach things to the studs"?
I skipped that up until now. The foam blocks have plastic or steel strips embedded inside them that you can attach things to (Fig. 1-11). Some people nickname these strips *studs*. Their technical name is **tie ends**, or just **ties** for short. I will explain much more about them later. You can sink a screw or nail into them pretty much the same way you do into the studs of a wood-frame wall. You can find a tie with a stud finder or by other methods and put your screw right through the wallboard. Again, Chapter 11 will give you the full story. By the way, for really heavy things like a wall-mounted sink or cabinet, you have the option of anchoring directly to the concrete. You can sink heavy-duty steel anchors into the concrete at the core of the wall. You can later attach whatever you're mounting to the anchors for a very high-strength

connection. That kind of thing is usually handled by the contractors when they're building the house.

Earlier you said that most ICFs are big, hollow blocks. Does that mean that there are different types of ICFs?
There's definitely a range of different types of ICFs. But I don't recommend that you spend a lot of time worrying about the details of this. Most of the differences are much more important to the contractor than to the homeowner. Some systems are easier for the contractor to install in certain situations. So the contractor picks the type of ICF that is best for his particular way of operating, or best for the particular house to be built. I generally don't suggest you get involved in this decision, any more than you would get involved in choosing what lumber company the contractor buys his studs from.

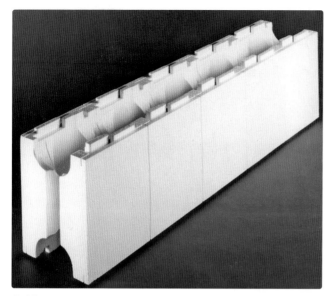

1-12. An all-foam block. (ReddiForm, Inc.)

Having said that, I know a lot of people are very curious about the details of ICFs. Plus, in a few instances it might make sense for you to discuss the issue with the contractor. So I will tell you a little about the varieties that are available.

Fair enough. What are the different types of ICFs?
Well, there are plenty of little differences between the brands here and there. But in my mind the main difference is the shape or "geometry" of the form. Another factor that can be important sometimes is the material the form is made of.

OK, explain the different shapes of ICFs to me.
I already showed you the main type. It's a big block with two layers of foam, and the layers are held an even distance apart by plastic ties. One of the main variations on these is the all-foam block; contractors call it a **screen block**, and if you really care why you can ask a local ICF contractor or distributor (Fig. 1-12). This is way too detailed for most homebuyers to be worrying about. Instead of ties made out of a separate material, the screen block is one molded piece of foam, including the ties. In fact, the "ties" aren't usually called *ties* in this block at all. Sometimes people call them **webs**. They are really just a different section of the block, not

a separate part that is assembled into the foam. The other main variation is called a **plank** system. It doesn't consist of blocks at all. It consists of flat pieces of foam that are connected together in the wall with separate ties that snap into place (Fig. 1-13).

What different types of material are the forms made of? I thought they were this EPS stuff.
About 90% of them are. But there are a couple of other options. Some plank systems use planks made of **extruded polystyrene** (also called **XPS**) instead of expanded polystyrene (EPS). It's a different variety of foam.

Some screen blocks don't use a plain foam at all, but instead use a **foam-cement composite** (Fig. 1-14). This is a mixture of cement, water, and little beads of expanded polystyrene foam. It's kind of like concrete that contains beads of EPS instead of sand and stones. When it hardens, you have a gray mass flecked with white beads that is somewhere between foam and concrete. It's heavier than foam but lighter than concrete, harder than foam but softer than concrete.

Which one of the different form shapes is the best?
That's kind of like asking what kind of HVAC equipment you should get. The answer depends on how big the house will be, what local fuels are available and are least expensive, how much energy efficiency

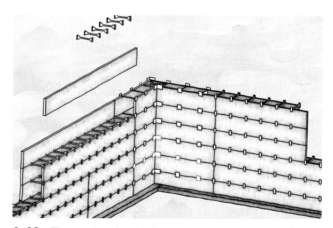

1-13. The parts of a plank system going into a wall.

1-14. Workers stacking blocks made of a foam-cement composite. (Perform Wall, LLC)

you want, and so on. Unless you are an expert, you shouldn't be making this decision by yourself. You should be hiring a competent HVAC contractor, explaining what you are looking for, and following the advice of the expert.

The fact is that the forms from any of the major companies make a good wall. There usually aren't a whole lot of differences between the walls once they're done. Most of the differences in the forms have to do with the way the wall is put together and what works best is really for the contractor to decide. You can take an interest in it if you want to, but I'd leave it to the contractor to decide which form to use.

There have to be some differences or they wouldn't make these different types. I really want to know what's different about the different types of forms and materials.
OK, I can tell you the main pluses and minuses people usually list for each of these.

Screen blocks require less concrete and the blocks themselves are often a bit less expensive. On the other hand, some people don't like that the wall is not a completely continuous layer of concrete. (The wall has the foam webs running through it every foot or so.) Plus the lack of ties means the crews have to resort to other methods to attach things to the wall.

Because the pieces of the plank system are all separate, they can be fit into a small space for shipping and storage. On the other hand, there is a bit more work to put them together because you have to snap the ties in one by one.

As you can see, most of the form differences are things that are more important to the contractor, so it makes sense for the contractor to use what works best for the crew and the particular design.

What about differences between different form materials?
Extruded polystyrene (XPS) has a slightly higher insulating ability than EPS, but it's a bit more expensive. Fiber-cement composite has a lower insulating value than either EPS or XPS and is heavier, but it is also harder and may be more durable. It's especially popular in the southwestern United States and is often used to

1-15. Southwestern style built with foam-cement composite forms. (Perform Wall, LLC)

create an adobe style of architecture with rounded corners (Fig. 1-15).

DISADVANTAGES OF ICF HOUSES

What are the disadvantages of ICF houses?
As much as I like ICFs, they do have a few disadvantages.

- First, they usually cost somewhat more to build. And since they're new, it might take some searching to find people who can build with them correctly.
- Also, outside at ground level, the foam needs to be covered with something hard, otherwise you could bang it up with the lawn mower or weed whacker and make gouges that need to be repaired.
- Depending on the type of foam system and the type of siding used, extra work may be required to install the siding. For example, strips of wood may need to be attached first to provide a place to nail the siding.

- Another point raised by some people is that ICF houses are "cast in concrete," making last-minute design changes, like moving a window, difficult and expensive once the concrete has set. Remodeling ICF walls presents similar challenges.

Are those all the disadvantages?
Pretty much. But these things may be important, especially the first two. I really like the benefits of ICF walls, and I have put down my own money to buy them. But even a few thousand dollars extra can be a big sacrifice for some people. If you're at the limit of what you can spend for your house, you may have to decide between the better walls and something like a hot tub, granite countertops, or a few dozen more square feet of space.

You can usually recoup the money you spend on ICF walls with things like the energy savings that the ICFs give you. Also, the cost of building with ICFs appears to be coming down as the manufacturers ramp up their production volumes and the contractors become more skillful at building with them. But in the foreseeable future you'll usually have to spend a bit more upfront.

How about the need to search longer to find qualified contractors? Is that such a big deal?
Usually not. But every now and then we still run across a town where there are no experienced ICF contractors or designers. In these places I advise you to think twice before proceeding with ICFs. As I'll explain later, without some people on the job who have a few ICF houses under their belt, you're running a greater risk of errors and inefficiencies in the project. And these are serious issues. As with any construction system, if the crew doesn't know what they're doing, you can get a real mess. You can also end up spending extra money and be stuck waiting for your house to be ready.

GETTING MORE INFORMATION

How do I decide if I want ICFs for my next house?
Read on. I'll take you through the costs and benefits, so that you can weigh those against each other. Then, if you think you want the ICFs, I'll tell you how to find and evaluate experienced contractors and designers, and work with them to get yourself a good house.

Is this book all I need to learn about ICFs?
There are other useful sources of information. When I believe that it's worthwhile for you to check those out, I name them. There are three in particular that I mention a lot. They are the three top Web sites for information on ICFs (see box titled "Top ICF Web Sites"). These have the very latest news, up-to-date directories of ICF companies and contractors, and some interesting discussions by actual contractors and homeowners.

Other than ICFs, are there any other ways to build a house out of concrete?
Absolutely. There are several. They are somewhat different from one another, but all of them share most of the basic advantages of concrete. I don't talk about them here because each one would be a book in itself. If you're curious about them I suggest you go to the www.concretehomes.com site and look them up. Another good source of information is a new division of the National Association of Home Builders (NAHB) called the Concrete Home Building Council (CHBC). It's been set up to keep builders and the general public up to speed on building with concrete, and to promote it. The CHBC is new and changing fast. You can contact the council through the NAHB Web site (www.nahb.org). That's about it for now. So please, read on and learn, and good luck!

Top ICF Web Sites

www.forms.org This is the Web site of the Insulating Concrete Form Association (ICFA). ICFA is the trade association that represents companies and individuals with a business or professional interest in the ICF industry. It has hundreds of members, including manufacturers of ICF forms, contractors who build with them, architects and engineers who design ICF buildings, and companies that supply related products and services. The site has a good, searchable directory of all ICFA members, which you can use to track down distributors, contractors, and others who can help with your project. It also has current news about ICFs and the industry, as well as information about major industry events.

www.ICFWeb.com This is an independently operated Web site that keeps running by taking advertising and selling various ICF-related services and publications. It has its own directory of companies and people involved with ICFs. It also has discussion forums for contractors and homebuyers who want to learn more about ICFs. Almost every conceivable subject is addressed, and you can start your own discussion about any subject that isn't covered. This site can be informative and fun to read. But, like a lot of open discussion forums on the Web, some of the comments are pretty off the wall and not entirely accurate. So, reader beware.

www.concretehomes.com This site is operated by the Portland Cement Association (PCA). PCA is the trade association that represents the suppliers of cement, which is a key ingredient of concrete. PCA provides information about most things involving the use of concrete. This site covers *all* the major systems for building homes out of concrete, including an excellent section on ICFs.

CHAPTER 2

Pluses and Minuses of an ICF Home

ICF HOUSES OFFER a lot of advantages to their owners and occupants (Fig. 2-1). These include some important benefits to living in the house as well as some long-term savings. But it is important to realize that there are some downsides to

Stacked forms.
(Arxx Building Products).

ICFs as well. Most of these involve the added costs, or the extra effort sometimes required to find good contractors. You should also be doing some extra checking during construction to make sure the job is done right. If you weigh these pluses and minuses, you'll be in good shape to decide whether an ICF house is right for you.

What are the most important benefits of an ICF house?

The benefits considered most important change from person to person. Often they will even change for the same person from time to time. In surveys of buyers who chose to build an ICF house, the most highly rated benefits of ICF construction were energy efficiency, resistance to disasters, comfort, and quiet. Others benefits mentioned were strength, durability, and design (see box titled "Top ICF Benefits").

Can I really get all these benefits from a house with ICF walls?

Yes, with some conditions. If you build your house with ICF exterior walls, you will get some measure of improvement in all these areas. In fact, by my standards the house is a much better house. However, most of these benefits also depend on other parts of the house,

2-1. ICF houses offer a number of important benefits.

too. For example, if you have ICF walls and a poorly constructed roof and cheap doors and windows, you won't have nearly as good energy efficiency or wind resistance as you could otherwise. It's a little bit like buying a Cadillac with a motorcycle engine under the hood. To get the full benefit you need good components all around.

The roof and windows and doors are key because they're the other parts of the house that separate the indoors from the outdoors. Building professionals call the exterior walls, the roof, and the windows and doors all together the **envelope** of the house because they make up the whole outside surface. I will talk many times in this book about how you should look after some of these other details—not just the walls—to get the maximum benefits in the areas of energy efficiency, disaster resistance, comfort, quiet, strength, and so on. For now let's summarize the situation as follows:

- If you build a house with ICF exterior walls and everything else of average quality, you can get a definite increase in all of these benefits.
- If you build a house with ICF exterior walls and higher-quality components for other critical parts of the house, you can get an even greater increase in most of these benefits.

- If you build a house with ICF exterior walls and poor-quality components for other critical parts of the house, you may get a little increase in most of these benefits.

ENERGY EFFICIENCY

Where does the energy efficiency of an ICF house come from?

It comes from a few things. The factor most people already understand is the high insulation value of the foam. This is known as the foam's **R-value**. R-value is a measure of the ability of a material to slow the passage of heat out through the walls (in winter) or in through the walls (in summer). Foam has a very high R-value, which means it does a good job of keeping the heat inside during the winter and outside during the summer.

Although the foam is key, the energy efficiency also comes from the airtightness and the "massiveness" of the concrete walls. The airtightness keeps excess air from coming in from the outdoors. This reduces the amount of cold drafts entering in the winter, and hot, humid air entering in the summer. In addition, the mass of the concrete keeps the temperature from fluctuating, much like being near a large body of water keeps the local climate a little warmer in winter and cooler in summer. I will discuss all of these things in much more detail later in the book.

How much money do you save on your fuel bill with ICFs?

This question is so complicated that it always makes my head spin. So I don't think it's a very good idea to go into too much detail here. The problem is that your savings can depend on a hundred different factors, including the type of windows and doors you choose, the type of roof you have, how large your window area is, what your local climate is, your lifestyle, and on and on. All these things can make a big difference, so it's almost impossible to simply throw out a single number.

But to give you a rough idea for the time being, home-owners usually estimate their fuel savings at something close to 20% to 40%. I've written a whole separate chapter on the ins and outs of energy efficiency for everyone who's interested in the fine points. So to get a little more scientific information on this, read Chapter 4.

What does the term "equivalent R-value" mean? I've heard some people say that ICFs have an R-value that's "equivalent to R-50."

Equivalent R-value is a complicated number that can be helpful or very misleading. You need to know a lot more about energy efficiency to understand it, so I'll defer that discussion, too. It's all in Chapter 4 if you want to spend the time to read it. And if you don't, do *not* go around using terms like this or accepting numbers like equivalent R-values from strangers. They're like industrial explosives. They're very useful if you know how to handle them, but very dangerous if you don't.

IN HURRICANES, TORNADOES, AND HIGH WINDS

So, do ICF houses resist disasters better than conventional houses do?

By and large, they do. For the most part, there's widespread agreement that they are safer in high winds, such as those you experience in hurricanes and tornadoes. They also appear to be safer in some ways during floods. For good disaster resistance you need to pay attention to other details, like the roof and windows and doors, too. But we'll get into these things later on.

ICFs can also provide greater resistance to fire, but you must be careful about what you conclude from this. Fire is still a big concern and you can't lower your guard just because your house has ICF walls. The properties of ICFs help reduce some risks from fires, but have little or no effect on others.

ICF homes seem to hold up well in earthquakes, too. However, there isn't quite enough data yet to say they're better or worse than frame houses in earthquakes. They're even known to be more resistant to explosive blasts, believe it or not.

Why am I safer with ICF walls in a hurricane or tornado?

There are two reasons. The house doesn't break apart easily, and the ICF walls don't let flying debris into the house as easily.

How do you know the ICF house won't break apart so easily in high winds?

Because engineers toured the devastation of Hurricane Andrew (in Florida) and Hurricane Iniki (in Hawaii) after they struck in the 1990s. Nearly all the reinforced concrete homes had most or all of their walls still intact, while a lot of the wood-frame walls had collapsed or broken apart (Fig. 2-2).

2-3. This house lost its roof in high winds, but the ICF walls remained largely intact. (Federal Emergency Management Agency)

2-2. An ICF house (at left) standing after a windstorm, flanked by the foundations of wood-frame houses that were destroyed. (Reward Wall Systems, Inc.)

Actually, the concrete walls in Florida and Hawaii were mostly made of reinforced concrete block. These are hollow blocks made of concrete—not foam—with reinforced concrete put in the hollows. Technically it's different from an ICF wall, but the way reinforced concrete walls act in wind is generally consistent from one type of concrete wall to the next, so many people think it's a good indicator of how ICFs will do.

From the reports, it appears that nearly 30% of the houses in the direct path of the hurricanes lost their roofs (Fig. 2-3). The wind simply tore them off. Following this, a good fraction of the frame houses were either pushed over or pulled apart. But almost all the reinforced concrete walls remained standing, even if they had lost their roofs.

The story was pretty much the same when the incredible string of four major hurricanes hit Florida in 2004. We don't have as much scientific data on the results of these storms yet, but the reports from owners pretty consistently confirmed that the reinforced concrete walls survived very well. This time around there were quite a few ICF houses in Florida as well as concrete-block ones, and all the stories I heard from builders and owners there said that the ICF walls appeared to survive intact.

Why can the ICF walls still remain standing after the roof that connects them has blown away? There are a couple of reasons for this. The first is weight. Concrete is naturally heavy, so the wind had a hard time moving it. The other is the steel reinforcement. The steel bars embedded in the concrete go from inside the foundation right up to the roofline. These bars are extremely resistant to being pulled apart.

The engineering on these houses also predicts that reinforced concrete houses will resist the wind. A good engineer can sit down with the house plans, run the calculations, and confirm the wind speeds that it can withstand.

But can ICF walls really stand up to a tornado?
Apparently. There are several stories about ICF homes that rode out a tornado without so much as bending out of shape. Yet next door a wood-frame house was pulled right off its foundation. Several of these have received local press coverage. But this isn't so surprising, either. The same properties that help an ICF house withstand the force of hurricanes help it withstand the force of tornadoes. While winds in tornadoes tend to be much higher than those in hurricanes, it is possible to "beef up" ICF walls to withstand even those higher wind speeds by adding more rebar.

Can the roof still come off an ICF house?
Yes and no. Certainly, wood-frame roofs can pop off reinforced concrete buildings in high winds. But there are ways to prevent this. If you live in a high-risk area, you should consider asking for things we call **hurricane straps**, whether the walls are ICF or wood frame. These are metal straps or plates that the contractor can embed into the concrete at the top of the wall or attach to a wood plate anchored to the concrete (Fig. 2-4). The contractors then attach the straps to the roof by nailing each strap into one of the roof trusses or rafters. These straps provide a much stronger hold than you get by simply nailing the roof trusses or rafters down to a wall. If the rest of the roof is also well built,

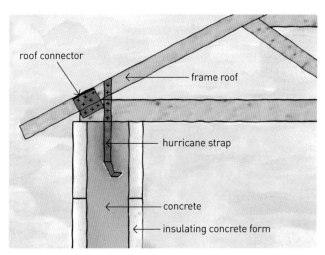

2-4. View of a frame roof connected to ICF walls with hurricane straps.

it can stay intact through much higher winds. I will also discuss this at greater length later in the book.

There's one more way to make the roof on your ICF house extra-resistant to the wind: Build it out of the new ICF roof systems (Fig. 2-5). This makes the roof reinforced concrete as well. When using these systems, the rebar runs from inside the foundation, through the walls, and all through the roof. This is more expensive than a conventional roof, but it definitely gives you an ultrastrong building. I'll remind you about this option later.

2-5. Workers pouring concrete onto an ICF roof.
(INSUL-DECK, LLC)

WITH WIND-BLOWN DEBRIS

You mentioned that ICFs also resist wind-blown debris better. What exactly is wind-blown debris?
Bricks, studs, tree branches, and other things that the wind picks up and throws through the air at frightening speeds. These flying pieces of debris can penetrate the walls of many buildings, threatening the occupants and the contents. In fact, according to some researchers, debris actually causes more total injury and damage in a hurricane or tornado than is caused by the collapse of buildings.

What happens when wind-blown debris hits an ICF wall?
For the most part, flying pieces of debris simply bounce off. Or they become lodged in the foam. But they very rarely are able to penetrate the walls. The ability of ICF walls and conventional walls to resist flying debris was tested by researchers, and the ICF walls performed extremely well (see box titled "Torture Testing of ICF Walls").

FIRE RESISTANCE

Now, how are ICF walls safer in a fire?
They're safer only in a few, specific ways. In other words, even though they will reduce some of the dangers of fire, there are still a lot of dangers that are just the same as with wood. The point is that you can't just forget your usual fire precautions.

Most of the safety benefit comes because the core of the wall is concrete. It takes much, much longer for fire to damage a concrete wall structurally. Thus, it will remain standing and reasonably strong through many hours of fire.

This is beneficial in a few ways. First of all, the walls won't collapse as soon as they would if this were a wood-frame structure. Therefore, if there are people trapped inside during a fire, it might give them more time to get out before things come crashing down

around them. This could also be a benefit to firefighters who enter the building to try to stop the fire. They often get hurt when buildings collapse, so this can give them more time before that starts happening.

Second, ICF walls help keep the fire from spreading *outside* the house and setting, say, a neighboring tree or the house next door on fire. This may not benefit the owners, but it certainly helps the fire department and the neighbors.

Third, if the fire starts *outside* the house, the concrete walls can slow the fire from coming *into* the house. This can be an advantage in areas where there are brush fires, such as the dry southwest United States. The concrete could conceivably stop a fire from consuming your house long enough to allow the fire department to arrive or long enough to allow the conditions outside to change and the fire to subside.

Why is the concrete so good in a fire?
Concrete is nonflammable. It does not burn any more than most common rocks will burn. If it is subjected to extremely high temperatures of thousands of degrees for a long period, it will eventually decompose—that is, become crumbly. However, these temperatures are far higher than any that occur in a common house fire. But remember, I can't stress enough that even with these advantages, you cannot get complacent. The important rules still apply—like not taking chances with fire, hitting the floor when you detect smoke, and having planned escape routes and a meeting spot for everyone to go to outside in the event of a fire.

Can you be specific about why there are still dangers from fire when I have ICF walls?
Sure. Most personal injury from fire occurs when a fire starts inside the house. The contents of the house—furniture, carpets, books, and so on—burn and give off smoke and toxic fumes that are extremely dangerous when inhaled. All of this can and generally does happen before the fire gets inside the walls at all. In fact, the wallboard we install over the inside face of the walls is there partly to slow down the fire from getting into

Researchers at Texas Tech University tested the resistance of different types of walls to projectiles similar to the wind-blown debris a building might face in a hurricane or tornado. The video of the tests is one of the more fascinating laboratory films I've ever seen. The researchers shot wooden studs out of a special contraption they called a *stud cannon*.

They aimed the studs at several different types of walls. Some of the walls were standard wood frame. These had fiberglass insulation between the studs, wallboard on the inside, and sheathing on the outside. Some of the frame walls had vinyl siding over the sheathing, and some had full, 4-inch-thick brick over the sheathing. Then there were ICF walls with wallboard on the inside. The ICF walls had no sheathing on the outside because ordinarily none is needed. Otherwise, the outside finish on the ICF walls was the same as for the wood—vinyl siding in some cases and brick in others.

The researchers shot these studs at all the walls, attaining speeds of over 100 miles per hour. This, they say, is about as fast as the wind drives debris in a tornado. The results were pretty clear. On all the wood-frame walls, the stud went completely through the wall. It shot a fairly clean hole through the exterior siding and the interior wallboard. This happened even when the siding was brick. None of the wood walls stopped the stud (Fig. 2-6a).

On the ICF walls, the results were totally different. The stud always bounced off the foam on the outside of the wall (Fig. 2-6b). When the outside finish was brick, the stud broke apart an area of brick, but neither the stud nor the shards of loose brick did much more than dent the exterior foam. Looking from the inside, you couldn't tell that anything had happened to the wall. The wallboard remained completely intact.

2-6. (a) In a wood-frame wall, the airborne stud shot clean through, breaking the interior drywall. (b) The same projectile bounced off the ICF wall covered with vinyl siding. [Portland Cement Association]

the wall. Officially, gypsum wallboard is considered a **fire barrier**. So you see, in this situation it doesn't much matter what the walls are built of. The contents of the house still burn and still give off toxic fumes. The occupants can get injured or killed whether the walls are ICF or not.

With enough time, a hot enough fire will get through the wallboard and start burning the contents of the wall. At that point the wood of a wood-frame wall can burn and add to the fumes. Foam can give off similar amounts of fumes when exposed to fire, although technically it may not exactly burn.

What do you mean, foam may not burn?
Well, the foam used in construction—including the foam in ICFs—is required to be **modified**. This means it has additives in it that prevent it from burning and acting as fuel in a typical fire. Labs are constantly testing this because regulators require that manufacturers of foam construction products provide evidence that their products meet fire-resistance rules. The labs take a piece of the foam and subject it to a flame. Where the flame touches the foam, the foam just melts away. As soon as you remove the flame, it immediately stops melting. The foam melts instead of catching on fire as, say, a wooden stud might.

However, most foam plastics can ignite or contribute fuel to a fire under certain conditions. For that reason, the foam should always be covered by drywall or by another fire-resistant material when it is used in a living space. Check with your local building department for specific requirements in your area.

Can the fumes from wood or foam be dangerous?
Yes, they can, just as the fumes from the other contents of a house can be dangerous. Once a fire gets into the walls, either of these materials can add to the fumes in the house. In any case, it is best to have all people outside the house before this occurs.

Let me ask some more about ICFs stopping outside fires from coming in. Is having an ICF wall the only thing I need to survive a brush fire?
No, that's not really enough. The experts usually recommend that you avoid having anything on the outside of the house that might catch fire. For example, you might want to avoid wood siding, wood trim—things like that. Instead, stick with sidings like stucco and brick, and roof tiles made of clay or concrete. You should even be wrapping any exposed eaves of a wooden roof with fire-resistant materials. In short, everything on the exterior surface of the house should be nonflammable. That way you can minimize the places where a fire burning on the outside can catch onto the house. And of course the concrete walls are a line of defense.

In fact, there's a famous case of a house built by the Kaw Valley Chapter of Habitat for Humanity, which is near Kansas City. It had ICF walls and, instead of wooden or vinyl siding, it had **fiber-cement siding**. With this type of siding and trim material, the boards are made with a fine concrete-type material. After the house was built, arsonists threw a firebomb against the front wall of the house. The bomb burned there on the ground, up against the wall, but almost no damage occurred to the house (Fig. 2-7). The Habitat volunteers cleaned the smoke stains off the siding where it had become black. There was a plastic soffit under the eaves of the roof that had melted from the heat, so the workers replaced it. That's about all they had to do to clean up. The foam was fine, the rest of the wall was fine, and the rest of the house was fine. The concrete walls were probably a good barrier to keep the fire from getting inside the house, but the concrete-based siding probably kept it from taking hold of the foam or any other part of the house in the first place.

How do we know exactly how much better the concrete walls are at surviving a fire?
There's a test for that. In fact, it's required for the types of walls that will go between the living units in an apartment or condo building. The idea is that the wall between families should slow down the spread of fire so that if a fire starts in one apartment, the people next door will have more time to get out and the fire

2-7. A Kansas City ICF house that survived arson. (Habitat for Humanity International)

department will have more time to come before it spreads. The test is commonly called the **fire wall test**.

How does the fire wall test work?

A laboratory builds a wall and puts a controlled fire on one side of it. The technicians start the fire off at a particular temperature, then gradually increase the temperature at a specified rate. They time the test, and when the temperature on the opposite side of the wall gets above a certain threshold, or if the fire breaks through the wall at any point, they stop the test and record the elapsed time. The amount of time it takes to reach the temperature limit across the wall, or for the fire to break through, is called the wall's **fire rating**. Of course, the higher the fire rating, the longer we expect the wall to hold back fire (Fig. 2-8).

How do wood and ICF walls compare on their fire ratings?

Well, for wood-frame walls it depends a lot on what the wall is covered with. The wood frame itself is hollow, or it has lightweight fiberglass between the studs, so it won't stop the spread of fire for more than a few minutes.

Usually scientists test a wood-frame wall with wallboard on each side. This is the type of wall that is generally found on the interior of a house. It's probably also reasonably representative of many exterior walls. In this case the wood walls routinely get a fire rating of half an hour to an hour.

On the other hand, ICF walls, even without any wallboard over them, routinely get a fire rating of two to four hours. That's about four times as long as a wood-frame wall (Fig. 2-9). Also, because the temperature in the test is continually increasing, they survived the extra time at much higher temperatures.

At the end of it all, the concrete walls are also in much better shape. By the end of a fire test, wood-frame walls typically are heavily charred or in flames. Structurally, they can't hold up much of anything. In a real house, frame walls that had been damaged to that extent would most likely collapse under the weight of the roof or the story above.

At the end of the test on the ICF walls, they are still strong and could continue to hold up big loads for much longer. The main reason the test is stopped on an ICF wall is that the heat eventually penetrates through the wall, making the temperature on the "cool" side go over the allowable limit. However, the layer of concrete is still intact, and flames are not passing through the wall.

2-8. Cooling a wall after a fire wall test. (American PolySteel, LLC)

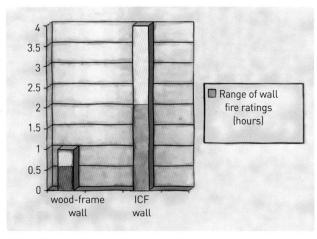

2-9. Chart of fire wall ratings. The top of the red bar represents the lowest rating received by that type of wall, and the top of the pink bar represents the highest.

EARTHQUAKE RESISTANCE

OK, so now we're on to earthquakes. How well does concrete do in earthquakes?

It appears that the modern reinforced concrete used in ICFs does just fine. Early in the twentieth century a lot of **unreinforced** concrete buildings were built. They had little or no steel reinforcing bar embedded in the concrete. These buildings did poorly in earthquakes. The shaking cracked the walls and eventually made pieces break off. Ultimately, a strong earthquake will bring unreinforced concrete walls down.

Nowadays nearly all the concrete walls built in high-risk areas of the country are required to have large amounts of rebar in them. According to engineering calculations, this is supposed to help the walls resist earthquakes because the steel gives the concrete **tensile strength**, which holds the walls together. Tensile strength is "pulling strength," a material's resistance to being pulled apart. And it appears to work as predicted. We don't have as much data from earthquakes as we do from hurricanes, because there are fewer of them. However, there have now been a few eyewitness accounts of tremors around ICF houses, and the houses have allegedly come through them as well as or better than their wood-frame neighbors.

FLOOD RESISTANCE

You mentioned floods. Do ICFs resist floods better?

Yes, in *some* ways. Both logic and experience suggest that ICFs help resist a lot of structural damage to a house. They may also reduce some of the water damage. But there are some types of damage that they can't really prevent. The situation with flood resistance is similar to that with other types of disasters—the walls definitely can help, but they can't do it all.

What do you mean by "structural damage," and why should ICF walls have less of it in floods?

Basically, structural damage means bending or breaking. If a wall gets bent or twisted out of shape or falls over, that's what we call structural damage. It can no longer do its job of holding up floors or the rest of the house.

ICF walls should survive a flood well structurally because the forces of rushing water are a lot like the forces of wind. The water pushes against the side of the walls with a high force. And, as we have discussed, the higher strength of ICF walls resists these forces well—measurably better than typical wood-frame walls.

A number of reinforced concrete homes (akin to homes with ICF walls, but built with conventional forms, rather than with foam) have survived floods impressively. One example hit the press recently. After Hurricane Katrina, the Federal Emergency Management Agency (FEMA) saw an interesting sight in a part of southern Mississippi that suffered a big storm surge. It was a house that was still standing with only some roof damage. All around it, wood-frame houses had been washed away. All that was left of the frame houses were their slab foundations and a few loose studs. On investigation, FEMA learned that the surviving house was made of reinforced concrete (Fig. 2-10).

To be fair, that house had other design features to help resist flooding, in addition to the reinforced concrete walls. But it showed rather dramatically how the strength of reinforced concrete can help stand up to floods.

OK, then what do you mean by "water damage," and how do ICF walls resist that?
By water damage I mean decay that comes from getting wet. When wood gets wet, it can grow mold and decay. This can make the indoors a pretty unpleasant place to be. In addition, the decay can eventually weaken the wood. In extreme cases it's not just a nuisance—the wood weakens so much that the home's structure is seriously compromised. Parts of the framing may need to be replaced or the house could start to sag or collapse.

An ICF distributor in Texas told me about a customer of his with a house on the coast. The house went through a flood, too. After the water receded, the interior woodwork, along with many interior finishes and furnishings, had to be thrown out. But the ICF walls were fine. They were dried out, cleaned off, and nothing else had to be done to them when the house was restored.

So in what ways don't walls built with ICFs help you in a flood?
In the aftermath of Hurricane Katrina, we all read accounts of the devastating property damage throughout New Orleans and southern Mississippi. The way I see it, many of the horrendous problems that the home-owners suffered would have been about the same no matter what their outside walls were built of.

I already touched on one problem with the example from Texas. That's damage to the *insides* of the house. In any really serious flood, the water will get inside even if the walls hold up. The water will break out windows or gush through vents. When it does, it will soak carpeting and food and newspapers and wood framing used for the interior walls and a dozen other things made of organic materials. These will get moldy and rot.

2-10. A reinforced concrete house that survived a storm surge from Hurricane Katrina, surrounded by the remains of frame houses that did not survive.
(Federal Emergency Management Agency)

On most ICF houses, the roof and some floors are still built of wood. If water reaches them, they have a chance of suffering structural damage and rot, just as wood walls do.

The exterior walls can't do much about rotted contents and wood framing. It's true that you might be able to dry out the walls and use them, but you would still have to clear out the damaged organic materials and replace them.

So you're saying that ICF walls can help a house resist flood, but they can't do it all?
Exactly. Building with ICFs can take care of the walls. But there are still important things that could go wrong with other parts of the house, as happens with other kinds of disasters.

Personally, if I lived in a flood zone I would consider that to be one more reason to build my house with ICF walls. On top of that, I would check into building my floors and roof out of concrete, too. That can be expensive, but I would at least look into it. I discuss this option more in Chapter 3. I would also consider using water-resistant materials in as many other parts of the building as I could.

How do I know what other things to do to my house to make it flood-resistant?

The experts, like those at the Federal Emergency Management Agency (www.fema.org) and the Institute for Business and Home Safety (IBHS; www.ibhs.org), are producing more and more detailed recommendations. To simplify them a bit, they center around four things:

1. Structural strength
2. Elevation
3. Foundation with a low-resistance profile
4. Water-resistant materials.

Structural strength refers to building the walls, floors, and roof so they're strong enough to keep the building from being pushed out of shape by flood waters. We've just discussed how ICFs can help with this.

The idea of **elevation** is to raise the main part of the house above the level that floodwaters are likely to get up to. Then, as long as the foundation is strong and water-resistant, the contents of the house are pretty safe. The trick, of course, is to know how high is high enough. Flood levels have a nasty habit of exceeding expectations every once in a while.

By **low-resistance profile** I mean a foundation that is streamlined so it is hard to knock over. This is important for houses that are very near the coast and therefore may get a high-force wave of water all at once. Such a wave of water is called a **storm surge**. Reinforced concrete walls can stand up to this better than conventional wood frame can, but the force of a storm surge can be strong enough to knock over even reinforced concrete. So the recommendation from experts is to build a foundation of **piers**. These are sort of like stilts for a house. They are columns planted in the ground, made of reinforced concrete or treated timbers, that support a house and raise it about 8 to 12 feet above the ground. The piers provide much less resistance to the force of the water, the way that a few posts get pushed around by wind a lot less than a wide board does. Sometimes there are walls constructed between the piers, to form an enclosed space inside. But these walls are supposed to be somewhat weak so that during a storm surge they will break away without taking the rest of the house down. Often I've seen people use this space below the house as their garage.

The purpose of the water-resistant materials is the same as I stated before. The less organic material you have in the house, the less mold and rot you will have after it gets wet, and the less cleanup and repair will be needed. Both FEMA and IBHS have plenty of guides that provide specific recommendations. I suggest you check out their Web sites if you are planning to build in areas that may get flooded.

What problems other than house damage should I be concerned about in a flood?

Let's face it: A lot of the problems brought on by Hurricane Katrina occurred because of things that happened outside of houses. The water became contaminated, the electricity was cut off, and transportation throughout the region was paralyzed. Residents would have suffered these disaster-related problems no matter what their houses were made of. It's true that ICFs can contribute to a flood-resistant house, but that doesn't mean you'll be 100% safe. As with fire, it's still important to follow the standard safety procedures, such as evacuating before disaster strikes.

RESISTANCE TO EXPLOSIONS AND IMPACT

Winds, fires, earthquakes, floods—is that it for disasters?

The only other ones I can think of are explosion and sudden impact. Explosion is mostly an issue for governments and the military. But it's interesting and impressive to hear how well ICFs survive a blast.

How do you know how well ICFs survive explosions?
Because the government has tried to blow them up. Every few years, government agencies run a set of blast tests on the grounds of the Marine Corps base in Quantico, Virginia. They set up various types of walls and other building products, put a charge of TNT next to them, blow the charge, and see how well the materials hold up.

And ICFs have been tested for blast resistance in this way?
Yes. There was a round of these tests in the spring of 2003, and another round in the spring of 2004. Included in the testing were some little ICF structures they called "boxes." They were basically cubes, 8 feet on each side, with one side open. They were shaped like a cardboard box with no top, turned on its side.

2-11. An ICF reaction box after explosion test. (Insulating Concrete Form Association)

How were the results of the blast resistance tests?
Pretty amazing, actually. The potentially most damaging blast was 50 pounds of TNT set 6 feet from the wall of one of these boxes. It flattened the foam against the concrete. However, the wall was not even slightly bent out of shape (Fig. 2-11). Upon closer examination, there were some thin cracks in the concrete, but the steel rebar held the wall together at those points. (Actually, that's the steel's job—to hold things together in the face of severe forces.) The wall appeared to have nearly its full structural strength, even after the blast, although testing would be required to confirm this.

When the test was over, workers clipped steel cables onto the top of the box, and a crane lifted it onto a flatbed truck to haul it away. According to one observer, when the box was picked up, "It didn't even creak." The other explosion tests on other ICF boxes had the same result.

Wow, concrete can stop an explosion, then?
Well, concrete and foam. Reinforced concrete does survive blasts fairly well. But, according to engineering calculations, if this had been a plain reinforced concrete wall with no foam on it, the blast would have created a hole about the size of a basketball.

It appears that the foam cushioned the blast—blunted it enough so that the concrete could take the impact without sustaining too much damage. It's sort of like having collapsible crash-protection bumpers on cars. They collapse in a controlled way, so there's less jarring of the car's frame, and the frame can survive more of a jolt without buckling.

But is this kind of resistance to explosion or sudden impact relevant to me?
Explosion resistance probably isn't too important to us ordinary citizens, but resistance to sudden impact might be useful in some rare cases. There was recently a report of a car smashing into an ICF house at high speed in an accident (Fig. 2-12). As you might guess, the car just bounced off.

This kind of thing happens to all types of houses now and again, of course. In fact, when that crash into

2-12. Results of a car colliding with an ICF house. (American PolySteel, LLC)

an ICF house occurred, some interested ICF suppliers looked through the newspaper reports to see if there were any stories about a car crashing into a frame house. Sure enough, they found a story from almost the same day. The big difference was that, with the frame house, the car didn't bounce off. It ended up inside the living room. I don't think most of us have to worry about cars careening into our houses very often, but these results confirm the high level of strength and protection that ICF walls offer.

COMFORT

So if that's the last type of disaster, what is the next thing on your list of benefits?
The next thing on my list is comfort. This is usually pretty important to the people who buy ICF houses.

What do you mean by "comfort"?
How comfortable the house is to live in. Some may consider this subjective, but that is not entirely true. ICF houses have specific, measurable differences from wood frame that affect the comfort of the people inside. First of all, many ICF homeowners in the survey I mentioned earlier said that their houses have a much more even temperature—more even over the course of a day and more even from place to place all around the house. Second, a lot said they have fewer drafts than they had in their previous, non-ICF homes.

Why would the temperature in an ICF house be more even?
The even temperature comes from two features of the walls—the continuous insulation and the mass of the concrete. The insulation of an ICF wall is the foam on each side. Over the length and height of the wall this foam is almost completely unbroken—except for the windows and doors—and well sealed against air leaks. The insulation of a wood-frame wall is the fiberglass between the studs. If done well, this can produce a good-performing wall. But when the insulation is poorly installed, as it often is, gaps in the insulation create cold cavities, leading to cold spots indoors. Also, walls poorly sealed against air leakage can permit air leaks to undermine the fiberglass insulation, and sometimes leak into the living space, creating cold drafts. To a lesser extent these problems can lead to hot spots in very hot weather.

But everywhere there is a stud, there is no insulation. In fact, if you add up the area of the typical frame wall that is wood—and not insulated—it is about 25% of the total area. So because the insulation is quite continuous throughout an ICF wall, there are fewer cold and hot spots in an ICF wall.

How does the concrete mass figure in making the temperature more even?
It evens out the temperature over time. In a wood-frame house, especially one that's older or poorly insulated, the gas or electric heat comes on in winter, and you feel warm. When it shuts off and the house cools down a few degrees, you may feel a bit chilly, and then the whole cycle starts all over again. The same thing happens with air-conditioning in the summer, but in reverse. You feel chilly for a while when the AC blasts through the house, and you feel warm when it hasn't been on for a while.

But with massive materials like concrete, it takes a long time for the material to heat up and cool down. So the temperature in a concrete house goes up and down more slowly than in a conventional house, and doesn't have the same high and low points.

Just before we moved into our new ICF house in 1995, my wife doubted my claim that it would be more comfortable. But after we had lived in it for a few months, we went to visit her parents on a cold November day. As you might guess, their house was an older wood-frame home. The heat cranked on and off and the temperature went up and down, just as I described. We were taking our sweaters off and putting them back on about every half-hour. "Wow," she said

afterward, "I guess there really is a difference." The difference would be less noticeable in a newer, better-insulated, wood-frame home. But buyers of ICF houses with neighbors who have newly constructed wood homes still say they can feel a marked difference.

What about the drafts?
The ICF walls are also more effectively sealed against air coming through. This is important because, in cold weather, a drafty house will feel cold no matter how high the thermostat is set.

A wood wall is made by nailing together a large number of pieces of wood that never fit together perfectly. As a result, the typical wood-frame wall has thousands of tiny gaps. Over time the wood expands and contracts over and over again because of heat and humidity. Things loosen up and the gaps increase in size. Air comes through, especially when there is wind. This can give you a cool blast in winter or a hot one in summer. But ICF walls rarely have significant gaps. The foam is nearly impermeable to air, and the blocks fit together tightly (Fig. 2-13). Most important, when the concrete is poured into the cavities, it fills any remaining gaps, sealing the wall. Air can still get through at other points, like through the roof or around the doors and windows, depending on the quality of the workmanship. But the walls themselves are nearly eliminated as a source of drafts.

2-13. ICF blocks fit tightly at their joints. (IntegraSpec ICF)

NOISE REDUCTION

What makes ICF houses quieter?
Sound passes through lighter materials, like wood and fiberglass, more easily than through heavy ones like concrete. So less noise outside comes through walls made of concrete than through walls made of wood.

Does this reduction in sound really make a difference?
Yes, it really does. Many homeowners said their biggest surprise in moving into an ICF house was the noise difference. Most of them had never been told that the

house would be quieter, or they didn't believe it would be a significant difference. They were happily surprised. One story that new ICF owners often tell is the "night storm" story. It goes something like this: The ICF homeowner bumps into his next-door neighbor one morning. The neighbor lives in a wood-frame house. They start talking.

Neighbor: Man, did you wake up last night, too?
ICF owner: Wake up? From what?
Neighbor: From the storm.
ICF owner: What storm?

Less noise got into the ICF house, so the ICF owner was never bothered by it. Many ICF owners have told a similar story.

Another common story is the "traffic" story. A prospective homebuyer takes a tour of an ICF house. He stands at the front window. After gazing out for a few seconds, he says, "Hey! I can see all the traffic on the road, but I can't hear it."

A contractor in Missouri who I met found he had good luck selling ICF houses near a local medical complex. It turned out that many of the medical personnel worked during the night and needed to sleep during the day. The sound-dampening walls helped them sleep more comfortably in daytime, and they gladly paid the extra cost for the ICF construction.

How much more do ICF walls block sound?

Scientists measure the amount of sound that penetrates a wall by the wall's **sound transmission class**, also called the **STC**. The STC for a typical wood-frame wall is 35 to 40 decibels, depending on exactly what finishes are put on each side. A few ICF companies have had their walls tested, and the results showed that ICF walls have an STC about 10 decibels higher than wood walls do: ICFs have an STC of about 46 to 52.

What does a higher STC mean?

Well, the STC scale is complicated, and it's not worth going into all the details here. But to make a long story short, an extra 10 points in the STC of a wall means

that the sound perceived through the wall is reduced by about 50% (Fig. 2-14).

Here's another way to explain the difference that may be easier to understand. A construction products company did a study of walls with different STC numbers, and how people *perceived* the sound reduction of each wall. According to the study, if there was "loud talking" on one side of a wall with an STC of 36, people on the other side of the wall considered the sound to be "audible but generally not intelligible." The STC of 36 is in the range for typical wood-frame walls. When the same people listened to the same talking through a wall with an STC of 45, they noted that they "must strain to hear" it. When the wall had an STC of 50, they considered the sound to be "inaudible." STCs of 45 and 50 are more typical of ICF walls.

So the sound that gets through an ICF wall is half as loud as the sound that penetrates a wood-frame wall?

That's correct for the *ICF* portion of the wall. But be careful here. All houses still have some weak points.

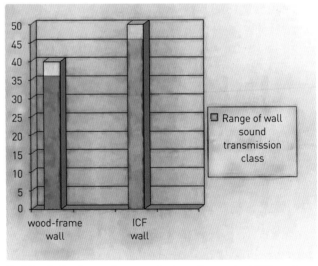

2-14. STCs (sound transmission classes) of ICF and wood frame walls. The top end of the light blue represents the high end of the range. The top end of the dark blue represents the low end of the range. The STC of wood-frame walls runs about 35 to 40, depending on the exact details of their construction; the STC of ICFs is about 45 to 50.

A fair amount of sound will still get through most windows and doors, and that can reduce the total difference in perceived sound between the ICF and the frame house. You still have to make sure you have good windows and a tight roof to gain the full benefit. Double-pane windows can make a big difference. They are the usual type of window installed nowadays anyway, but if you are concerned about sound, you want to make sure that they are what you will be getting.

STRENGTH AND DURABILITY

What's so great about the strength of ICF walls?
Well, it's very high. Usually much, much higher than the minimum you need to hold the house up. That's one reason ICFs do so well in disasters, as we discussed before.

How is strength different from disaster resistance?
I've listed it separately, because there are other things about the strength of ICF walls that people tend to like, beyond the resistance to disasters. One is that there is less vibration. If you slam the front door in a house with ICF walls, chances are you'll feel much less vibration than you would in a wood-frame home. Usually in an ICF house, you still have a wooden floor. This will still have almost as much bounce as in any house because of the flexing of the wood. However, that bounce is *slightly* less in an ICF house because the floor rests partly on the rigid concrete walls.

The house will squeak and groan much less in high winds or over the course of the day. In my parents' old home in Florida, every evening when the temperature dropped, I could hear a series of creaks as the wood cooled down, shrank a little, and shifted in the walls and the roof.

One woman who had lived in an ICF house for a year or so described the overall feeling of being in an ICF house by saying, "It feels very . . . well, *solid*. Yes, that's the word to describe it. Just being in the house, it feels very solid." I suspect that what she was noticing was a combination of the quiet and the lack of vibration.

What about durability?
The concrete structure of the house is likely to age better and shift less over time. Concrete does not rot, rust, or burn. It also doesn't shrink or expand nearly as much as wood does.

When my wife and I were house hunting, we saw a lot of old frame houses that were nice except that a wall here or there was tilted. Or a floor had become so sloped that if you dropped a marble on it, it rolled happily to the far wall. (We actually did that.) Apparently, the foundation and framing had shifted and settled over the years. This sort of thing is less likely to occur in an ICF house. Reinforced concrete walls are so strong and rigid that they are very resistant to settling or shifting. If you have wooden floors they can still sag, but where they are held up by the concrete wall that sagging should be reduced.

RESISTANCE TO TERMITES

What about termites—can ICFs resist those, too?
The short answer is yes. But there's some important detail behind this. Simply put, termites can't do any damage to concrete. But even in an ICF house there are ways that termites could get to the wooden parts of a house and do damage to the wood. Therefore, the building codes now require that houses built with ICFs in high-termite areas have some anti-termite precautions.

Can you explain how ICFs can be resistant to termites, yet you may need to take precautions to protect the wood from termites?
Sure. Termites cannot eat concrete, so your structural ICF walls are safe from them. Also, foam does not provide a food source for termites. They can chew it, but they can't live on it. But there has been concern that termites could get into the foam of the ICF and cause mischief. We know that termites will sometimes tunnel into or behind foam that is in contact with the ground. But now there are new building codes that require special antitermite measures if you are going to

put ICFs in the ground in high-termite areas. Common measures include using ICFs made of a special foam that is poisonous to termites, or putting a heavy waterproofing membrane over the foam on the outside that termites can't eat through. These are designed to prevent termites from tunneling into the foam (see the box titled "Termite Prevention Strategies").

If termites can't eat concrete, why be afraid of them getting into the foam?

The fear some people have is that termites will get into the foam underground, then tunnel through the foam until they find wood, and begin eating it (Fig. 2-15). If they were traveling in the foam, you wouldn't be able to see that they were going up the wall, and it would also be hard to hit them with insecticide.

What wood could a termite reach in an ICF house?

There are different possibilities. Some people build just their basement out of ICFs, and the house on top of it is wood frame. If the termites got into the foam underground at the basement, then tunneled up to the main house, in theory they might start eating it just as they would in any other wooden house.

But what if all the outside walls were made of ICFs?

In theory, it is possible that termites might still get to some wood somewhere. In many houses with all the outside walls built of ICFs, there is still a little wood around windows and doors. The floors and roofs are usually still wood as well.

A couple of people I trust told me about houses where this has happened. Termites got into the wooden roof of a one-story ICF house, and no one could see how, so they assumed the bugs had gone through the foam. But as best as I can tell, this is very rare. Now with these new termite-prevention measures in place, you have an extra margin of safety.

So that's why building codes require protection from termites?

Yes, as a precaution. In areas where termite risk is high, building codes require some extra steps to stop termites and make sure the critters won't cause a problem.

In what areas does this requirement for adding termite-prevention measures apply?

By and large, the places where termites can be a significant problem are the coastal states of the southeastern United States, most of California, and Hawaii (Fig. 2-16). Other locations are mostly too cold or too dry for termites to thrive. The building codes have maps that show it exactly.

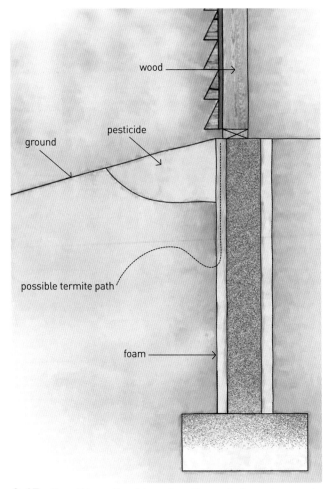

2-15. Possible path of termites through foam to wood.

DESIGN

You mentioned design earlier. How is that an advantage of ICFs?

Well, ICFs are quite flexible as far as design is concerned. You can make your ICF house look like just about anything you would want.

Can an ICF house look like an ordinary house?

Yes. In fact, nine times out of ten it looks the same as every other house on the block. It can be constructed in the same styles and with the same finishes. If an ICF house does look different, it's because the owner wanted it to. About the only way you can tell that it's not wood frame is that the windowsills are deeper. This clues you in that the walls are thicker than they would be with a normal wood-frame home.

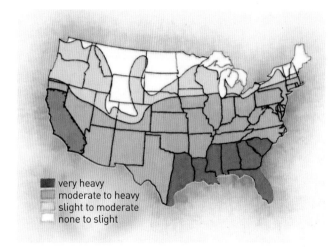

■ very heavy
▨ moderate to heavy
▧ slight to moderate
□ none to slight

2-16. Map of areas of termite risk in the United States.

Termite Prevention Strategies

Your builder should know the approved ways to handle termite prevention in your area. There are basically four options, with more being developed.

No wood. If you build your house with no structural wood, the building codes don't require you to do anything else because there's nothing for the termites to eat.

Structural wood is any lumber used to hold up the house. This includes lumber in the exterior walls, floors, roof, and sometimes an interior wall or two. Some people build their outside walls of ICFs, and their interior walls, floors, and roof out of steel framing instead of wood. Since these houses have no structural wood, most building codes don't require any termite-prevention measures.

Treated foam. The second option is to use an ICF with a special foam that is made with borates in it. Borate compounds kill termites when the pests eat them, but these compounds are considered harmless to humans and animals.

Waterproofing membrane. The third option is to put a special type of waterproofing membrane over the ICF below the ground (Fig. 2-17). In addition to stopping water from seeping into the home, this membrane has been shown to be too tough for termites to burrow through.

Steel mesh. A fourth option is a special fine steel mesh developed especially for termite protection. The mesh is put over the ICF, much like the waterproofing membrane is. These are the major options now available. However, there are plenty of companies coming up with other termite treatments. In coming years there will probably be many more.

2-17. Applying a termite-prevention membrane over an ICF foundation. (Polyguard Products, Inc.)

What finishes can you put on ICFs?

Anything you put on wood houses—wood siding, vinyl siding, stucco, brick, hardboard, whatever. All the finishes go on about the same way and at about the same cost.

Stucco may even be a little less expensive to put onto ICFs. When you put stucco onto a frame wall, you usually have to put a layer of building paper or some other membrane over the house first to keep the stucco from making contact with the wood. This prevents it from getting the wood wet, and from bonding to the wood, which could lead to cracking. With ICFs the membrane is unnecessary—you can put stucco right over the foam.

Another finish that goes onto ICF walls less expensively than onto typical frame walls is what some people call *synthetic stucco*. Some of the manufacturers have also started calling it a **textured acrylic finish**, or **TAF**. This is similar in some ways to stucco, but contains different ingredients. It is now popular because of the many bright colors it can have and the interesting moldings and details that workers can create with it. It is formulated to adhere directly to foam. On a wood-frame building the crew must first wrap the walls with a layer of foam, then apply the finish material. On an ICF wall they skip the first step because the wall surface is already foam. For more on TAFs, see Chapter 9.

Wooden shingles are usually more expensive to put onto ICFs. With ICFs you normally only attach things at the ties, which occur every 6, 8, or 12 inches along the wall. Because separate wooden shingles require nailing at random points all across the wall, you may have to attach a layer of plywood or horizontal wooden strapping first to provide something to nail to where you need it.

For everything else, the methods and costs are about the same for either type of wall. I'll talk more about this when we get to the chapters on the planning and construction of the house.

What about the shape of the walls of the house— corners, curved walls, funky window openings—can those things be done with ICFs?

Again, pretty much anything that you can do with wood you can do with ICFs. A few things are easier and cheaper to do on ICF buildings, and a few are more expensive.

What sorts of design features are less expensive to construct with ICFs?

Things like odd angles, curved walls, and odd-shaped openings can be faster to build and less expensive with ICFs (Fig. 2-18). This is because the foam is fairly easy to cut and paste into just about any shape you want. Curved walls are still more expensive than straight ones, but curving a wall on an ICF building may be less expensive than curving a wall on a frame building.

What features are more expensive?

The one main thing that can be more expensive with ICFs is constructing upper-story walls that don't line up vertically with the lower-story walls below (Fig. 2-19).

A good example from where I live in New England is the **garrison**. This is a second floor that hangs out an extra 16 inches or so over the first floor in front of the house. It provides extra space on the second floor and also creates an overhang for people at the front door. As a different example, there are house designs in which the second floor is smaller than the first. In either of these cases, you have outside walls on the second floor that "float" in space instead of resting directly on the first-floor walls.

Why are second-story walls that don't line up harder to do with ICFs?

Because when you pour the concrete into the ICF walls on the upper story they become very heavy. Since they won't be strong enough yet to support themselves, the contractor will have to build a lot of temporary shoring to hold everything in place until the concrete hardens. This costs time and money. After the concrete is hard, it's possible that the upper-story walls will be strong enough

2-18. A curved ICF wall. (Portland Cement Association)

to hold themselves up even though there is no wall below supporting them. I have seen houses where the engineer specified a certain type of concrete and certain rebar so the walls could do exactly that. It's feasible, but the cost of constructing it is more. It's also possible that you'll need to add something extra to help hold the concrete wall up permanently, such as a steel beam. This costs money as well.

Does this mean that I can't have an ICF house with lower- and upper-story walls that don't line up? No, there *are* ways to do all these things. They just add some cost to the project. I discuss them more in Chapter 7. But usually people opt to take this kind of

2-19. Nonaligning first- and second-story walls.

feature out and save the money. There's only a small minority of house designs that have this type of feature anyway, and most people don't miss it if they cut it.

FINANCIAL BENEFITS OF ICFS

Now what are the "miscellaneous financial benefits" of ICFs you cited as an advantage? First and foremost, almost everyone living in an ICF home has a lower utility bill because the walls make for a more energy-efficient house. How much lower varies, but you can get more information on this by reading Chapter 3.

It should also be possible to put a smaller HVAC system in your house because the house is more energy efficient. This saves some money up front, partly making up for the higher cost of the walls. Getting this savings depends on having a good HVAC contractor, however. I discuss that more in later chapters.

Most people living in an ICF home can also save on homeowner's insurance. Insurance rates are based on the odds that a house will suffer damage—the less likely the damage, the lower the premium. Since houses built of concrete are stronger and can stand up better to disasters like hurricanes and fire, insurance companies calculate that they will tend to suffer less damage. So many of them will give you a lower insurance premium.

It's also possible to get better mortgage terms. For example, mortgage lenders will only lend you so much money to buy a house, based on your income. This is because if they lend you more, they reason that there is a good chance you won't be able to repay it and they'll be stuck with a money-losing loan. But if you have an ICF house, you can often demonstrate that it will be more energy efficient so you'll save money on your fuel bill. The way the lender sees it, this frees up more of your income to pay the mortgage premium, so the lender might be willing to loan you a little more money. These deals can be a bit hard to track down, but may be worth searching for. And there is one brand-new economic benefit. In 2006, the U.S. government passed a new energy bill. In it are provisions that give a contractor a tax credit of $2,000 for each energy-efficient home that he or she builds. In other words, if your contractor builds you an energy-efficient ICF house, the contractor might pay $2,000 less in taxes. You won't see this benefit directly because the savings go to your builder. But it could mean that the builder gives you a little better deal on your house. Just like the smaller HVAC system, this might partly make up for the higher cost of the ICF walls. I cover these benefits in greater detail in Chapter 8.

DISADVANTAGES OF ICFS

So what are the disadvantages to building with ICFs? You mentioned cost at one point. That's a significant one for some people. The exact cost of building with ICFs, just like building with anything, will vary depending on a thousand different factors. The rule of thumb I use is that a house built of ICFs will cost somewhere around 1% to 5% more than one built out of wood frame. So a house that you might have built out of wood for $200,000 might cost you $202,000 to $210,000 if it were built with ICFs.

Although ICFs may cost more now, this difference is likely to shrink in the future. The cost of the ICF blocks should gradually drop as they're manufactured in larger and larger quantities. The labor cost should also decline as crews become more efficient. However, this won't happen overnight. The cost could be essentially the same as wood in a decade or so. It is already the same—or very nearly so—in an occasional house here and there.

But by and large ICF houses do cost a bit more and are likely to for at least several years. Honestly, it would make little sense for you to say, "I want an ICF house but I want to pay less. I think I'll wait a year or two until the cost comes down." For now, just figure that you'll have to pay a little more.

Is the higher cost of an ICF house worth it?

That's totally up to you. Personally, I think it is—that's why I had my house built of ICFs. But other people will have different preferences. That's why I wrote this chapter—so you can look over all the pluses and minuses and decide if ICFs are for you.

Could all the cost savings that can be realized in an ICF house ever outweigh the extra construction costs?

I've heard a few people claim that their energy and insurance cost savings were large enough that they more than made up for the extra money on the mortgage bill. They claimed that using ICFs led to lower total monthly bills, including mortgage, fuel, insurance, and so on. Whether that will happen in your case is hard to figure without more information. I give you a worksheet in Chapter 7 that you can use to estimate and compare your costs.

What about other disadvantages? Earlier on you mentioned that you might have to do more work searching for qualified contractors.

That's right. Depending on where you're located, you might have to put in some serious time to find someone who can do the job for you—and do it right. In most places nowadays, that's not too much of a hassle. However, in some areas there still aren't many contractors who have enough experience with ICFs to do a really good job. So it is possible that your search may go on for a while.

Chapter 6 tells how to find good people. One key is to have a good "leader" of the construction project. The other is to have a crew doing the ICF work that have ICF experience and do quality work. It's nice for the project leader also to have ICF experience, but that's not critical.

Does that mean that all I have to do is find the right people to build the ICF house, and then it will turn out fine?

I wouldn't say that for any house. You should always check up on the work being done. I go over ways to do this in Chapter 9. You should plan on spending a bit more time learning about the construction techniques specific to ICFs and checking details than you would if it were a conventional house, because ICFs are new and different.

But, having said that, you are much less likely to run into problems and get into arguments if you use people who have a good track record and are experienced with ICFs.

You also mentioned that hitting the corners of your walls with your lawn mower could be a problem. What about that?

Well, I did mention this as a possible disadvantage at one point. However, it's so minor that I'm not sure it's worthy of being discussed with all the other things in this chapter. Here's what I can say about it.

In warm climates, where houses are often built on a slab foundation instead of a basement, there is typically less exposed foundation so the exterior wall finish comes closer to the ground. If you hit the wall with something like a lawn mower, you will probably damage the finish material about the same amount, whether the walls are ICF or wood. In fact, the actual structure of the ICF wall will most likely hold up better just because concrete is harder than wood.

If you're in a cold climate, underneath the first floor you usually have a basement or a crawl space. This is ordinarily built of concrete, no matter what the walls above are. You see this on many houses; the band of concrete jutting out of the ground, underneath the finished walls. With ICF walls, there is a layer of foam on the outside of the basement or crawl space walls instead of just plain concrete. Since you don't want the foam to be exposed, the part of the basement or crawl-space walls that is above the ground but below the first floor is usually covered with something hard. A favorite choice is a thick-coat stucco or a similar product. If you hit this hard enough, you can put dents in it, and you will probably want to repair it. And, yes, damage that needs a repair is less likely if you simply had a basement or crawl space with walls built out of conventional, naked concrete. But in practice this type of damage isn't very frequent and isn't hard to fix. In my view, it's a minor consideration.

What about bad installation? I thought I read somewhere about an ICF house with crooked walls.

Good installation is important for any type of construction—wood, ICF, whatever. There have been some bad ICF jobs, just as there have been some bad wood-frame jobs. As far as I can tell, there is no greater chance of problems in building an ICF house than there is with any other new house. The critical con-sideration is the same as it is for any type of house: pick a good contractor and monitor the work wisely. I emphasize this throughout the rest of the book. I also suggest a lot of specific steps for contractor selection and project supervision. When you're having an ICF house built, however, you should plan to spend a bit more time monitoring the work, since a serious mistake in concrete can be difficult to fix. But follow my recommendations and you should be fine.

But isn't there a bigger chance of problems because contractors have less experience with ICFs?

There is if you hire an inexperienced contractor. But would you hire a contractor who had never built a frame house before? I would certainly hope not. You shouldn't hire a contractor who has never built an ICF house before either. That's why I tell you to find expe-rienced ICF installers, and if you can't, then stick with some other form of construction. Fortunately, as I mentioned before, in most places you'll now have a few good contractors to choose from.

2-20. A completed ICF house. (IntegraSpec ICF)

What other potential problem areas should I be asking about?

That's about it. Make sure to weigh the benefits of ICFs against the cost and (in some areas) the availability of qualified contractors. If you want to get into more detail on energy and energy savings, I cover this in Chapter 4. If you're worried about things like indoor air quality, I cover that in Chapter 5. Although this can pertain to ICFs, it's more a question of how you design your HVAC system and how you maintain your house.

The big questions on pluses and minuses have all been addressed here. You should have a pretty good idea now about whether or not ICFs might be right for you. The next three chapters should help you finalize your decision (Fig. 2-20).

CHAPTER 3

What to Build the Rest of the House Out Of

WHEN PEOPLE TALK about an ICF house, they usually mean a house with all its exterior walls built of ICFs. However, many other arrangements are possible, too. It's possible to build only some of the exterior walls out of ICFs; you can build

Casting a floor slab.

all the exterior walls *and* other elements (like interior walls, floors, and the roof) out of ICFs. It's also possible to build some of these out of totally different materials —neither wood nor ICFs.

HOUSE CONSTRUCTION 101

This sounds complicated. Can you start at the beginning? What parts of a house can get built out of what?

OK, let's start with conventional construction. In warm climates the typical house is built on a slab of concrete that rests on the ground. This slab is usually about 4 inches thick. It's sometimes called the **floor slab** because it serves as the floor for the first story (Fig. 3-1). It is also technically the foundation of the house because the remainder of the house rests on it. The rest of the house is usually built out of wood. The exterior walls are wood frame, the interior walls are wood frame, and the roof is wood frame.

By the way, on a two-story house, the second floor is sometimes called a floor deck. It is technically a deck because it is raised up, not resting on the ground, as the floor slab does. Sometimes roofs are also called decks, especially when they are flat.

3-1. A floor slab, with ICF wall construction under way on top. (Arxx Building Products)

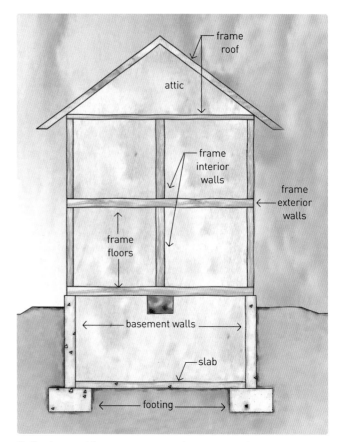

3-2. A wood frame two-story house on a basement.

How are houses in cold climates different?

They have foundations that are dug down into the ground. In cold climates the ground freezes. If you just put a slab on the top of the ground, the earth underneath will freeze and thaw during the winter months. As the ground freezes and thaws, it will rise and settle. This up and down motion of the ground will lift up the slab unevenly and crack it. The house will potentially end up in pieces, with walls bent and crooked. Not a pretty picture.

Therefore, in cold northern climates we usually dig down about 6 feet and build walls out of concrete. This far down, the ground doesn't freeze, so the house rests on a stable base. Actually, after digging down, we first build a thing known as a **footing**. This is basically a ribbon of concrete about 8 inches thick and 16 inches wide that extends all the way around the perimeter, underneath where the walls go. The concrete walls sit on top of the footing. We also pour a slab of concrete on the ground between the walls. The footing, walls, and slab together create a basement. The slab is the floor.

All these parts of the basement are built out of concrete for a couple of reasons. First, concrete is very resistant to water, insects, and vermin. That's critical below ground, where things are wet and critters do lots of burrowing. Second, especially when it is reinforced with steel, concrete is strong enough to support the weight of the ground pushing against it without breaking or bending over time.

In a typical house of the cold North, the contractor builds a wooden floor deck on top of the basement walls. This is the first-story floor. Then the contractor builds wood-frame exterior walls on top of the floor deck. If the house is to be only one story, the roof goes on top next. If it's two stories, next come the second-story floor deck, the second-story exterior walls, and then the roof (Fig. 3-2). And, of course, interior walls built of wood frame are installed along the way. As you might guess, the basement is technically the foundation of the house.

Does this cover all the main types of houses?
Almost. In moderate climates, such as North Carolina or Missouri, it's not always necessary to dig down 6 feet or so to get below the depth where the ground freezes. Sometimes 2 to 3 feet is enough. So here we dig down a few feet, put in a footing, and build concrete walls on top that are 3 to 4 feet tall—just enough for the walls to rise above the ground. The house is then built on these short walls. Usually there's not even a slab poured between the walls, as there would be in a basement. The short walls are often called **stem walls**, and the footing and stem walls together create an area under the house called a **crawl space** (Fig. 3-3). The stem walls and footing act as the foundation for the house. There are other variations on these basic types of houses, but this covers the vast majority of homes in the United States and Canada today.

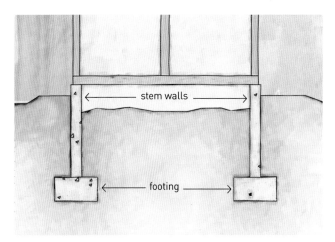

3-3. A crawl-space foundation.

ICF BASEMENT

Can ICFs be used for just one part of the house?
Well, most of the very first houses built with ICFs used them for the basement walls only. A standard frame house then went on top of the ICF basement. By using ICFs for the basement walls, the builder could provide a basement with concrete walls and a layer of foam on each face.

Why would someone want just a basement built with ICFs?
It can make a lot of sense if you intend to use the basement for living space at some point. If the walls are ICF, the basement is already insulated, and they're ready for attaching electrical wiring and wallboard. You get a nice space without too much extra work. If you do not plan to finish a basement, ICFs may not be a good choice, since most codes require the foam to be covered by a fire-resistant material such as drywall when used in a basement or other living space. Really, the benefits are mostly the same as they are when you build the above-grade walls out of ICFs. It's just that you only get them in the basement. Let's look at Table 3-1, a chart of the advantages I discussed in Chapter 2, and see which ones apply to the basement.

Table 3-1

Comparison of an ICF Basement to a Traditional Concrete Basement	
Energy efficiency	Higher with ICF basement
Disaster resistance	Same with both
Comfort	Higher with ICF basement
Quiet	Same with both
Strength	Same with both
Durability	Similar or lower with ICF basement
Design flexibility	Higher with ICF basement
Financials	Maybe a tad better with ICF basement

The two layers of foam give you an energy efficiency and comfort level that's going to be hard to match with a conventional concrete wall. To finish a conventional basement, contractors usually build a wood-frame wall inside the concrete walls. This is sometimes called **furring out** the wall. Then they put fiberglass insulation in the wall and cover it with wallboard. This provides a reasonably well-insulated wall, but doesn't match the insulation of the ICF wall.

The features based on strength and durability are about the same for both because either way the structure of the basement walls is reinforced concrete. Those walls will have about the same strength whether or not they're encased in foam. I would even rate durability a little lower for the ICF basement walls because the foam on the outside needs something hard put over it so it doesn't get dented by lawn mowers and the like. But, as I said before, that's pretty easy to take care of.

Design flexibility is usually higher with ICFs because you can cut and paste the forms to create unusual features like curves and angles. Some people care about this in the basement and others don't. It might be necessary in the basement if you plan to have unusual walls in the upper stories. The walls above may need to be supported by a basement of the same shape.

The financials benefit because of your lower energy bills, but you probably won't get lower insurance premiums or better mortgage terms just because the basement is ICF. That's too small a part of the house to make a lot of difference on the total energy bill or disaster resistance.

You need to weigh these advantages against the usual disadvantages of higher cost and sometimes a greater effort required to find a qualified contractor.

STEM WALLS

Does anyone ever build just stem walls out of ICFs?
Sure. This is sometimes done for energy efficiency. You can often lose heat (or cold) through the stem walls, too. It can travel down through the floor, into the crawl space, and out the stem walls.

Also, sometimes ICFs are used for stem walls just because it's faster and easier for the contractor. Tossing a few light foam blocks in the back of the truck to build some stem walls can be easier than moving the heavier removable forms that are used for conventional concrete walls. And when you're done, you don't need to strip off the forms and haul them away. For this reason it's even possible that in some cases you'll get a better price on stem walls built of ICFs. But there isn't a lot more benefit from ICF stem walls to the owner. The crawl space won't be occupied, so things like comfort and sound reduction aren't so important.

EXTERIOR WALLS

So what's the next step up from just a basement built of ICFs?
Generally speaking, it's all the exterior walls built out of ICFs, right up to the roof. They could be built on a basement, on stem walls, or on a slab. When ICF upper-story walls are built on a basement or stem walls, those foundation walls are almost always built of ICFs, too. It doesn't make much sense to build conventional concrete walls for the foundation and

3-4a & 3-4b. ICF house under construction (a) and the finished house (b).
(Arxx Building Products)

put ICF walls on top. You would initially save some money on building the foundation, but overall you would probably lose much of it because of the extra time and cost involved in switching between two different types of construction. You would also lose the benefits of the ICF foundation. Normally, when we say "ICF house," this is what we mean—a house with all its exterior walls built of ICFs (Figs. 3-4a and b).

MIXED ICFS AND WOOD WALLS

Do you ever build some of the upper walls out of ICFs and some out of wood frame?

Every now and then you hear about a house with a first story built out of ICFs and a second story built out of wood frame. Usually this doesn't make much sense because you only get the benefits of ICFs on half the house. If they were worth it on the first story, why aren't they worth it on the second? The total benefits for the house are reduced.

However, this arrangement can make sense if the second story will have walls that don't line up with the first-story walls. For example, this combination may be used with the garrisons sometimes built in my part of the country. In that situation, the wood-frame walls can be constructed to overhang the lower story economically. But in this type of situation it's still most common to construct *only* the second-story walls floating in space out of wood frame. You still build the walls that line up over the first-story walls out of ICFs.

Some crews prefer to build the second story out of wood if it will be more "cut up" than the first story. That means it has more odd windows and irregular details like dormers. They are more comfortable constructing all those odd angles and things out of wood. However, this doesn't really make a lot of sense to me. Most of these things are just as easy to create with ICFs as they are with wood. If the crew is not very experienced with ICFs, it may be easier for *them* to use wood. However, once they are more experienced, they will probably be just as comfortable building all these wall sections out of ICFs.

OTHER THINGS BUILT OUT OF ICFS

What can you build out of ICFs besides the exterior walls of the house?

I'm glad you asked. Nowadays you sometimes find people building interior walls, floors, and roofs out of ICFs as well.

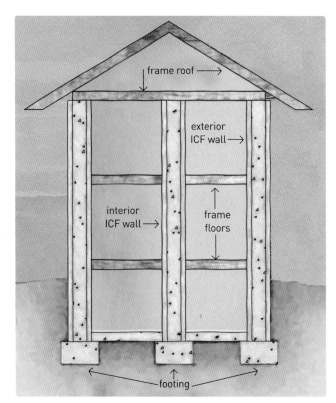

3-5. Aligned walls on the basement, first, and second stories.

Why would you want an interior wall built out of ICFs?

Usually it's for specialized reasons. Some people like to build the walls of a media room out of ICFs because they stop the sound from going into the rest of the house. Sometimes you may also need an extra-strong wall running down the middle of the house to hold up a heavy floor. This may be the case if you have a concrete floor above.

Another specialized use of ICFs for interior walls is the **safe room**. This is a room inside the house built with high-strength walls like ICFs for people to hide in during a hurricane or tornado. Usually it's a large, walk-in closet. When it's built of ICFs, the ceiling above it is ICF, too, and the one door is usually made of high-strength steel with a beefed-up latch. The occupants of the house run into the safe room during the storm, lock up, and ride it out.

Who uses a safe room?

Mostly people in the part of the country nicknamed Tornado Alley. This includes Oklahoma, northern Texas, and parts of Arkansas, Missouri, and Illinois. They can get a measure of safety from high winds by building just one room with high-strength materials.

But you said it's difficult to have ICF walls that aren't on top of another ICF wall below them. How can you just put these interior walls and safe rooms wherever you want?

Good question. You can't easily have an ICF wall that isn't directly on top of another ICF wall or concrete wall below. The reason is the same one I gave before—it's hard to create a concrete wall that's suspended in space. In fact, most of the interior ICF walls you find are in the South, where the homes are mostly built on concrete slabs sitting on top of the ground. So they just build the ICF wall on the slab, where it's well supported.

What about in the North?

It's the same story, just down one level. It's easy to build an ICF wall in the basement. It just rests on the ground. Actually, it will probably require its own footing underneath, but that's really not a problem because the crew can just build that footing when they build the usual basement footing. An interior wall on the first story is practical if you have one directly below it in the basement. And a second-story wall is practical if you have first-story and basement walls lined up below (Fig. 3-5).

Are there any other walls you might build out of ICFs?

One other type that pops up every now and then are the garage walls. Those are actually exterior walls, but most people don't think of them when I say "exterior walls," so I mention them specifically.

Do I want my garage walls to be built out of ICFs?

That's up to you. Some of the advantages of ICFs don't really apply to a garage because it doesn't have people

Table 3-2

Comparison of ICF Garage Walls to Wood-Frame Garage Walls	
Energy efficiency	Higher with ICF, but only matters if you heat or cool your garage
Disaster resistance	Higher with ICF, which keeps the car safer
Comfort	Better with ICF, but only matters if you'll be spending time there
Quiet	Quieter with ICF, but only matters if you'll be spending time there
Strength	Higher with ICF, but not always important
Durability	Better with ICF
Design flexibility	Higher with ICF, but most garages are simple boxes anyway
Financials	More expensive with ICF

living in it. Then again, some advantages do still apply, especially if you plan to insulate the walls and finish the interior for, say, a workshop. Let's consider the list of ICF benefits again (Table 3-2), to see what you might gain by building your garage out of ICFs instead of wood frame.

The advantages are still there, but the question is this: How important are they to have in the garage? A lot of people who build the exterior walls of the house out of ICFs do the garage with them as well. Often it's not all that much extra money because the crew is already set up to do the ICF work. However, you can certainly build the garage out of wood frame if that saves significant money.

FLOORS

So what can you build out of ICFs besides interior and exterior walls?

The other main things built with ICFs are floors and roofs.

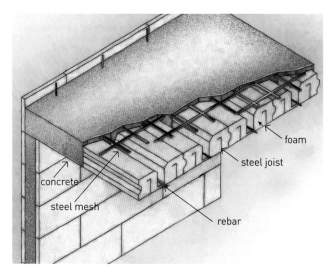

3-6. Cutaway view of an ICF floor deck.

it. Since there's only one layer of foam, it's more of an "open-faced sandwich" than the "full sandwich" that you get with the wall forms (Fig. 3-6).

Is that all there is to it—foam and concrete and steel reinforcement?
No, there's a little bit more. Embedded inside the foam, running parallel to the trenches, are light steel studs, called **joists** by builders since they run horizontally. These help keep the forms stiff so they can hold up the concrete when it's still wet. Also, they give you something to attach the ceiling to when you install the wallboard to the underside.

You mentioned that sometimes you might build an interior wall out of ICFs to hold up a floor. How does that come into play?
If the distance from the front wall to the back is very long, it may be tough for the concrete floor to span that distance. A special wall in the middle can help support that floor. In fact, this is true for all types of floors—wood, concrete, and steel.

Consider a wood-frame floor. When the distance that the floor has to span gets too long, the wooden pieces that support the floor (called **joists**) will flex and eventually sag. To make sure this doesn't happen, you use taller joists, which gives you a thicker floor that will span the distance with less flex. There are also specially constructed wooden assemblies called **trusses** that you can use instead of joists to do the job. But for longer and longer distances, you find that you have to create thicker and thicker floors and spend more and more money. After a while it becomes impractical. So you build a strong wall about halfway between the front and back of the house below the floor deck. The floor rests on this, so it only has to span half the distance on the front, and half the distance on the back. This way, you can get away with a shallower floor built in two parts, and it turns out to be less expensive.

It's the same with an ICF floor. If your house is, say, 40 feet from front to back, you can build a concrete floor to span that distance but it has to be quite thick and expensive. Somewhere before that distance, it often

How do you build floors and roofs out of ICFs? Can you turn the blocks sideways?
No, you don't use the same forms at all. Floors and roofs are what we call **decks**—flat, horizontal structures raised up above the ground and resting on something else. Constructing decks presents a challenge because they extend over great distances without support below, yet they are quite thin. Nonetheless, some years ago inventors came up with a way to create a deck with foam forms.

Let's look at the ICF floor first. ICF floor forms are long (up to about 40 feet), narrow pieces of foam that can be a foot thick. The workers set them on top of the walls at each end, so they span the house front to back. These narrow forms are set side by side. They have long, narrow trenches in them, so the whole set of formwork looks a little like it's corrugated. It's braced with special supports below to hold it in place until the floor is done.

When it's all in place the workers put steel reinforcing bars in place in the trenches of the forms. Reinforcing also goes on top, just above the top surface of foam. Then they pour concrete over it all. After the concrete hardens, the floor will stand on its own, so the braces below are removed. This creates a layer of strong, reinforced concrete with foam beneath becomes more practical to build an extra-strong wall out of ICFs in the middle of the lower level. Then you can rest the concrete floor on this. It really becomes more like two floors that span 20 feet, not one spanning 40 feet.

Could this center wall be built out of wood?
Yes, and it often is when the floor is wood. But when the floor is concrete, the weight on the center wall will be much greater. So an extra-strong wall is necessary to hold up the floor, and concrete makes more sense. You could do the center wall out of wood, but it might tend to compress over time from the weight. A concrete wall will compress much less.

Why would you want your floor to be built out of ICFs?
Well, a lot of the ICF advantages still apply. Let's look at Table 3-3 to see how we benefit by using ICFs for a floor deck instead of wood.

To start with the easy stuff, qualities related to strength (disaster resistance, strength, durability) will tend to be better with an ICF floor deck. The rigid concrete floor ties the walls together and supports them. You can prove this to yourself with a simple demon-stration. Get an empty cardboard box, take the lid off, and push against one of the sides. It bends. Now put the lid on and tape it to the sides all the way around. Push the side again. It will not bend nearly as easily. The top is a "deck" that helps stiffen up the sides by connecting them to each other. Another thing to note is that concrete floors tend to be more rigid. This means you will get less vibration and "bounce" with them.

Energy efficiency is a different issue. Usually you heat or cool the whole house, so having insulation in your floor isn't much of a benefit. But if you heat or cool your stories in *zones*—that is, if you keep the first floor at a significantly different temperature than the second floor—then the ICF floor can help a little. It insulates each story individually, so it's easier for your heating and cooling equipment to maintain different temperatures on different floors.

Table 3-3

Comparison of an ICF Floor Deck to a Wood-Frame Floor Deck	
Energy efficiency	May be higher with ICF if you zone your heating/cooling
Disaster resistance	Higher with ICF
Comfort	May be higher with ICF if you zone your heating/cooling
Quiet	Quieter between stories with ICF
Strength	Stronger with ICF
Durability	Higher with ICF
Design flexibility	About the same
Financials	More expensive with ICF
Bonus: Radiant heating	Easy to install in-floor radiant heating with ICF floor decks

Comfort is similar; however, the ICF floor can help if you maintain separate heating and cooling zones. But there is another way that the ICF floor can enhance your comfort. With the floor made out of massive concrete, it can help to keep the indoor temperature even more stable than it would be if only the exterior walls were made of concrete. It takes a while to move the temperature of that much concrete up or down. So once you get the house at the temperature you want it (say, 71°F), the concrete won't easily change temperature, either up or down. The indoor temperature will shift only very gradually. This can be a problem, however, if you want to quickly raise the temperature, say, after setting back the thermostat overnight or when coming home from a vacation.

What about quietness with a concrete floor?
On that, a concrete floor may give you a big benefit. It depends on your circumstances. The concrete floor will reduce the amount of sound that goes from the second story to the first, and vice versa. Say you have kids who make a lot of noise in their rooms upstairs, or down in the rumpus room in the basement. In that case a concrete floor that separates them from you on

What's a decorative concrete floor? Pretty much what it sounds like. There are now a lot of concrete pigments and "stamps" that contractors can use to give regular concrete different coloring and texture. Concrete floors can look like large slabs of stone or they can have their own unique color washes. They can look like exotic tile, cobblestones, or even brick (Fig. 3-7). And it's a very durable finish, of course. But the quality of the work very much depends on the skill of the people doing it. It's a highly specialized craft, and some craftspeople are a lot better at it than others.

There are many ways to create these finishes, and concrete "artists" are inventing more all the time. Some of the photos you see nowadays are stunning. Sometimes the decorative work is done by the workers who pour the concrete floor. They do the decorative work when the concrete has just gone down and is still wet. They know the look they are supposed to produce in advance and they have everything ready. They throw powdered pigments onto the concrete in the correct pattern. Those pigments soak into the concrete and color it. Then, if the concrete is to have a texture or relief pattern, they lay rubber "stamps" on the top and push them down. It's like the old wax seals on envelopes, on which a ring was used to make an impression in the hot wax. This is how they get a surface texture like stone or brick.

There are also designers, artists, and interior decorators who do some very fine and original work. They usually come in after the concrete is hard. They use stains to color the surface and maybe saws and grinders to create some subtle indentations.

3-7. A decorative concrete floor. (Distinctive Concrete Boston, Inc.)

the first floor can give you a lot more quiet. Or if you are entertaining on the first floor, they can sleep better on the second.

What about durability and design with a concrete floor?

A concrete floor will generally be more durable because it's less prone to sagging. Like concrete walls, it is also highly resistant to rot, rust, and insects. Most concrete floors are also very durable in a fire. As we noted before, this won't save the occupants from smoke inhalation, but it will hold the structure together longer. This may help someone who has survived smoke inhalation, but is late in getting out of the building. It might also help reduce property damage until the fire department gets there.

In most ways the design flexibility with ICF floors is not different from that with wood. By and large, floors are flat, and you can make a flat floor out of either material. You can make openings in either type. You can put all the usual coverings over either type of floor—hardwood, vinyl, carpet, tile, and all the rest. But there is one decorative feature that you can do a bit more easily on a concrete floor: produce a decorative concrete surface (see sidebar, "Decorative Concrete Floors").

So now what about financial benefits with ICF floors? Well, you might have a slightly lower energy bill than you would with ICF walls and wood-floor decks. That's discussed in greater detail in Chapter 4. But to be honest, having an ICF floor probably won't make a huge difference once you have the walls built of ICFs.

You probably won't get any bigger break on your insurance or better terms on your mortgage just because you have a concrete floor deck. You already get most of that from building the walls out of ICFs.

At the bottom of Table 3-3, you also list a "bonus" for ICF floors called radiant heating. What is that?
Well, a concrete floor like an ICF floor is a convenient place to install a type of heating distribution system called **in-floor radiant heating**. The conventional house has a system of hot-water radiators or air ducts; its heating and cooling system sends hot water through the radiators or air through the ducts to warm the house in winter, and cold air to cool it in summer. But in-floor radiant heating warms up the house differently: The heating system pumps warm water through tubing in the floor. With a concrete floor, there are actual plastic tubes that are set on top of the forms before the concrete is poured (Fig. 3-8). After the concrete cures, the tubes are inside there for keeps. When the warm water goes through the tubing, it warms the floor and that warms the house.

What's so great about radiant in-floor heating?
Comfort and efficiency. People who have it swear by it. The heating is very, very even and gentle. No hot spots, no cold spots, no noise, and no drafts. It also tends to be more energy efficient. With hot-air distribution, you usually get some leaks, and you have ductwork running through some cold areas where some heat is lost. Radiant heating generally gets the heat where it's going with only modest losses and doesn't leak.

I'm glad you brought up leaks. Doesn't the radiant tubing sometimes start leaking in the floor?
It really doesn't. The design and installation of radiant in-floor heating systems are geared toward preventing leakage. Pipes in the floor slab have been a regular practice in houses in the South for decades. Once in a while they get a leak in an old house or a poorly done

3-8. Tubing (white) in place for radiant in-floor heating before pouring concrete. (IntegraSpec ICF)

job. If it's bad, someone might have to come in, chip away some concrete, and fix the damaged pipe. But again, this is rare.

Can't I get radiant heating in a wooden floor?
You can. In that case the tubing is fastened to the underside of the flooring with brackets. The limitation of this arrangement is that you don't have that mass of concrete to warm up and evenly spread the heat. Many people still feel it's better than hot-air distribution, but not as good as when the tubing is embedded in concrete.

What if I don't want in-floor radiant heating?
No problem. If you have a concrete floor you don't *have* to install in-floor radiant heating. In fact, most people don't—they just stick with regular radiators or air ducts. Certainly, conventional heating systems are usually less expensive. But if you want radiant heating, a concrete floor has the advantage of accommodating it well.

I get the advantages of a concrete floor deck. What are the disadvantages?
As with walls, there are the cost and availability of crews to do the work. Concrete floor decks almost always cost a significant amount more than wood floors. The extra cost is usually in the range of $5 per

3-9. Forms and steel reinforcement in place for a sloped ICF roof. (Lite-Form Technologies)

ROOFS

You also mentioned roofs. How can you build a roof out of ICFs?
Pretty much the same way you build a floor deck. You use the same special forms. In fact, if you make a flat roof, you do it almost exactly the same way you build a floor. You set the deck forms on top of the walls, add reinforcement, and cast your concrete. The only real difference is that no one sets more walls on top afterwards because you're already at the top of the building. An ICF roof can also be sloped. To create a sloped roof, the crew sets the forms at an angle and adjusts the braces underneath to hold them that way. The rebar goes above, and then they cast the concrete (Fig. 3-9).

But what about gravity? Doesn't the concrete slide off when you pour it on a roof?
Gravity definitely limits how steep a pitch you can get. Crews can readily build a roof sloped up to about 20 degrees. That's what a contractor calls a *4-in-12* roof, because it rises up 4 feet for every 12 feet that it extends in the horizontal direction (Fig. 3-10). The workers pouring the concrete just use a stiff mix and

square foot or more. In some cases it is much more. But you'd have to get an exact quote to know what it is for your particular job.

There actually are lots and lots of concrete floor decks built, and there are plenty of contractors who do them. However, they are typically used in commercial buildings rather than houses. Finding contractors who do them on the small scale of a house may take some work, depending on where you are. Actually, many contractors who do ICF walls can also handle floors, or at least are in contact with other contractors who do them. I go over all this in Chapter 6.

Are there other disadvantages?
Some people don't like the feel of a naked concrete floor. This is a matter of taste. Some people feel the floor is too hard; others like that it is "firm." Much like a tile floor, it can also feel cold to the touch. But in the South this issue doesn't come up very much—there the floor on the first level is usually concrete anyway because it's a slab on the ground. So people are used to it. Besides, if you have a floor covering (like carpet, hardwood, vinyl, or tiles) on top of the concrete, that will determine the feel of the floor more than the concrete underneath. And the vast majority of concrete floor decks in a house have a floor covering over them.

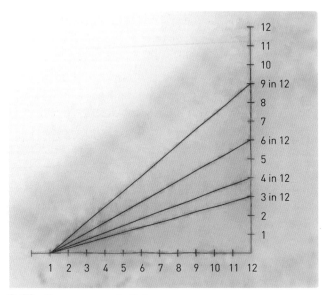

3-10. Common roof pitches.

use their trowels to push it into position. If they do it right, the concrete stays in place long enough to harden. For any steeper slope, it's difficult to keep the concrete in position long enough for it to harden in place. It has been done, but only with extra measures used by highly skilled crews.

So why would I want a concrete roof? Is the strength the attraction?

Actually, there are a lot of benefits. The roof helps enclose the house, just as the exterior walls do. So most of the advantages of ICF walls apply to an ICF roof, too. And the amount of improvement can be significant. Let's look at Table 3-4 to compare the roofs.

Once you build the walls out of ICFs, the roof becomes one of the main remaining "weak points" of the house. The ICF walls block heat transfer (for energy efficiency), resist disasters, keep the temperature even, muffle sound, and hold the house rigid. But the standard wood roof doesn't help as much as an ICF roof would to further these benefits. Building the roof out of ICFs buttons the roof up, too.

For example, with ICF walls you will get a reduction in heat transfer and air infiltration between the inside and outside *through the walls.* That saves energy. But you will still get quite a bit of heat loss through the roof if it is not well insulated and sealed against air leaks. A lot of heat loss can result from air leakage where wires, pipes, chimneys, and other building components penetrate the ceiling. And the point where the roof connects to the walls is often poorly insulated in conventional construction. Once you add an ICF roof, air leakage is greatly reduced and the connection between walls and roof is virtually seamless. So those energy weak points in the house are sealed.

The same goes for the other benefits I mentioned. In high winds, concrete houses are highly resistant to being bent out of shape or torn apart by wind. But the major exception is the wood roof. In hurricanes and tornadoes, wooden roofs are still pulled apart with some frequency. But once you put a concrete roof on top, the chances of the roof yielding drop sharply. In

Table 3-4

Comparison of an ICF Roof to a Wood-Frame Roof	
Energy efficiency	Somewhat higher with ICF
Disaster resistance	Higher with ICF
Comfort	Higher with ICF
Quiet	Quieter with ICF
Strength	Stronger with ICF
Durability	Higher with ICF
Design flexibility	Lower with ICF
Financials	More expensive with ICF

addition, putting a rigid concrete "lid" on top of the concrete "box" stiffens up the structure a lot. The concrete roof plugs one of the remaining holes in the blocking of sound from the outside.

What about durability?

In principle, an ICF roof should be more durable, too. The roof will be less subject to rot, to shifting over time, or to destruction by termites. Decay in roof structures can be a big problem, particularly in cathedral ceilings, which are difficult to ventilate properly. These are no longer a problem with concrete.

Why do you rate design flexibility lower with concrete?

Because it's harder to make very complex, ornate roofs with concrete. But I doubt that is much of a consideration for most people. If you look at a lot of new high-end homes, they have very complex roofs with lots of ins and outs and valleys and gables. These are interesting to look at, but complicated to build. And it's going to be even more complicated to build these intricate roof designs with ICF roof deck systems. However, it can be done. It will just increase the labor hours and the overall cost.

Then there's the issue of roof slope. If you want a steep slope (more than about 20 degrees), that's difficult to get with ICF decks. I've heard of crews who can go higher, but you'll probably have to pay a premium for it—that is, if you can find someone to do it.

So the question is going to be how important these things are to you. I'd guess that 80% of all roofs built on houses in the United States can be done with ICF forms without these complications cropping up. But for the other 20%, you might find the costs mounting fast.

Why do you rate the "financial" advantage only a little different compared with wood roofs?

Because I expect you'll get most of the financial benefits from doing just the walls out of ICFs. An ICF roof might give you a bit more of a bump. Energy savings should go up over and above what they were with ICF walls alone. But I doubt you'd get a bigger break on your insurance rates. Insurance companies give you a higher rating when you build the walls of ICFs, but they don't have an even higher rating than that to hand out for the all-concrete house. More on this in Chapter 8. And I doubt you'll get any better mortgage terms. Most of the superior mortgages that you can qualify for with ICFs are what are called *energy-efficiency mortgages.* But as with insurance, most of the mortgage plans that reward energy efficiency have one simple cutoff. If you beat their energy standards, you get better terms. The lender won't give you even better terms because you beat the standard by a *lot*. In fact, the real challenge with energy-efficiency mortgages is finding a lender that hands them out at all. That will be your major task. There is more on this in Chapter 8, too.

Do the usual disadvantages of ICFs apply to roofs as well?

Yes, they do. And, I must admit, even more so. ICF roof decks will be more expensive than wood roofs. And, for that matter, if they have a slope they will be even more expensive than ICF floor decks. And there are not yet many crews capable of building them, although the number is growing. It's exactly the same situation as for the ICF floors, because the roofs are built about the same way, out of the same products, and by the same people.

How do you put the roof shingles on an ICF roof?

That's a good question. Any common roof covering— including shingles—can go on an ICF roof, but the methods may be a little different from the way they go on a frame roof. Let's start with how you cover flat roofs, because that's easier to explain.

Over a flat roof, workers either brush on a hot, tarlike substance or they lay on a heavy rubber membrane. This waterproof layer may go directly on the roof.

These types of roof covering are the same as they are for conventional flat-roof construction. Flat roofs are common in commercial buildings, and the "hot-applied" tar and rubber membranes are the typical methods of finishing them. One additional task involved is to put some drains on top of the roof. Drains take the water off, and that prevents the water from building up, which might put undue weight on the building or might create so much constant pressure on the membrane that the water eventually breaks through and creates a leak.

Of course, this type of roof is not commonly built on houses, so it's important to get a crew that is experienced with it. I talk about that more in Chapter 6.

How do you put the covering on a sloped roof?

Most of the roof coverings that are commonly put on a sloped roof are nailed on. In the United States and Canada, the common coverings are asphalt shingles, clay or concrete roof tiles, slate, and special metal sheet. Each of these is nailed on in some fashion. Of course, it is difficult to drive nails directly into concrete. Therefore, the contractors need to come up with some alternative, and there are a variety of them. Perhaps the most common one is to attach strips of wood (called **strapping**) to the concrete, and then nail the roofing to the strapping. They may attach the strapping by embedding it when they pour the concrete, or by attaching it with special concrete fasteners later on.

If you live in an area prone to violent storms, consider building a flat concrete roof that is covered with a sloped wooden roof. I call it a safe ceiling because it has some similarities to a safe room. Like a concrete safe room, the ICF safe ceiling is covered by wood framing. In this case, however, you get the benefits of a safe room for the whole house except the attic (Fig. 3-11).

The house will be a very strong "box" that will resist disasters well. In high winds, it is possible that the upper roof built of wood may be torn away and may have to be replaced, but the occupants and the main house should be well protected. In addition to safety, the entire house below the attic will enjoy all the benefits listed above in the section on sloped ICF roofs. The house will be very well insulated and energy efficient. It will also have all the comfort, quiet, strength, and durability characteristics of a house with a sloped concrete roof. The design flexibility of the roofline should actually be the same as with a standard wood-frame roof because it's built out of wood frame. And the financial benefits should be the same as with a sloped concrete roof—that is, a tad better than if you had only a frame roof.

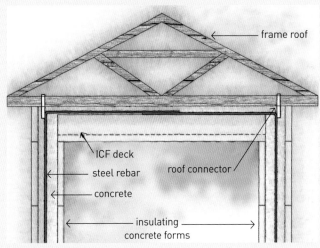

3-11. Diagram of roof area, showing a safe ceiling below roof.

Does this limit what types of roof covering I can have installed on a concrete roof?
No. Any roof covering that can be installed on a frame roof can be installed on a concrete roof. In fact, the tar and membrane types of roofing that go on flat roofs can be installed just as easily and inexpensively on an ICF roof. In some cases they can even be installed on sloped ICF roofs.

But on a sloped roof it is most common to use a nailed roofing. On an ICF roof, the cost of using a nailed roofing will be higher. This is because the contractor must do the extra work of installing the strapping to concrete and must pay for the strapping material. Like most cost issues, your best course of action is to get a price quote from a reputable contractor and decide based on that.

In any case, it is important that you decide what roof covering you will use before the roof is built. Anything can be put on, but the cost and efficiency of installing the covering will be much more favorable if the crew knows what the covering will be and can plan for it. I discuss this more in Chapter 7.

It sounds like building a concrete roof is not much of an option unless I want to spend a lot of money.
You can always price it and check. A flat roof is definitely a less-expensive roof deck to build with ICFs, compared with a sloped roof.

But what if I really want a sloped roof, or I need a sloped roof because I'm in a climate with a lot of snow, and I don't have a lot of money?
That's a good question. Flat roofs are definitely risky in homes. They are harder to seal effectively and prone to leaking. If you really want a concrete roof, there's a good compromise solution that gives you about 75% of the benefits of a sloped concrete roof and may not be too much more expensive than a conventional roof. I call it a **safe ceiling**. Some contractors call it a **two-part roof**. It's essentially a flat ICF roof with a

conventional wood-frame roof built on top (see sidebar, "Disaster-Resistant Ceilings").

That sounds like a pretty good idea, but won't it still be a lot more expensive? It seems like you're really building two roofs instead of one.

Yes, it will definitely be more expensive than just a conventional wood frame roof. But it won't necessarily be terribly expensive if it's done efficiently. Once you have a concrete top on the box, engineering studies confirm that the roof above it doesn't need to be as strong or have as many pieces. The opportunity to build the framing with less wood could save some money. And you don't have to worry about how you will attach the roof covering—it just goes on the usual way.

But, as always, you really have to price it. The safe ceiling is new and different. The wooden part of the roof *can* be built with less wood, but that doesn't mean you can find contractors who know *how* to build it with less wood, or that your local building officials will let them do it. When something is new, people may be uncertain about how to do it correctly, and they don't want to build or approve a house that might have problems because they will get blamed. So it might be a chore to find contractors who know how to build a lighter, wood-frame roof. And there might be some delays and costs while the contractor explains things to the building officials. All this is tough to generalize about. The best you can do is ask your contractor.

Are there any other ways to get concrete floors and roofs beside ICF deck systems?

Sure. Actually there are quite a few ways to build concrete decks. A few of these ways work quite well in small buildings. They can be even less expensive than the ICF deck systems. The main difference is that they have no built-in insulation. However, this is often not important for a floor deck. All the other advantages are pretty much the same. For the roof, insulation is more important, of course. In that case you would want to be sure that a good layer of insulation was added somehow.

How can I find out more about these other types of concrete floors and roofs?

The same contractors who do ICF walls and ICF floors and roofs often know about these other types of concrete floors, too. Many of these contractors will give you a choice. They will build you decks either out of ICF deck forms or out of one of these other systems. They should be able to help you decide what's best for you.

Are there any other details I should be thinking about with an ICF roof?

Yes, there is one more important one. If you have ICF exterior walls and an ICF roof, you will have what is called a very "tight" building envelope. That means that very little air will leak in and out. That's a good thing in terms of energy efficiency, avoiding uncomfortable drafts, and giving you good control over your indoor air. I discuss this a lot more in Chapters 4 and 5.

But if you're going to build a really tight house, you need to think through ventilation and air-quality issues. Many contractors recommend some fans or air inlets in your heating and cooling system to get a controlled amount of outside air brought in.

Is house ventilation something special that has to be considered?

Nowadays this is very much on everyone's radar, so you probably won't even have it bring it up yourself. All houses are gradually being built tighter and tighter, because of the push for energy savings and the desire to keep outdoor air contaminants from entering randomly. To make sure we still get a controlled amount of fresh air, the general trend is to build some type of ventilation into the HVAC system. If you build a house with all ICF walls and an ICF roof, you definitely want to make sure someone is looking out for this. It's a good idea to have a ventilation system on any house, and many good contractors already know what to do. I'll talk more about this in Chapters 5 and 7 when we get into indoor air quality and design and planning.

STEEL FRAMING

Are wood and concrete the only materials used to construct interior walls, floors, and roofs?
There are all sorts of alternative building materials. One that is very popular for these other parts of an ICF house is steel.

Steel? How do you build these parts of houses out of steel?
A lot like you do with wood. There are steel pieces that are shaped and sized a lot like the lumber pieces used for wood framing. They're made of fairly thin sheets of steel that are bent and folded into shapes that are something like a hollow piece of lumber. Many people call them **light-gauge steel** or **cold-formed steel**. These are technical terms that refer to how they are manufactured, but what they tell you is that these parts are relatively lightweight as steel goes.

The contractors connect these pieces in almost exactly the same patterns that they connect pieces of wood. Building this way is called **steel framing**, just as its wood counterpart is called wood framing. The pieces of steel need to be connected with screws instead of nails (Fig. 3-12). That's about the biggest difference. After the house frame is up, it gets covered with plywood and wallboard pretty much the same way wood frame is.

If it's so much like wood frame, why should I use steel frame?
Because it's often about the same total cost and it has a few added advantages. In fact, some of these advantages are the same advantages that lead people to choose ICFs over wood. So a lot of people who choose ICFs for their exterior walls opt for steel for other parts of the house.

What are the advantages?
In a nutshell, they are strength, durability, and consistency. Steel pieces are precisely manufactured to be straight and of consistent dimensions. Wood nowadays is often warped a bit. That can make the walls and

3-12. Light-gauge steel frame wall inside an ICF house. (Phil-Insul Corp.)

floors a tad warped, too. This can get worse over time as moisture and temperature changes make wood expand and contract. Steel pretty much starts straight and stays straight. And, of course, termites can't do much to steel.

Does steel have disadvantages?
The prices of the steel parts and of lumber both fluctuate, but usually they are about the same. The total installed cost of the framing (which includes labor and materials) runs about the same, if you can find crews experienced with steel in your area. This is the same kind of availability issue you have with ICFs. If local crews do steel framing on houses, you should be fine. If not, you may have to work to find someone to do the construction, and you may have to wait longer and pay more. The other disadvantage that appears in some cases is energy efficiency. Heat moves faster through steel than through wood. A lot faster. So with exterior walls built of steel frame you'll have to do more heating or cooling to keep the inside comfortable.

That makes sense if the exterior walls are built of steel frame. But I'm building mine out of ICFs.
That's exactly right. That's one reason ICFs and steel make a good combination: ICFs are on the outside,

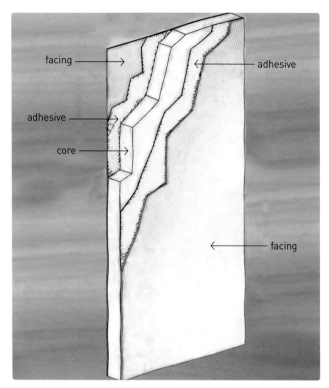

3-13. Cutaway view of a structural insulated panel.

and steel can be on the inside. But you do still have to think about this if you want to build the roof with steel framing.

What do I do about energy efficiency if my roof is built with steel frame?

You should take some extra steps to insulate the roof a bit more than you would with wood frame. This is done differently in different places. One popular option is to put the usual fiberglass insulation between the steel rafters, and then put a thin layer of foam over the rafters for good measure. Your local contractors should be able to advise you.

STRUCTURAL INSULATED PANELS

Are there any more of these alternative materials that I should consider in my house?

There's one more option for the roof that I would give serious thought to. That is something called **structural insulated panels**, SIPs for short. An SIP is a panel that consists of a layer of foam, with a layer of wood sheathing glued to each face. It is also a "sandwich," with foam in the center and wood layers on the outside (Fig. 3-13). The foam is usually 4 or 6 or 8 inches thick. The sheathing is either plywood or what is called **oriented strand board**, also known as **OSB**. OSB is a modern substitute for plywood. The sheathing is adhered to the foam with high-strength permanent adhesives. The resulting panel is surprisingly stiff and strong.

What's so good about building my roof out of SIPs?

SIPs can be used for all sorts of things, but one of their better uses is as a roof. The foam gives them a tremendous R-value (see page 62 for more information on R-value). Because the panels are large, there are few joints, so air infiltration is generally low. Their strength is high, so they are resistant to sagging or being pulled apart by wind. They can be left entirely open underneath, making it easy to have high cathedral ceilings in every room below, if you want. Because they have a layer of sheathing on each side, it is easy to nail any finish roofing material to them without requiring any special measures or preplanning. Perhaps best of all, an SIP roof can often be had for only a little more money than a conventional frame roof. So you get some of the advantages of a concrete roof, but at less cost.

What are the disadvantages of an SIP roof?

The major one is the same one that applies to all these alternative materials. Crews experienced at installing SIP roofs are not available everywhere. You may have to hunt for a while to find one, and you may end up paying more to get one than you would in areas where there are a greater number of experienced installers. But SIPs work well in combination with ICFs and are becoming more widely used. I know a couple of contractors who build almost nothing but houses with ICF walls and SIP roofs. The other "disadvantages" are things that an SIP roof may not do quite as well as a concrete roof would. The energy efficiency of an SIP and an ICF roof should be close. SIPs don't have the same thermal mass as an ICF or other concrete deck, but they have even more foam for a higher R-value, and if the joints are sealed properly, they should be comparable in air infiltration.

SIP panels should hold together in strong winds. They won't pull apart the way the sheathing sometimes pulls off a conventional frame roof. The connection of the panels down to the walls will be critical, but there are metal straps that could be used to make this connection effectively. SIPs probably won't stop projectiles as well as a concrete roof does, but I would expect them to stop projectiles better than a conventional roof would because they have a foam cushion and two layers of sheathing, not one. Comfort should be good because of the continuous insulation and the low air infiltration (although, again, you don't have the thermal mass of concrete).

The ability of SIPs to stop sound is supposed to be better than that of conventional frame roofs, but it is unlikely to be quite as high as a concrete roof's. Overall strength probably won't be quite as high as a concrete roof. SIPs are a somewhat new product, but some were installed decades ago and durability appears to be good.

Design flexibility should be a bit higher than with a concrete roof because they are light and a bit easier to cut into pieces and reconnect than some of the concrete forms. All in all, SIPs give you a lot of the benefit of a concrete roof at a lower cost. They're definitely worth a look if they're available in your area.

OK, are those all the materials and uses to consider?

For the alternatives to wood in the structure of the building, this is about it. As I've said, there are dozens of alternative building materials that are used here and there. And there are lots of other parts of the house to build. But for someone who is considering building a house with ICFs, these are the options that are most likely to be of interest. I'll discuss all of this a bit more in Chapter 7, when we get into planning and design. In the meantime, there are plenty of other things to learn.

4

More on Energy, for Fanatics

INCREASED ENERGY EFFICIENCY is the reason people cite most often for having their houses built with ICFs. And it certainly is a big benefit of using the system. Unfortunately, it's not a simple subject. Even trained engineers cannot

Walls up and ready for the roof.
(Quad-Lock Building Systems, Ltd.)

answer straightforward questions like "What will my fuel bill be on this particular house?" with as much accuracy as we would like to have. There are a lot of forces at work, and even the numbers that sound so simple depend on many factors. For that reason, the details really involve a lot of discussion with a lot of qualifications.

That's what this chapter is for. It goes over the details, at a finer level than you really need in order to plan and build an ICF house. If you're curious about these things, you may want to read through it. There is actually a lot of good information here, which will help you fine-tune your house for energy efficiency, if that's what you're looking for. If this information isn't important to you, then you can skip it without missing anything that's crucial in most cases.

If you want really precise answers to questions like "How much will I save in heating and cooling if I build my house with ICF walls?" you're out of luck. If most experts can't do it, I can't either. Just know that, by reading through this chapter, your understanding of energy issues and the quality of the decisions you make in designing your house will be greatly improved.

SAVINGS

Why can't you tell me how much energy I'll save if my walls are built of ICFs?

How much gas will you save if you buy your car with a four-cylinder engine? You can't tell me and neither can your automobile dealer or the EPA officials who do the mileage ratings, or anyone else. It all depends on a large number of variables. Are you putting this engine in a subcompact or an SUV? Will you drive it mostly in the city or on the highway? Are you comparing your mileage to what *you* would have gotten with a larger engine if you drove the car exactly the same way, or are you comparing it to how some other driver with an eight-cylinder engine drives? Are you getting any other optional features, like traction control or fuel injection? Remember, all those things have an

impact on mileage as well. And they can change the amount of the savings in mileage you will get if you change the engine.

It's the same with the energy savings from ICF walls. A hundred little things affect how much you will save. If you build a house with ICF walls that is tall and thin with a lot of walls and a small roof, then you'll save more than if the house is a ranch (one story) with low walls and a big roof. In the case of the one-story house with a big roof, the walls are just less of a factor at holding the heat in (or out), and the roof is more of a factor.

As another example, if you have a lot of kids who are constantly going in and out and leaving doors open, then ICFs will save you less in fuel costs because more energy will leak out through the doors, and the ICF walls can't help that. The list of important factors goes on and on. ICF walls will always help save energy, and in almost every case it will probably be a substantial amount. The problem is pinpointing exactly how much.

But what if I really need an exact number for my energy savings? Maybe I need it for some energy subsidy I'm applying for, or because I need to make a precise cost savings estimate before I decide to build with ICFs.

The one way I know of to get a reasonably accurate estimate of the fuel bill for a particular house is to hire an expert. Some people call them **energy auditors** or **energy analysts**. They do this kind of thing for a living. They have special software and they ask detailed questions about the design and construction of the house, the local climate, and everything else they need to know. They feed the numbers into the software and come back with an estimated fuel bill. You can ask for energy bills for different situations, and compare them. For example, you could hand them a design and tell them to estimate the fuel required with frame walls and again with ICF walls. This would allow you to compare the energy bills. But more than likely you'll want to get their advice, too. They're often full of recommendations for how to adjust your building design and materials to boost energy savings inexpensively.

What will I pay for an energy expert?
Anywhere from a few hundred to a couple thousand dollars. It depends how much work you have the person do.

If I wanted to hire an energy expert, how would I find one?
One option is to talk to a local member of the Residential Energy Savings Network (also called RESNET). Its members are **energy raters**. These are people who estimate the energy efficiency of houses for a living. The RESNET Web address is **www.natresnet.org**.

If you want to go with the most highly trained specialists, look for a good **mechanical engineer**. These are the engineers who estimate the heating and cooling needs of a building. Most of them concentrate on commercial buildings, where they get paid to figure out how to build the heating and cooling system. But some also do work on houses for a fee. Finding one who does houses is definitely harder. You have to search through phone listings, call a number of them, and ask. Another way to find help is to ask your ICF contractor or local distributors of ICF products. They have often worked with an energy expert in the past, and can get you in touch. I explain how to find ICF distributors in Chapter 6.

But what if I don't want to spend this kind of money to get an expert's estimates of what my energy bill will be? Or what if I just want a better understanding of the energy issues?
Despite all my protests, I can throw around some numbers that give you some rough ideas of possible savings.

Okay, then, what are your rough estimates of energy savings from ICF walls?
Estimates for the amount of energy you'll save by opting for ICF walls instead of frame walls vary widely.

I've seen numbers anywhere from 5% less for heating and cooling to 70% less. But personally I don't believe the extremes. I think the real numbers are somewhere in the middle.

Wow, that is a big spread. Why don't you believe the energy savings estimates of 5% or 70%?
Well, some of the lowest numbers come from so-called "scientific" studies. These studies are either based on energy calculations or on side-by-side tests of two actual houses. The "calculations" are usually computer simulations or calculations of how much heating and cooling a particular house will require. They run the numbers once for a wood-frame house and again for the same house with ICF walls, then they compare. I guess you could think that they must be accurate because they're done by engineers.

The trouble is that I know too much about how these calculations are done. There are a lot of simplifications—otherwise the whole thing would be too complicated. And the most questionable assumption is that the wood-frame walls will be essentially "perfect." The wood is rarely assumed to be warped, there are not assumed to be any gaps between the pieces, the insulation is assumed to fill up the cavities perfectly, and so on. But if you visit a typical construction site, you know few of these things go exactly as planned. Some of the wood is warped and twisted. There are little gaps here and there. In some cases, the insulation crew has stapled the insulation to the sides of the wooden studs (instead of stapling it to the face, where it's designed to be stapled) and compressed it. This reduces its insulating value. In some spots the insulation does not fill the wall all the way up to the top or down to the bottom.

These simulations and calculations typically compare ICFs to perfect wood-frame construction. But, unless a wood-frame house is built by a crew experienced in energy-efficient building techniques, the actual energy performance of a wood-frame home is likely to be somewhat less than was predicted by calculations.

What are the studies of actual side-by-side houses like?

These studies compare one house built with standard frame walls to another one built with ICF walls. This is a little better than the computer simulations because it compares real construction to real construction. These studies have shown a savings of anywhere from 7% to 20%. But I'm inclined to think that these may be a little on the low side as well.

Why do you think these estimates from real, side-by-side houses are on the low side?

Basically, these studies, like the simulations, give wood frame the benefit of the doubt. The frame houses they use to calculate the measurements are unrealistically perfect. There are two reasons for this.

First of all, the houses have usually been built especially for the energy studies. And the researchers make sure that the materials and the workmanship are all exactly "according to the book." So, again, the wood is nice and straight, the insulation is cut and fit to fill every cavity perfectly, and so on. But this isn't the way frame houses are usually built in real life, and there's no way to get one built close to this standard unless you find a very conscientious builder who specializes in energy-efficient construction. You will have to pay extra for this level of work and, even then, you may need to personally inspect the workmanship to ensure that it is done correctly.

Second, they always take their measurements on the houses when they are new. Usually they do all the testing on the fuel bill in the first year. They really have to do it this way to get clean measurements. They can't be taking measurements on the two houses with owners in them who might have different habits on things like opening and closing windows and taking vacations and lowering the thermostat when they go away. So they do everything the same on both houses for a year or so and take their measurements. Then they sell the houses and let the new owners do what they want with them.

The point is that they check the fuel bills on both homes when they are still in their best condition.

Over the years, the energy performance of all homes deteriorates somewhat as window and door seals come loose, caulks and sealants fail, and gaps open up. These effects are likely to be stronger in a wood-frame home as the wood expands, contracts and shifts over time. Because of an ICF structure's inherent stability, energy performance should remain more constant over time.

But be fair. The researchers must give the same breaks to the ICF houses.

I'm convinced that the "breaks" given to ICF construction are a lot fewer. Consider the quality of construction. There's almost never a significant gap in the ICF insulation. And there's a reason for that. If workers on a wood house have some gaps in some of the frame or the insulation, they can simply keep working, and they do. I worked on a framing crew, and when you're dealing with twisted lumber and bad weather and a tight deadline, at some point you just have to say that the work is "good enough." But with ICFs, if you have any gaps in the foam insulation, when you pour the concrete you get leaks and blowouts and you have a real mess on your hands. So you make darn sure to get it right the first time. Unlike with wood, screwing up the ICF insulation actually costs you *more* time. So for your own selfish interests, you work very hard to keep that insulation completely in place.

Of course, it's possible to do some bad ICF work, but it's in the contractor's own interest to get the foam right. You can and should know key things to look for when your house is built, to check up on the quality of construction. I discuss this a lot more in Chapter 9. But, more than likely, missing insulation or gaps in the wall will not be among any imperfections that you find.

Why don't you believe the highest estimates of energy savings?

Would you believe them? Saving 70% on your fuel bill just by changing what the walls are built from sounds too good to be true. The logical conclusion is that it probably is.

Most of these claims of ultrahigh energy efficiency come from ICF homeowners who compared their energy bills to the bills of a neighbor with an older, leaky, wood-frame house. I actually got the chance to check up on claims like this once by getting fuel bills for an ICF house and its frame neighbor, and talking with the owners. The ICF house did indeed consume a lot less energy. But after a few questions it became apparent that the house had a lot of other energy-saving features besides the ICF walls. Some of the other features it had were special superinsulating windows, lots of extra insulation in the roof, a very high-efficiency heating system, and so on. This makes sense. The owner was an energy bug, so he chose ICFs for the walls and other energy-saving features for other parts of the house. But you can be pretty confident that the ICFs alone didn't save all that energy.

It doesn't make sense that you could save two-thirds of the fuel to heat and cool a home just by changing what the walls are built of. You don't even lose that much through the walls—a lot goes through the roof, the windows, and so on. So even if you somehow miraculously cut *all* your losses through the walls, you still couldn't save two-thirds.

OK, so I can get some significant savings, but probably not cut my fuel bill in half just by using ICF walls. Is that all there is to know?
Definitely not. If you're reading this chapter, it's because you have a particular interest in energy efficiency. And if you have an interest in energy efficiency, there's more you should know to make sure you get it in your house.

First, you should understand the mechanics of fuel use for a house. Then you should arm yourself with information in order to sort out all the wild energy claims people make, so that you don't get taken. And finally, you should know what other components are available to complement the ICF walls and make the house very energy efficient (if that's what you want).

BASIC ENERGY PRINCIPLES

So what's there to know about fuel use for a house?
Let's start with basic principles. Energy is an issue because the outdoors is cold and you want to keep the indoors warmer (in winter), or the outdoors is hot and you want the inside to be cooler (in summer). Consider the case of winter. You can warm things up inside with a furnace or a fire or any other source of heat. But the heat leaks outside over time, so you have to add more fuel inside to keep things from getting chilly. I'm sorry to state things so simply, but it's important to start at ground zero because it gets complicated as we go into greater detail. We need to keep things straight.

OK, I'll bite. Explain how the heat leaks inside and outside.
Scientists identify several different ways that heat goes through the envelope of a building. (*Envelope* is just a fancy word for the walls, windows, doors, and roof—the things that separate the inside from the outside.) But for our purposes we really only have to talk about three ways heat travels through the envelope.

The first is called **conduction**. This is just heat moving by contact. In other words, if something hot touches something cold, heat moves from the hot thing to the cold thing. That's why a bowl warms up when it's filled with hot soup and your hand gets cold when you hold a snowball. The heat in the soup travels into the bowl, and the heat in your hand travels into the snow.

So if it's warm inside the house, as the air makes contact with the walls it warms them up. In fact, some heat is moving from the air into the walls. On the other side, the warm walls warm up the cold outdoor air. So the heat goes out into the world. More and more heat gradually transfers through the walls until the inside air is as cold as the outside air (Fig. 4-1). The heat travels the opposite way in the summer: outdoors to indoors.

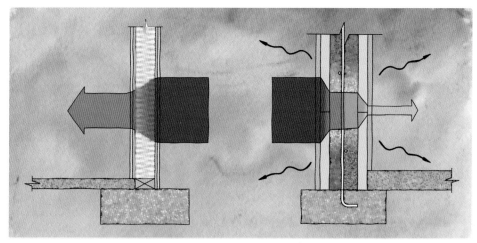

4-1. More heat (red arrow) is conducted through a typical frame wall (left) than through an ICF wall (right). When it's cold, heat stored in the thermal mass of the concrete emanates from the ICF wall (black arrows).

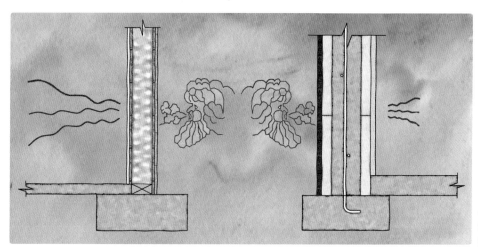

4-2. Air infiltration is greater through typical frame walls (left) than through ICF walls (right).

You said there are three important ways the heat moves. What's the second?

It's called **infiltration**, or, to be more precise, **air infiltration**. This is the actual movement of air through holes—even tiny ones. This is pretty obvious. If you have leaks in your house's envelope, some cold air will come in during the winter, some of the warm inside air will leak out, and things will get cooler inside (Fig. 4-2). And believe me, every house has some leaks.

What's the third way heat moves?

It's **radiation**. This is heat coming in with the light, as when the sun comes through a window, hits the floor, and warms it up. This is usually much more important in the summer. Sun coming in makes the house even hotter, and you have to run air-conditioning to compensate for the added heat. In the winter, incoming sunshine can actually reduce the amount of heating you have to do by helping to warm the interior. Some houses are specially designed to harness this so-called **solar energy**, reducing the amount of extra heating necessary by about 50%. But in the typical house, incoming sunshine has only minor effects in the winter. Radiation can occur through ways other than sunshine, but that's the one with the biggest impact on home heating and cooling.

So what do these different methods of heat transfer mean when it comes to building with ICFs?
It helps us break down the savings from ICFs into parts. And once we do that we can understand what kinds of energy savings are possible, evaluate companies' claims of energy efficiency, and figure out what we can work on besides the walls to make the house energy efficient.

All right. Break the savings down for me into these different methods of heat transfer.
Once again, there are no exact figures. From the energy experts I've talked to, the figures for heating in the winter run something like this. About 20% to 25% of the heating is to make up for heat lost through the walls by conduction. Maybe 30% or more is for heat conducted through the roof, and maybe from 10% to 20% is to replace heat lost through conduction through the windows and doors. Lastly, about 20% to 40% of the heat lost from a typical frame house is thought to be from air infiltration.

In summer a big chunk of the heat entering the house is in the form of radiation—basically, sunshine coming through windows. Over 25% of the cooling done in the summer in a typical home is due to the heating effects of incoming sunshine. The rest of the incoming heat is through the same things that let heat out in the winter: conduction through the walls, roof, and windows, and air infiltration, but each of those will be slightly less important to the big picture because the radiation heat contributes so much.

How do the ICF walls reduce these heat transfers?
They cut the amount of conducted heat through the walls because of the foam. Foam is a good insulator. **Insulation** is really just a name that we give to any material that only allows heat to move through it very slowly. And foam slows down the movement of heat considerably.

But wood frame walls have insulation, too, right?
Right. Ninety-five times out of a hundred it's fiberglass insulation. "Blankets" of fiberglass are placed between the studs. The studs are the wood-framing pieces running vertically in the wall.

Doesn't fiberglass insulate as well as foam?
Not really. The frame wall is much less well-insulated than the ICF wall for several reasons. To go into that you have to understand the meaning of R-value.

R-VALUE

What's R-value?
It's the standard measure of insulating ability. The actual units are pretty complicated, but the basic idea is not too tough.

Let's say scientists can test any sheet or wall of material in the lab to see how fast heat conducts through it. (In fact, they *can* do this, with good accuracy.) The scientist tests one sheet of material under a very specific set of conditions that are always the same no matter what materials he is testing. If the scientist finds that exactly 1 unit of heat goes through the material every hour, then we say that that material has an R-value of 1. If it only lets through one-half unit of heat every hour, we say it has an R-value of 2 because its insulating ability is twice as good. If it lets through only a third of a unit of heat every hour, we say it has an R-value of 3, and so on.

This all may sound a little arbitrary, but once you get the scale set up, it's an extremely useful way to compare the insulating ability of different materials. A layer of insulation with an R-value of 20 is twice as "good" an insulator as one with an R-value of 10, because it lets through only 1/20th of a unit of heat per hour in the standard test, as opposed to 1/10th of a unit.

An inch-thick layer of fiberglass insulation has an R-value of about 3 to 4. An inch-thick layer of most of the foams used in ICFs has an R-value of almost exactly 4. For comparison's sake, the R-value of an inch-thick wooden board ranges from 1 to 1½, depending on the type of wood. Inch-thick steel has an R-value of about .003, depending on the exact

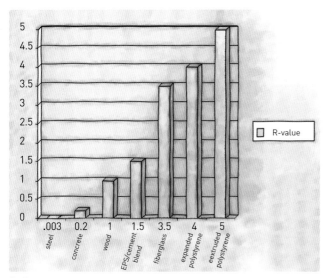

4-3. R-values of common materials.

ingredients. Steel is considered to be a very poor insulator (Fig. 4-3).

Note that as the thickness of a sheet of material goes up, so does the R-value. For example, a 2-inch-thick layer of fiberglass has an R-value of 6 to 8, or double what an inch-thick layer has. Likewise, 2 inches of foam has an R-value of about 8. In other words, double the layer of insulation and you have half the movement of heat through it. Triple the thickness and you reduce the heat movement to a third, and so on. Therefore, one way to reduce the heat conduction of a wall (and increase the energy efficiency of the building) is to increase the thickness of the insulation.

That's all fine, but the R-value you gave me for the fiberglass insulation in a frame wall is almost the same as the R-value for the foam in an ICF wall. So isn't the frame wall as energy efficient?

That would be the case if the insulation in the two walls were arranged the same. But it isn't. In an ICF wall you typically have about 5 inches of foam total on the wall—around 2½ inches on each side. That makes for an R-value of 20. Sometimes it's a little more, sometimes a little less. The concrete in the middle also adds to the R-value, but since concrete is a poor insulator, the concrete only adds 1 to 2 points to the R-value. In general, the average R-value for an ICF

wall, including both foam and concrete, is around 20 (Fig. 4-4).

The majority of new frame walls in northern states use 2×6 studs with a 5½-inch-thick cavity for holding insulation. The fiberglass insulation put into it usually has an R-value of 19. In southern climates, 2×4 walls with a 3½-inch cavity are more common. The fiberglass insulation put into it usually has a total R-value of about 11. In some cases a premium ("high-density") fiberglass is used that has an R-value of about 13. *But,* that doesn't mean the whole wall is R-11, R-13, or R-19. You see, there are a lot of spots in the wall that have no insulation at all—only wood. In fact, the wood framing takes up about a 25% of the wall area for a 2×4 wall and about 22% of the area of a 2×6 wall. At those points heat can pass through the wall faster because the wood isn't as good an insulator. The wood

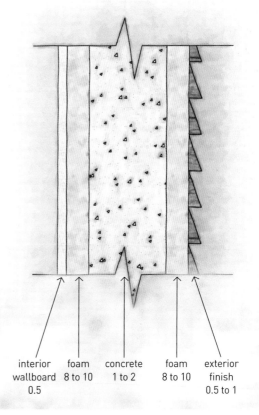

| interior wallboard 0.5 | foam 8 to 10 | concrete 1 to 2 | foam 8 to 10 | exterior finish 0.5 to 1 |

4-4. R-values of the materials in an ICF wall.

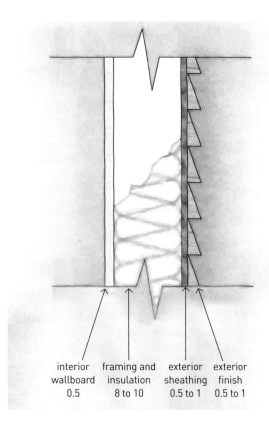

4-5. R-values of the materials in a frame wall.

interior wallboard	framing and insulation	exterior sheathing	exterior finish
0.5	8 to 10	0.5 to 1	0.5 to 1

at those points has an R-value of only about 4½ for a 2×4 and 7 for a 2×6 (Fig. 4-5).

When the laboratories test a complete typical frame wall—not just the insulation by itself—they usually measure an R-value of about 10. So a 2×4 frame wall really has only about half the R-value of the ICF wall. Even a 2×6 wall, when all the framing is included, has an effective R-value of only about R-14, still quite a bit less than an ICF wall.

AIR INFILTRATION

Well, then, do ICFs reduce any other kinds of flows of heat through the wall?
Yes, they reduce the other big one—air infiltration. Remember, air infiltration can account for 20% to 40% of your heating and cooling costs. ICFs are very airtight.

How much do ICFs cut the total air infiltration in the house?
Again, that varies widely. The testing on new ICF and wood-frame houses side by side suggests that air infiltration in an ICF house is reduced by about one-sixth. But as you might guess, I expect these figures are a tad low because the frame houses are constructed more tightly than the typical frame house. Also, as I mentioned earlier, they are tested when the house is new and the framing pieces haven't yet started to shift or loosen up.

Some ICF houses have been tested and shown to have air infiltration rates only about one-quarter as much as a typical wood-frame house. In other words, the rates were about three-quarters *lower* than the rates for average wood-frame houses. But I don't consider these very accurate numbers because these houses generally had specially constructed roofs that were unusually airtight, as well as other special features that reduced air infiltration in other parts of the house.

THERMAL MASS

So ICFs may cut the conduction losses through the walls by as much as half, and the air infiltration of the house by as much as a third. Are these all the ways that ICFs save energy?
There's one other way. But it's a complex concept to grasp, and the amount of savings is controversial. It comes from something most people refer to as **thermal mass**. This is a property of materials. It's basically how much heat you need to raise the temperature of the material. For example, if you put a pot of water on the stove it will take maybe ten minutes to boil; boiling occurs when water reaches 212°F. But if you put the same amount of marshmallow cream in the pot it will reach 212°F in less than five minutes. It took less heat energy from the stove to raise the temperature of the marshmallow cream to 212°F, so we say the marshmallow

cream has a lower thermal mass, and the water has a higher one.

Likewise, if you let the two pots cool, the water will give off more heat and stay warm much longer. The water has more thermal mass, so it took more heat and more time to bring its temperature up. Likewise, it will give off more heat and take longer for it to cool down.

What does thermal mass have to do with my home's energy efficiency?

If your house is made of something with a lot of thermal mass, it can cut a few percent more off your bill. My favorite example of this is the adobe homes that the Native Americans of the Southwest built. In the desert, the daytime temperature can reach over 100°F, while at night it can drop down into the 40s. This could make things pretty uncomfortable, but these houses had the benefit of being built with a material that has a lot of thermal mass—namely, thick walls of mud. During the day the sun beating down on the walls would warm the building up, but only very slowly. So inside the temperature stayed cooler. The house's shell would be quite warm by the evening, but by that time the outside air was getting cool. Over the course of the night the warm walls and roof would "buffer" the inside from the cold outdoors, keeping the interior warmer. Come morning the house might be getting cool, but by then the sun would be out and the cycle would start all over again.

How does thermal mass work in a house today?

Concrete walls have a lot of thermal mass. So, like those adobe homes, when the outside air is hot they soak up some of the heat and when it's cold they give some of it off. This can buffer the indoor temperature from the outdoors, keeping indoor temperatures more steady and increasing comfort. This can also reduce the amount of fuel needed by a few percent.

This sounds good for times when the days are hot and the nights are cold. What if I live someplace where it's always cold for much of the year? Or how about in the Deep South where sometimes it doesn't get below 75°F for months?

To be honest, you would definitely get the most savings in places like Phoenix or Atlanta, where daily temperature swings are the greatest and the temperature cycles around 70°F for a lot of the year.

But how does this work when you have insulation on both sides of the concrete? With adobe homes, the massive part of the wall is exposed to the air so the air can warm it up and cool it down.

That's a good question, and engineers definitely predict that the savings from thermal mass vary depending on whether insulation is used and where it is placed. Concrete insulated on both sides is not as effective as concrete insulated only on the exterior, but it still produces significant savings in some climates. Exactly how much isn't known. That's where the controversy comes from. Some people see the insulation and say that there will be no thermal mass effect. However, the engineers who have studied it all say there will be *some* savings from thermal mass. The heat still conducts through the foam and into the concrete. As it does, it will warm up the wall a little and later the wall can give off that bit of heat. Although the insulation slows this process down and reduces the thermal mass effect, it doesn't eliminate it.

So how much will thermal mass reduce my fuel bill?

Nobody knows for sure, but engineering estimates for an R-20 wall with the insulation on both sides and heavy thermal mass in the center usually come out with 4% to 8% savings. That's extra savings beyond what you would have gotten just from the high insulation itself. You're likely to get closer to the high end of the range in a moderate climate, and closer to the low end in a climate that stays constantly hot or constantly cold for long periods of time.

SOME MORE CONSIDERATIONS

Is that basically all I need to know about energy efficiency: R-value, air infiltration, and thermal mass?

Those are the three major "mechanisms" through which ICF walls can lower your fuel bill. But as long as you're considering energy efficiency, there are some other things I'd recommend you look into so you're well informed and you can get the best possible house for your money.

You should know about R-value and how it's determined. Although it is confusing, there are actually different methods to determine the R-value of a wall. These different methods may yield different numbers, and if you aren't aware of this, you can be misled. You should know about how the size of your furnace and air-conditioning system are determined. If it's done incorrectly, you can end up paying too much and getting a system that does a poor job. And you should know about other things you can do to make the home energy-efficient. The ICFs pretty much take care of the walls, but if you want a really energy-efficient home you should consider taking a few simple measures in some other parts of the house, too.

Wait, all that stuff you told me about an inch of foam having an R-value of about 4, and fiberglass having an R-value of about 3 to 4—isn't that true?

Yes, you can count on that information. The R-value of insulation materials is pretty easy to check in a lab, and the Federal Trade Commission is aggressive about taking insulation companies to court if they haven't had their material tested or if they report inaccurate numbers.

Most of the trouble comes when you have a wall that's made of pieces of different materials. Remember when I said that fiberglass insulation usually has an R-value of about 11 or 13, but a frame wall with fiberglass insulation in it usually tests in the lab at about R-10? A typical wood-frame wall is about 22% to 25% wood; the rest is fiberglass. The wood allows more heat to transfer through the wall, and this brings

the overall R-value of the wall down to maybe 8 or so. Then the crew adds wallboard on the inside and some sort of exterior finish to the outside. This usually takes the R-value back up to 10 or so.

So why not just test all the different kinds of wall and give us their R-values?

That would be nice, but it's just too expensive. It's a lot harder—and costlier—to test a whole wall than a thin slab of an insulation material. On top of that, there are millions of possible ways to build a wall. Once you figure in all the exact different materials that could be used and how they could be arranged and what finishes could be put on each side, you realize that it's impractical to test them all just to figure out an exact number for each particular wall. Instead, most manufacturers *estimate* the R-value of the walls their products appear in. But there are different ways to do the estimate, and which one is most accurate can vary from case to case. So a lot of times you'll get R-values from two different manufacturers and can't really compare them because you're not comparing "apples to apples."

Then how do I check the R-value of the products I'm looking at?

You really know enough now. Generally speaking, the ICF wall itself is about R-20. Two-by-four wood frame is closer to R-10, unless you do additional things to it to beef it up. If someone is making odd-sounding claims for a particular product or wall, you know enough to do a reality check. How many inches thick is the insulation? What's the R-value per inch of insulation? Is there anything like wood or steel that breaks all the way through the insulation at any points to lower the R-value?

I've heard some people say an ICF wall is "equivalent to" an R-50 wall. Does that make any sense?

It may make some sense, but it probably doesn't mean what you think it means. Fifty is *not* the standard R-value of any ICF wall, except a few special-purpose walls that have over 10 inches of foam for

The easiest way I know to explain equivalent R-value is with a story. Suppose Joe is an ICF salesman. Joe tells Bob, a homebuyer, that the ICF walls will be R-20. And Bob realizes that wood-frame walls would be about R-10. Bob says, "So if I beefed up my frame walls so that they were R-20, I could get the same energy savings as with ICF walls."

Joe, of course, doesn't want to lose the sale. So he says, "Well, it would be hard to get frame walls up to R-20. You'd have to do a lot of special things and that would increase the cost and slow down construction. But *even if you did* build frame walls that were R-20, your house still wouldn't be as energy efficient as a house with ICF walls. ICFs reduce energy costs further by letting less air infiltration through. They also have thermal mass, which cuts the energy even more. Frame walls will still have higher air infiltration and lower thermal mass even if you double the thickness of the wall and add twice the insulation."

Bob sort of understands, but he can't get over the idea that the R-values will be the same. So Bob builds his house out of wood and Joe loses the sale.

Joe is disappointed by the loss of the sale. Then he comes up with an idea. Suppose he estimates the total energy bill for a house with ICF walls. Then he estimates what the bill would be if he built exactly the same house with frame walls. *Then* he estimates the bill if he increased the thickness of the frame wall to make it R-20. It would still be higher than the bill for the ICF house because the frame house doesn't have the savings from higher thermal mass or lower air infiltration. *Then* he keeps estimating fuel bills for frame houses with more and more insulation in the walls until he finds a set of frame walls that would give the frame house the same total energy bill as the house with ICF walls.

Joe does this calculation and he finds that the frame walls would have to be R-50 before the frame house would have as low an energy bill as a house with R-20 ICF walls. Simply put, because you don't get much air infiltration or thermal mass savings from the frame walls, to get the same total energy savings you have to keep building the walls out with more and more insulation to cut the conduction energy losses to make up for it. And that can take a lot of extra insulation.

"Wow," says Joe. "This will open some eyes!" So on his next sale, he tells the homebuyer, "You'd have to insulate your wood walls out to *R-50* to get the same fuel bill you'll get with ICF walls." The homebuyer is impressed. Joe told him the story in a simple number that he's familiar with, an R-value. And it's a darn big R-value. The ICF walls must be good!

You're probably wondering if an R-20 ICF wall is really equivalent to an R-50 frame wall. The answer depends on a lot of factors and involves a lot of number crunching. Engineers have run these numbers; by their estimates, you would need frame walls anywhere from R-30 to as high as R-50 to get the same total energy savings as you get with R-20 ICF walls. It varies from climate to climate, though. In some places the equivalent R-value is less; in some it's more.

very energy-sensitive projects like freezer buildings. Some people say that an ICF wall has an **equivalent R-value** of as high as 50. The equivalent R-value may also be called something like the **mass-corrected R-value**. The number is higher because it tries to take into account not only the higher insulation value of the ICF wall, but also the energy savings from the thermal mass effect (see sidebar titled "What's an Equivalent R-Value?").

Why is the equivalent R-value different from place to place?

Because the thermal mass savings are estimated to be different from place to place, as I mentioned earlier. In moderate climates the savings from thermal mass are estimated to be higher, so the amount you'd have to insulate frame walls to get the same savings will be higher. In extreme climates, the estimated thermal mass savings are less, so the equivalent R-value of ICF walls is less.

What about the air infiltration factor? Does that vary, too?

The truth is that air infiltration isn't usually figured into the calculation of equivalent R-value. That's why they sometimes call it the mass-corrected R-value. They "correct" the R-value only to account for the additional savings specifically from the thermal mass effect.

Do you mean that I would need something like R-50 frame walls to get the same savings as an ICF-type wall, but that does NOT even include the air infiltration savings?

That's what I mean. If you figured in the air infiltration savings from ICF walls, too, then you'd come up with an even higher number. Some people have talked about doing that calculation, but I've never seen it done.

So how am I supposed to interpret the equivalent R-value number when someone gives it to me?

Just take it for what it is—a convenient way to say that ICF walls will save even more energy than R-20 frame walls would save. But don't take it to mean something it doesn't. It does *not* mean that the ICF walls are R-50. They're still only around R-20. The rest of the savings come from other things. And it does *not* mean that your fuel bill will be cut by a factor of five. The number just means that the ICF walls cut your fuel bill by an amount equal to cutting the *conduction* losses through the *walls* by a factor of five.

The big misunderstandings arise when the speaker doesn't make it clear that he's giving you the equivalent R-value, or you don't know what that means. For example, you might hear that one ICF is "R-50" and another is "R-20," when actually they're the same because the R-value you heard for the first one is the *equivalent* R-value and the R-value you heard for the second one is the *conventional* R-value. You have to know which number people are giving you so you can compare apples to apples.

Generally you don't have a lot of business getting into this level of detail on the products in your walls, anyway. I'll talk about this later, but you really need to find a good contractor whom you can trust on these fine points. All the major brands of ICFs are around the same R-value. You should leave it up to the contractor to pick the brand that works best for his crew and your house.

HEATING AND COOLING EQUIPMENT

When you discussed other things I should know about energy efficiency, you also mentioned a problem with heating and cooling equipment. What is that?

The problem is that an energy-efficient house like an ICF house should by rights have smaller HVAC equipment installed in it because it doesn't need as much heating and cooling. But most HVAC contractors aren't familiar with how to size the equipment for such efficient houses. The result can be that you end up with a furnace, heat pump, or air-conditioning system that is much larger than needed for your house.

Is that really such a problem?

It's not horrible, but it's definitely not ideal. First of all, you pay more than you have to. On an average house, the extra cost of the bigger equipment could easily be a thousand dollars. For most of us this is enough money to be concerned about.

Second, oversized equipment can actually operate *worse*. Consider heating. If your furnace is bigger than you need to heat the house, when the house gets a little cool the furnace comes on and blasts in warm air and brings the house back to a comfortable temperature in only a few minutes. It then stays idle for a while before turning on again. When it does turn on again, that is only for a brief time once more. A heating and cooling expert would say that the equipment is **short cycling**. Short cycling is less energy-efficient and it's hard on the equipment. It's something like using a race car for stop-and-go driving. You could be in for more frequent repairs.

There's even more to this problem on the air-conditioning side. In most climates we count on our air conditioner not only to cool the air, but also to *dehumidify* the air. Modern air-conditioning takes moisture out of the air, which helps us feel more comfortable. If your air-conditioning unit is larger than you need, it will only come on for short spurts because it can cool the house down in that time. However, this may not leave it running long enough to dehumidify the air adequately. So when you have too large an air-conditioning compressor, you may feel cool inside your house, and yet feel muggy at the same time.

How do I make sure I get the right size of heating and cooling equipment in my house?

This depends a lot on getting a good general contractor for the house—someone you can trust, and then trusting him to do the job. I talk a lot about this later on. A general contractor experienced with ICFs will know about this issue and will find an HVAC contractor who can size the equipment accurately.

Why is this even a problem? Can't you just tell the heating and cooling contractor to make sure the equipment isn't too big?

Most of them don't have experience with such highly energy-efficient houses. They have good judgment on the size of the units to put into a *conventional* frame house. They've often developed this through years of experience. But houses with super-insulated walls are unfamiliar to them.

Can't the contractor just look things like this up in a book to figure out the right size for the HVAC equipment?

Not really. Now there's new software for sizing the heating and cooling equipment in energy-efficient houses. But that depends on getting a contractor who uses modern software. Most of them don't. At some point this stuff may become reduced to a few simple tables that anybody can read. In the meantime you need to find someone who has good judgment from working with other energy-efficient buildings, or someone who uses modern software.

Can't we just hire someone to figure out the right size for the equipment and tell the heating and cooling contractor?

Yes and no. You can definitely hire energy analysts to estimate how much heating and cooling your house will need. And they can almost always recommend the size of the equipment to install. And their recommended size should be pretty accurate. But some contractors may still resist following their recommendations.

Why wouldn't the HVAC contractor listen to an expert?

It can be risky for the contractor to install smaller equipment. Suppose you tell him to put in a smaller furnace than he's accustomed to, and he does it. Now suppose that six months later you complain that the house isn't warm enough in winter. He has a dissatisfied customer, and might even get pushed into replacing the furnace at his expense. This kind of thing has happened to some contractors before. From their point of view, it's a lot safer to put in equipment that might be a little on the large size, and avoid getting angry calls later on.

So what can I do to get my HVAC equipment sized accurately?

We've covered the best options. Get a good general contractor who can find and work well with a good HVAC contractor. Some people hire energy analysts for a variety of reasons. If you do this, you can get the analyst's recommendation on equipment size and that should help put the contractor at ease. I've presented you with all the worst possibilities here—usually things get taken care of pretty well without a whole lot of work on the homebuyer's part. But it's good for you to be aware of these issues so you know better how to deal with them in case they do arise. I talk a lot more about this in Chapter 6.

OK, now what else can you tell me about the heating and cooling equipment and how it can affect my energy efficiency?

There are definite grades in energy efficiency available for heating and cooling equipment. Where I live in the northeastern United States, the standard furnace is about 80% efficient. That means for every 100 units of heat available in the fuel, the furnace actually puts out about 80 units of heat. But for not too much more you can get a 90% efficient furnace. Basically, you save about 10% on your heating bill just by buying the better furnace. More recently, furnaces with estimated energy efficiencies as high as 97% have become available.

The same sort of thing goes for air conditioning, too. The government has established energy ratings for many types of home appliances and air-conditioning equipment. The measure they've established for this is the **SEER**. This stands for **seasonal energy efficiency ratio**. To oversimplify a bit, this ratio tells you how much heating or cooling you get out of the equipment for every unit of energy put into running it. Air conditioners with a SEER of 10 used to be pretty standard. But now units with SEER ratings of 13 are becoming standard, and higher ones are available. You can clip 20% or 30% off your air-conditioning energy bill just by springing for a better piece of equipment. The high-SEER units are more expensive, but if you are interested in energy efficiency, they are one of the easiest ways to get it.

Is there anything more to be concerned about in my HVAC system?

Yes, one of the more troublesome problems is leakage from your air ducts. Most new HVAC systems these days spread the heating or cooling around the house by **forced air**. This means that they heat or cool air at a central location (the furnace or air conditioner), then blow it with fans through ducts that snake around the building. The ends of the ducts open into the rooms of the house to blow warm or cool air in.

However, the ducts tend to have leaks. They are made of pieces that are connected to one another, and the connection points often have small gaps in them. So some of the heated or cooled air never gets to its destination. This is not much of a problem if the leaks are located in parts of the house that have to be heated or cooled anyway. But often the heater or air conditioner is located in an attic or basement that is not insulated and is not intended to be heated or cooled. In that case, leaks in the ductwork send air into a part of the house where it is not useful and the heat or coolness leaks mostly to the outside.

How do I reduce my energy losses from leaky ductwork?

There are ways to seal the connections of ductwork more precisely. So one option is to find an HVAC contractor with good sealing procedures to do the work on your house. However, this may be easier said than done. Not many contractors have tightly controlled procedures for duct sealing, and even if they do it is easy to make mistakes in the field. It is almost necessary to inspect the installation work to make sure it is done well. But few of us have the time or expertise to do that.

A reasonable alternative is to run all the ductwork in the living spaces of the house. When you plan the house, put the furnace and air conditioner in a closet on one of the main floors, not in the basement or the attic. Or insulate the basement or the roof of the attic (instead of the floor of the attic), so the equipment and the ducts are in an insulated space (Fig. 4-6).

Fortunately, if you are building your house out of ICFs and you are putting the HVAC equipment in a basement, the problem is pretty much solved for you. You will be building the basement out of ICFs, so it's well insulated. With the HVAC equipment in the basement, the ducts leading up to the rest of the house will be in an insulated area. For that reason, loss of heat or cooling to the outside will be less. It's still nice to have tightly sealed ducts to direct the conditioned air up to the main living areas. However, the results of duct leaks are not as bad. The same sort of logic goes for putting insulation in the upper side of the attic and the equipment in the attic.

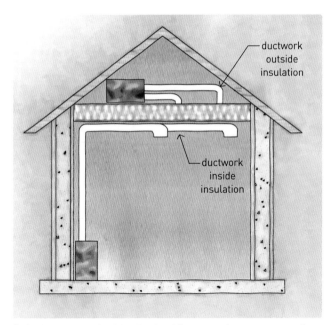

4-6. Ducts run inside the building envelope are usually more efficient than ducts run in uninsulated basements and attics.

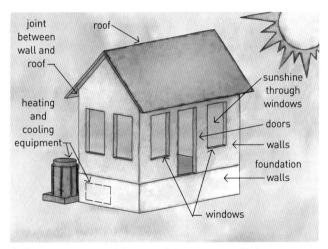

4-7. Potential "trouble spots" for energy efficiency.

All of these measures require that attention be paid to ventilating the HVAC equipment properly. Fortunately, most contractors have installed HVAC equipment inside the living space before and are familiar with the correct procedures.

OTHER WAYS TO INCREASE ENERGY EFFICIENCY

Moving on to the next topic you raised, what are some other good ways to increase the energy efficiency of my house?
There are a lot of them. I can go over a few of the major ones here, but if you really want to get into detail on this and get some careful recommendations, hire an energy analyst. That's what they do, and many people find it worth the cost. But in general, if you're building your walls out of ICFs, you want to concentrate on other parts of the house's envelope (Fig. 4-7). With ICFs you've got your walls about as efficient as they can be.

OK, what do I look for in these other areas to increase my home's energy efficiency?
I can only give you a few clues because the products are always changing and things that are appropriate in one part of the world might not work so well in another. The general rules on windows are to look for double-pane windows. The more energy-efficient ones nowadays have things called **low-E coatings** and are argon-filled between the panes. But all that may be old news in a few years. You also want windows with frames that don't conduct heat readily. There are all sorts of things they do to frames to raise their R-value. You'll have to talk to your contractor and maybe some window distributors if you want to get into detail on this.

In hot climates you can pick up a lot of excess heat from the sun shining through the windows. This seriously raises the air-conditioning bill. One solution is to not put too many windows on the south or west sides of the house, or to use awnings or large overhangs to shade the south glass in summer. There are also coatings that go over the windowpanes that cut the amount of heat coming in. Some windows come with this preinstalled. On others it can be added later.

You don't have to worry much about air infiltration with quality windows these days. They are mostly designed to fit very tightly.

What should I do to the roof to gain energy efficiency?

For energy-saving purposes, you want the same sort of things in a roof that you have in the walls—high R-value and low air infiltration. Thermal mass is nice to get if you can, but that can be difficult to have in a roof.

Can't I build an ICF roof?

Yes, and that would certainly take care of all three items. The foam has good R-value, and there are few if any breaks in it. When you cast the concrete, you basically seal the roof against air infiltration. This includes the joint between the walls and the roof. That joint is a big spot for potential leakage when you have a wood roof, but casting concrete all the way from the bottom of the walls to the top of the roof pretty much eliminates it as a concern. You would also get some good thermal mass. But ICF roofs cost more, and for most people they would be too hard on the budget.

You might also remember from Chapter 3 that there is another good option. That is a structural insulated panel (SIP) roof. It should give you nearly the same energy efficiency as an ICF roof, at a lower cost.

What if I stick with a frame roof?

There are ways to increase the efficiency of a standard frame roof. This is a good thing to talk to your general contractor about, since the best way to do it is going to be different in different cases. You'll need to rely on the general contractor's judgment.

One technique I've seen on a frame roof is to fill it with the usual fiberglass insulation, then put a continuous layer of foam insulation underneath (Fig. 4-8). This adds R-value, it even covers over the wood pieces (which are a weak spot for transferring heat), and the foam layer helps stop air infiltration. But this can be tricky, especially if you will be running lights and ductwork in the ceiling. It also has costs.

But *beware!* Exactly how you build this type of roof will vary. I believe that in hot, humid climates it is actually better to put the layer of foam *outside* the roof,

not inside. That is the sort of thing a good contractor will know.

An extra layer of insulation over the framing is almost a must when the roof is steel frame. The steel transfers a lot of heat, so you should be very wary of building a steel-frame roof with insulation placed only between the steel pieces and none running over them.

Another alternative that some people are turning to is using spray-in foam insulation instead of fiberglass. It usually has a higher R-value, and it seals the roof against air infiltration. But this also costs more, and you may not have contractors trained to do this in your area.

TROUBLE SPOTS

Is that all I need to know to make my house energy-efficient?

There are some other potential trouble spots, but we're starting to get into small details. Doors are usually quite energy-efficient these days. Solid wood doors actually have a poor R-value, but most exterior doors these days are steel or fiberglass with a core of insulating foam in the center. Those are very energy-efficient. If you have a door that has a lot of glass

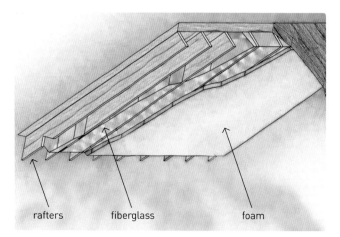

rafters   fiberglass   foam

4-8. Frame roof with a layer of interior foam sheathing.

you want it to have the same sort of energy-efficiency features as a window. Sliding doors are often a big problem because they usually aren't very air-tight. A lot of air gets through between the door and the frame. So either don't use sliding doors or pay for the newest, most energy-efficient type.

Recessed lights can also be a problem, especially the cheap ones, which can leak a lot of air through the ceiling. Some more expensive ones are specially sealed to prevent this.

If you have a house with lots of glass—huge picture windows and such—you just have to accept that you'll have a higher energy bill. Even the best windows don't have nearly the R-value of an ICF wall, so if you have a lot of windows you'll let a lot of heat through them.

A dozen other things could be important, but I believe we've hit the high points. If you put a high priority on reducing your energy bill as much as possible, this is something you should be discussing with your general contractor.

Are there any other things that have to do with energy efficiency that I should be asking about? The one other thing I can think of is the relationship between energy efficiency and indoor air quality. When you start building these really airtight houses, you want to be sure you have the proper controlled ventilation installed in them. I go over this in more detail in the next chapter.

Other than that, I think we've covered this issue. If you are curious to go into more detail, you should probably get a book just on energy or start hanging out with mechanical engineers. For the rest of us, it's time to get on to the next subject.

5

More on Health, Mold, and Other Things We Worry About Nowadays

HOUSES TODAY ARE getting tighter and tighter. By that I mean that they are constructed to reduce the air infiltration through the envelope. This has two advantages. It reduces the possibility of unwanted airborne contaminants entering

Painting the new home's interior.

the house. It also reduces the costs of heating and cooling the house, as we discussed in the last chapter. This trend of tightening up the house goes for all types of construction. ICF walls do a lot to cut the air infiltration of a house, but builders of frame houses are gradually finding ways to cut it in their houses, too. The flip side of this trend is that designers and builders must now make some effort to ensure that a house gets *enough* new or filtered air coming in. If it doesn't, there could be some problems.

What kind of problems can occur if my house is too tight?

There's no guarantee that anything negative will happen, but with a very tight house it is a good idea to take a couple of precautions to guard against the buildup of indoor air contaminants and the potential for mold to grow.

INDOOR AIR CONTAMINANTS

What are indoor air contaminants?

These are gases and particles that can accumulate in the air. They may only cause the air to smell bad. But if they become extreme, some might aggravate respiratory problems or make occupants nauseated or ill.

Where do these indoor air contaminants come from?

There are a number of possible sources. Some things in the building might contain substances that evaporate and mix into the air. This is sometimes called **off-gassing**. Cooking, fires, marking pens, paints, and certain building materials—all sorts of things—can put foreign substances into the air. If the building is very tight, these things can build up indoors to unpleasant or sickening levels.

Why weren't people worried about indoor air contaminants before?

I suppose partly because in times past there were plenty of other things that could make them sicker,

and they worried about those more. But—and maybe more importantly—houses used to be built much looser, so there was lots of air infiltration from the outside. This had the disadvantage that it could bring in unwanted things from outdoors and it made the house drafty and energy inefficient. But it also flushed out the bad stuff from the indoors constantly so it couldn't build up to high levels.

I've heard that the things the house is built of can give off contaminants. Is that true?

Building products are sometimes made with substances that can off-gas and produce an unpleasant or unhealthy environment. However, this is rapidly declining. A lot of carpeting had this property at one point, but the manufacturers are finding alternative ways to produce their products, which reduce indoor air problems. Certain wood products have also long been treated with formaldehyde, which can evaporate and build up in the air. But that too is being reduced.

What about ICFs? Can they give off anything dangerous?

Apparently not. This has been tested numerous times. The foam used in ICFs is made of a plastic called **expanded polystyrene**. That's sometimes abbreviated EPS. Some people thought that this foam might give off bits of the polystyrene material and that these might accumulate in the air. So German scientists went into houses that had a lot of foam insulation and tested the air. They had scientific instruments that they modified to make them ten times more sensitive to the polystyrene material. They ended up finding nothing. There were *no* measurable polystyrene particles in the air.

I've heard that foam contains a gas of some sort. Can that come into the house?

Not really. Expanded polystyrene foam is manufactured with pentane. Pentane is a flammable gas, similar to the natural gas used to heat homes. But nearly all the pentane escapes from the foam during the manufacturing process and is vented away inside the plant. The rest continues to escape while the foam sits in the plant before shipping. By the time the foam gets to your job site, there is virtually no pentane left.

MECHANICAL VENTILATION

But from what you say I may still have some indoor air contaminants from all sorts of sources. How do I make sure my indoor air quality is good?
Most people seem to be moving to **mechanical ventilation**. This is a fancy term for bringing in controlled amounts of outside air from specific locations and mixing it with the indoor air. This flushes out the inside air several times a day with a minimal chance of bringing in other things that you don't want (Fig. 5-1).

Mechanical ventilation is what most construction authorities recommend, and more and more houses are being built with it. That includes *all* kinds of houses—not only wood frame or ICF. In fact, there are now proposed regulations that, if adopted, will require mechanical ventilation in most houses. Some people are opposed to these regulations because they increase the cost of a house. But even though it's not required yet, a growing number of owners are asking for it, and a growing numbers of builders are installing it in all their houses, whether it's requested or not.

How can I get mechanical ventilation installed in my home?
This is another thing to ask your general contractor. The GC should be able to explain your options.

What should I be asking for to get the right ventilation?
Ask what kind of ventilation can be put in the house to make sure you get enough fresh air from outside. Some people use the term **air exchange** to mean the same thing. Almost every house has at least *some* mechanical ventilation. Even a bathroom fan, for example, provides some. There are a lot of different products that provide mechanical ventilation and they're always changing, so I can't generalize much here about which is best. For advice on how much ventilation you need, see the sidebar "How Much Ventilation Is Enough?"

How Much Ventilation Is Enough?

There's no hard and fast rule for residential ventilation requirements, but there are a few general guidelines. Some proposed regulations would require that all houses have at least 0.35 **air changes per hour (ACH)**. This is sometimes abbreviated 0.35 ACH. Other proposals use a more complicated formula based on the house's square footage and number of occupants, but the result is usually close to the 0.35 ACH level.

One air change per hour (or 1.0 ACH) means that each hour, an amount of new air comes into the house that is equal to the total amount of air sitting inside the house. You can think of it as "replacing" all the inside air with fresh air about once per hour. So, basically, 0.35 ACH means that in an hour you replace 35% of the air in the house.

With a new ICF house that has no extra mechanical ventilation, you're often right around this border of 0.35 ACH. If you really button up all the other parts of the house (windows, roof, and so on), you'll almost certainly be well below it, and you should consider taking a serious look at adding mechanical ventilation.

If you're interested, you can have your house tested after it is built. Or, if you're hiring an energy analyst, you can give the analyst the house's specifications and get an estimate of the air infiltration along with your estimated fuel use. But most people don't bother. They decide whether they want mechanical ventilation based on their own preferences and discussions with their contractor.

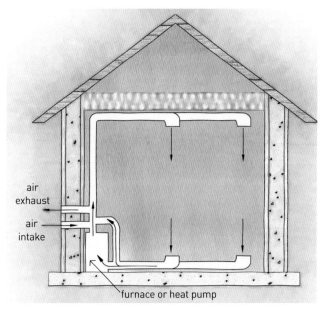

5-1. Mechanical ventilation attached to the heating and cooling system brings in outside air.

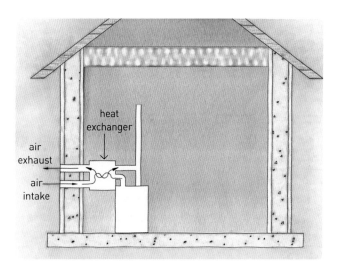

5-2. An air-to-air heat exchanger takes some of the heat or coolness from outgoing air and puts it into the incoming air to keep from losing it all.

Does mechanical ventilation waste energy?

That's a good question. Compared to a tight house with no ventilation, it will increase the energy bill, but only a little if done properly. However, compared to a house built leaky, a well-designed mechanical ventilation system will probably use less energy. And you will have much better indoor air quality since the amount of air exchange and the distribution of the fresh air are controlled rather than left to chance, such as how windy it is on a given day.

One fairly popular option is an **air-to-air heat exchanger** (Fig. 5-2). It's also called a **heat recovery ventilator**, or **HRV**. This device brings in outside air and exhausts out inside air. It uses a special mechanism to keep some of the heating (or cooling) from going outside, too. We did this on my house, and it worked well. We got fresh air and still had very low fuel bills.

Then why not always put in a heat recovery ventilator?

It costs more, for one thing. Outfitting a typical house with this might cost in the range of $2,000. There might also be less expensive or better ways to provide

air exchange in your case. That's why I recommend talking to your general contractor. I'll remind you about this in Chapter 7.

FILTRATION

You said most people are moving to mechanical ventilation. Is there another option?

I have heard of another option from some very good mechanical engineers. Mechanical engineers are the people who figure out what type of heating and cooling you need for a building. They mostly work on commercial buildings, but a few of them work regularly on houses.

The option they sometimes recommend is to filter the air in the house instead of bringing in outside air. They point out certain advantages to filtration. It's more energy efficient, since you don't have to heat or cool the outside air as it comes in. You don't need a heat exchanger. You don't bring in any air contaminants that might be outside. And you don't bring in humidity from the outdoors that would have to be removed by your heating/cooling system.

So why don't I just use filters instead of all the mechanical ventilation and heat exchangers?

The problem is finding someone qualified to design a system like this. It's a different way to do things, and there aren't too many specialists who are doing it. And if you can't find one of them, it probably isn't a good idea. You can't just throw a few filters onto a regular heating/cooling system. You have to know what you're doing. Also, these systems may be expensive to install and require regular maintenance or expensive filter replacements to remain effective. Some experts recommend this approach for individuals who need especially clean air for health reasons.

MOLD

How does mold fit into all this?

The way mold fits into this discussion is that the ventilation and the indoor air quality can affect the growth of mold in the house. The general public has become concerned that mold might be a bad indoor air contaminant. In the past, mold has been found in some buildings and blamed for various health problems. Mold gives off tiny particles called **spores**, which are basically the mold's seeds. Most of the concern about mold is that breathing in these spores may harm us. So people are looking at ways to prevent the growth and spread of mold spores.

How serious are the effects of mold?

I have seen presentations by several experts on the subject, and at this point they are mostly scratching their heads. They appear to have no ironclad evidence that breathing in mold spores in the air can really hurt most people's health. They do say that it is possible that high concentrations of mold may be harmful to individuals with severe respiratory problems. But currently most of the concern seems to be coming from private citizens who have health concerns and are blaming them on mold in their homes or offices. The experts are scrambling to see whether there might be a link, though they didn't know of a significant one before.

As a separate matter, mold can eat away at organic materials. Some people have opened up old wood-frame walls and found that long-term growth of mold has severely eaten the wood (Fig. 5-3). This could dangerously weaken the wall. However, this is quite unusual. And it's nearly impossible in ICF walls because they have little or no wood.

I've heard that there is a variety called "toxic mold." Is that a really dangerous kind?

There are thousands of varieties of mold, just as there are thousands of varieties of flowers. One variety has the scientific name **stachybotrys**. Reporters started calling this toxic mold because some people believed it

5-3. Mold growth on old wood.

was causing problems and was particularly harmful to humans. It can definitely be very ugly looking. But in the presentations I've seen, the experts don't think it should be considered particularly harmful. Some scientists have said that, to the extent that mold is harmful, they would expect several other varieties to be *more* harmful than stachybotrys.

How does mold get inside a house?
Mold can get just about everywhere. The spores spread out and settle on virtually any surface. Anywhere that has the right set of conditions, mold can survive, live, and grow.

What conditions does mold need to grow?
The main conditions are: a moderate temperature, organic matter, and high humidity. Most molds live best at room temperature. They can't survive great heat or cold, much like us. They also have to have something organic to eat. Wood, paper, natural fabrics, and the like are usually good food for them. They also need fairly high humidity because they often get the water they need from the air. They generally need a humidity level that is higher than most humans feel comfortable with.

So how do I stop mold from growing?
Avoiding high humidity is the easiest way to control mold growth. If we keep the indoor air at a humidity level humans are most comfortable with, mold won't be able to gain a foothold. That's one of the reasons we're getting away from letting outdoor air enter the house randomly. In humid climates, outdoor air will bring in moisture and possibly create conditions for mold growth. So instead we limit the amount of outside air that comes in, or we only bring in outdoor air when and where we want it. Then we can run it through the air conditioner or other equipment to dehumidify it. That keeps the moisture in the air low, and helps prevent mold from growing inside.

So it's simple, right? We just keep our houses dry and mold can't live there.
Yes, but only up to a point. The problem is that it's hard to keep every nook and cranny at low humidity. Plumbing that runs through floors and walls may have tiny leaks, or moisture in the air may condense on the pipes. These things will raise the humidity inside that floor or wall right around the plumbing. Bathrooms as well as kitchens can also be humid—anywhere we use water. Wet basements and crawl spaces, due to poor drainage around a building, are major sources of mold in buildings. Also, the insides of exterior walls and roofs can sometimes become humid because they're the "border" between warm and cold air. Warm air that gets in can hit the cold side, and the moisture in the air might condense. So you can control mold by controlling humidity. But it's not reasonable to think that you will ever eliminate mold completely.

What about the food? Can I take away the organic materials and eliminate the mold that way?
Again, you can to a point. That's another argument for reducing the use of wood in the house. Mold can't live on things like concrete and foam for long. But you can never take all the organic material out of your home. Do you just throw out the cotton quilt your great-grandmother gave you? Force yourself not to use wallpaper? Never file away old papers? Even the wallboard we use has paper on its surface.

So I should use my heating, cooling, and ventilating system to keep the humidity down. I can try to use nonorganic materials where possible. Is there anything else I should do to control mold?
Those are definitely the key tactics. The other important thing to remember is not to let the ventilation shut off for prolonged periods. This is especially true now that we are building our houses tighter and tighter. I heard of a man with a vacation home who shut off the AC and ventilation and locked everything up tight as a drum all summer. He came back to find it had a lot of mold inside. The indoor environment had stayed warm

and humid for a long time—a perfect environment for mold.

Indoor air contaminants, like mold—should I be worrying about these things?

That's like asking if you should be worried about hurricanes, floods, or fires. Really harmful ones are rare events, although they can be more frequent under certain conditions and in certain locations. I would say you should be aware of them so you can take prudent precautions to be able *not* to worry about them. Specifically, you should consult with your contractor to make sure that someone is thinking about the ventilation of your house. It may well be that no special equipment or measures are needed—most people still don't install ventilation systems in ICF houses or in houses in general, and by and large they do fine. But it's worth someone with knowledge giving this some thought.

Note that adding ventilation is usually handled by the HVAC contractor. So at some point your general contractor may be discussing options with this person. And, as you are probably beginning to gather, between the sizing of the heating and cooling equipment, the type of heating and cooling equipment, and the possible use of ventilation, there is plenty to talk about with the HVAC contractor.

In conclusion, I can say that, fortunately, ICFs are pretty inert. They don't appear to give off anything harmful. They are pretty much unaffected by water or any moisture that might happen to build up in close proximity to them. But they're also part of the trend toward tighter and tighter houses. This can be good because it saves energy and helps control which airborne substances come inside. But it makes it important for us to think a bit about what we should do to keep the inside air fresh.

CHAPTER 6

Finding the Right People for the Job

HOME BUILDING IS one of those activities that requires the efforts and cooperation of a lot of different specialists. This includes the general contractor, dozens of subcontractors for all the different parts of the building, and sometimes an

Man inserting rebar in holes in the footing with adhesive. (Simpson Strong-Tie Co., Inc.)

architect or even an engineer. If these are competent, dedicated people, the house will likely be high-quality (Fig. 6-1). So, first and foremost, you want to make sure you have good people working on your new home.

Is it really all that complicated to get the right people to build your ICF house?

The basic requirements are simple. The person supervising the crew who actually install the ICFs, and preferably the crew members themselves, need to have ICF experience one way or another. It's best to find a general contractor who has experience building ICF houses, but it's not absolutely essential as long as the person directly supervising the crew can make up for the GC's lack of knowledge about ICFs. Either way, a general contractor who is a competent, quality-minded person is a must. If you hire an architect, the same thing applies: ICF experience is important, but overall competence is most critical. Also, it really helps to have certain subcontractors with some special ICF experience; this is most crucial for the heating, ventilating, and air-conditioning contractor. But even though the basic

idea is simple, it may take some legwork and some discipline to find these people. You should not settle, however, until you do.

GENERAL CONTRACTOR

OK, so there are maybe a few different people I need to get lined up to build my house. Where do I start?

As you might have noticed, I put a lot of emphasis on the general contractor. Nine times out of ten, this is the person who leads the project and has the most influence on how well it comes out. So I recommend putting a lot of effort into hiring a good one.

Exactly what is a general contractor?

The general contractor is also sometimes called the *GC* or just "*the general*" for short. The GC is the person who handles all the construction and has responsibility for seeing that the work is done right. And when I say *responsibility,* I mean formal, legal responsibility. The general contractor registers with the local building department when the construction is about to start. The building department sends inspectors out to the job site at key points during construction. If anything serious is wrong, the inspectors require the general contractor to get it corrected. If he doesn't, the department shuts the project down until things are set right. The general contractor is the person they hold responsible for making sure that all the workers are complying (Fig. 6-2).

The general contractor also has formal responsibility to you, the homebuyer. The two of you sign a contract upfront for the construction of the house. (In fact, this is where the term *contractor* comes from.) The contract lays out a lot of details about how the building will be built, in addition to how much you will pay and a raft of other details. If anything isn't going according to contract, you can complain to the GC. If things aren't made right, you may have the right to withhold payment.

6-1. An ICF home.

6-2. Choose your general contractor wisely.

In work terms, the general contractor runs the show. The GC typically works with the homebuyer at the beginning to finalize the design of the house, submits the formal papers to the local building department to get permission to build, finds subcontractors to carry out the different tasks of construction, supervises the subcontractors and pays them, finds and buys the materials, and deals with the building department if there is a problem. Ultimately, the GC is responsible for delivering your house to you in good, final order.

How does the general contractor fit in with all the other people working on the project?

This can vary from house to house. Let's start with one of the most common arrangements. Say you found some land that's ready for a house. You buy it. Then you ask around and hear about a general contractor who is supposed to be good. You meet and are comfortable with the GC. You get some house plans that you like. You discuss a few modifications you would like to make, and the GC suggests ways this can be done. You agree on a price and sign a contract.

The general contractor files papers with the building department and lines up subcontractors to do the work. In some cases, the GC personally works at the job site, perhaps with a few regular employees. But most of the time he is scheduling various subcontractors in and out, getting the key materials for the job, coordinating the subcontractors, checking their work, dealing with the building department, and generally making sure everything comes together properly.

SUBCONTRACTORS

Subcontractors get their name because they sign separate contracts with the general contractor. Some people call them "*subs*" for short. There are usually separate subcontractors to dig the hole for the foundation; build the foundation; construct the structure (walls, floors, roof); install the electrical lines and equipment; install the plumbing; install insulation; put on the exterior wall finish; put on the roofing; install the HVAC equipment; install the wallboard over the insides of the walls; put down flooring; paint inside and out; and put in the trim, kitchen cabinets, and other interior finish items. And this list is far from complete. Some subcontractors do more than one job, but still a typical house will involve 10 to 20 subcontractors.

Various other specialists may be brought in for minor jobs without a contract. They simply submit a bill when they are finished. But, again, the GC generally finds and deals with these people as needed.

Does it always work this way?
No. There are many variations on this common pattern. What I've just described is the classic **custom home** construction. You buy the land, and then you find a GC to build it according to your own, custom specifications.

In some cases, you don't own any land but you find a general contractor who does. GCs often buy up lots for new houses and offer to build you a house on it and sell you the whole package. In this case you usually get a little less choice in how the house is built. You

have to accept the general contractor with the land, and that GC probably does things in certain ways. In my area of the country, this kind of arrangement is called **build-to-suit**. Some other areas call it **semi-custom home** construction.

DEVELOPERS

In another common arrangement, businesspeople buy larger tracts of land, then do all the paperwork with the local government to get permission to divide up those tracts and build houses on them. These are called **developers**. Some developers are also general contractors; they take responsibility for building the houses, hire the subcontractors, supervise all work, and so on. And some hire a general contractor to do that work and build homes for the public. A few developers even sell the plain lots to general contractors or homebuyers like you and me.

If the developer will sell off the lots and let you build however you want on them, this is just a variation on custom homebuilding—you simply got your land from a specific source. If the developer requires that you have the developer or the developer's chosen contractor build the house from a limited range of house plans, this is a classic semicustom arrangement. Such semicustom construction is common in large developments, especially in the southern and western United States. The developer has a large tract of land that he subdivides into lots. He also has a book of standard house plans. You pick a lot, pick a house design you like, and choose from a list of allowed options (like a choice of paint colors, bathroom fixtures, etc). There are standard prices for every lot, every design, and every option. In three months, voila! Your house is done. It's almost like buying a new car.

Is there any way to build or buy a new home that isn't "custom" or "semicustom"?
There is **speculative** homebuilding. Most contractors call the house built by this arrangement a **spec home** for short. A spec home is one that a general contractor

or developer builds without having a buyer yet. The GC or developer buys land, gets the permits from the municipality, and builds a house of a style that will probably appeal to local buyers. Then he advertises it for sale and hopes that a buyer will come along soon. Sometimes it will be advertised for sale even before it is finished; in this case the builder will often let the buyers choose what specific finishes they want—paint colors, styles of trim, and so on. But anything that is already done is locked in and you have no choice.

Can I get an ICF house built any of these three ways—custom, semicustom, or speculative?
You will probably *not* be dealing with spec home-building if you want an ICF house. The odds that a builder has chosen to construct a spec house out of ICFs are very low. When they build spec houses, they typically choose the most common materials and styles and colors. Expect spec houses to be wood frame with a conservative floor plan and the finishes that are most common in your area.

If you want ICF walls, you will need to specify them before construction starts. Generally speaking, that puts you into custom homebuilding. You find the land, then find the builder who will build the house the way you want. Occasionally, you can find a semi-custom builder or developer who is flexible enough to use a new and different wall system. Most of them are not, but if you find a semicustom development or lot that you like, you can always ask.

Are there really no developments of ICF homes?
Well, okay, nowadays there are a few. Some developers have decided that ICFs will be popular in their area. So they offer to build your house on one of the lots out of ICFs. Usually this is an option. They don't build *all* the houses out of ICFs—they leave the choice up to the buyer of each house. You might stumble on a development like this.

ARCHITECTS AND ENGINEERS

But where do all those other people you mentioned figure in? What about architects and engineers?
Architects may be involved, too. Most people however, don't hire an architect for their new house. They pick standard plans they find in books, or the GC supplies some typical plans and the buyer chooses one of those. If these buyers want to change things a bit, they can work that out with the GC. If you're considering hiring an architect, see the sidebar titled "Why Hire an Architect?"

Engineers also work on only a small percentage of houses built nowadays. For most conventional houses, the contractors and the building departments know how to build the house so that it's strong enough to meet the structural and safety requirements. For example, for wood-frame houses the size of lumber you need and how you have to arrange it is mostly worked out in a series of tables that cover typical sizes and styles of homes. The same goes for ICFs: There are now tables for the building details that determine the structural strength of the walls (like the thickness of the wall, the size and positioning of the steel reinforcing bar, and so on). So the contractors and the building officials can just look in the tables to make sure everything is being done soundly.

But sometimes people build houses that aren't covered by the tables. Perhaps they're unusually large or they're made with unconventional materials. In that case, the building department may require that an engineer design the structural parts of the house to make sure everything is okay. It's up to the person who is paying to have the house built to find and pay the engineer. However, if you are dealing with an architect or general contractor, that person may recommend an engineer and coordinate the work. If you hire an architect to handle the whole project, the architect usually supervises the engineer so that you don't have to.

Years ago, when building departments were not yet very familiar with ICFs, most of them required buyers to hire an engineer to design the structural parts of the house. But that is becoming less and less common. The

Maybe 5% to 10% of homebuyers hire an architect. This may be especially attractive if the house is to be highly original, unusual, or creative. Some buyers want a house design that is very artistic or very precisely tailored to their individual needs and preferences, and are willing to pay more for that. Of course, you hire an architect only if you are building a custom house.

In the standard arrangement, you hire the architect and the architect supervises both design and construction through to the time the house is finished. At the beginning you discuss your needs and preferences, and the architect draws up preliminary designs. You review them, and the design goes through some revisions until everyone is more or less happy. The architect may recommend a general contractor, but you choose and hire the GC. The architect reviews the construction work as it is being done, and attends to a lot of day-to-day details so you don't have to. You pay both the architect and the GC.

Other arrangements are possible as well. When my wife and I built our house, we picked a standard plan out of a book, then hired an architect to change the floor plan to meet our needs better and jazz up the outside look a bit. Then we took the plans and handled things from there. It was less expensive than having the architect create a complete set of plans and manage the construction process, and we were happy with the results. Things like this can be worked out with many architects.

6-3. The architect may visit the job site.

structural design of ICFs has now been reduced to tables for common house sizes and styles. These tables are in the most commonly used building codes, which are the regulations that building departments use to make sure that construction is being done correctly. So in most cases the building departments are happy to let you build an ICF house without an engineer. But you should still have an experienced general contractor.

ACTING AS YOUR OWN GENERAL CONTRACTOR

I've heard that sometimes the homebuyer can act as the general contractor (GC). What if I want to build my own house this way?

Yes, it can be done. Some local building departments allow you to sign your name and be the general contractor. The house still has to go through all the inspections and you still have to hire qualified subcontractors; in most towns the electrician, the plumber, and a few others have to be licensed. In short, you have to meet all the requirements that a regular general contractor must meet.

There are a lot of books that are very encouraging and give advice on how to do this. I even did it myself. But now that I have this experience under my belt and I have seen other people do it, I generally wouldn't recommend it (see "Lessons Learned on My Own House," page 89).

Why wouldn't you recommend acting as your own general contractor?
I think most of the benefits that people expect don't usually pan out. As best I can tell, most people want to act as their own general contractor because they think they will save money or they think they can better control the details and quality of the house. In my experience, those things don't really happen.

You pay a professional general contractor because this person has experience in building a home efficiently. When you do it yourself, the job is almost always done much less efficiently. This costs money, and the savings can evaporate. You can even end up paying more (see sidebar titled "Why Not Be Your Own Contractor?" on page 88).

But what about quality? Won't I make sure my house is built better because I care about it more?
There is something to this. But if you do your work in finding a *good* general contractor, you'll have one who cares about quality, too. Some are just out to make a buck, but some got into the business because they love building things, and they love building them right. Frankly, you often don't know *how* to build with high quality. You'll be likely to do some things that are overkill and pay more than you have to, and do other things wrong and actually make the quality of your house lower.

So if I'm my own GC I may spend a little more money and have a couple of glitches in the house. Is there anything more that could be a problem?
Yes. You could have to commit almost six months to a year of your time to building your house. And you may even end up moving into your house much later than that.

You have to be on constant call when your house is under construction. If the job is really going to be done right, you have to come out almost daily to inspect the work. You have to arrange to get supplies as they're needed or your workers will sit around with nothing to do for days at a time. You have to be available to answer questions as they come up. You're the only one who knows what the house is supposed to turn out like, so only you can make the important judgment calls.

And even if you keep on top of everything, the house will most likely still be finished later than if you had a general contractor take care of it. Your mistakes and all the rework will drag things out. When your subcontractors have another job to work on and don't show up for a few days, you have very little clout to get them back. They know you have no real pull and that you have to wait for them. A professional general contractor will tell them that they'd better get back to the job or they won't get any more work with him again. And if they're still slow in responding, he can call up two other good crews he knows to take over the work.

But what about acting as my own general contractor if I already know a lot about construction?
OK, you've got me there. If you're already an experienced general contractor, all the arguments against serving as the GC on your own house go right out the window. This is probably so even if you're an experienced architect or subcontractor with broad knowledge of homebuilding. But I've seen engineers, building inspectors, and very good "handymen" serve as general contractors on their own homes, and the results were not very encouraging.

If you think you'll have fun and you're willing to spend more and take longer, then your expectations are realistic and I say go right ahead.

Why Not Be Your Own Contractor?

Many first-time homebuyers think they can save money by acting as their own general contractor. Many books and magazine articles make it sound easy. But it's rarely easy and the savings often don't materialize.

Let's list the more common things that inflate the costs. First of all, you're building only one house. Professional general contractors typically complete at least a half-dozen houses each year. When you hire subcontractors to bid on the job, they will almost always charge you more than they would charge a professional GC. They have never worked with you and they don't know how demanding or how reasonable you'll be. For all they know, you will throw a lot of late changes at them, and they'll have to spend time redoing things. Also, you can't give them any future work. They're much happier with someone who will keep them busy month after month.

Buying materials is much the same story. A professional general contractor gets a discount on most things because the suppliers sell a lot to this same person without much hassle. This is economical for them. Selling to a new customer means they have to spend a lot of time setting up accounts, learning the person's needs, and so on, and they will only sell product to the person for a few months, then never again. You can argue all you want that this doesn't make sense—but they usually won't give you the discount.

Then there are the mistakes. Some things you will build bigger than necessary or with more expensive materials because you don't know any better. That costs. Other things you will have built wrong, and you will have to pay for extra materials and pay the subcontractors to rip out the work you just completed and redo it correctly. General contractors make fewer mistakes, and if they do make them, they have to pay to fix them. That's part of the contract—they are responsible for the finished product. Without a GC, you're responsible for the house, and you pay to get it right.

You may wonder how so many mistakes can take place. First of all, building a house is much more complicated than people assume, and no two houses are exactly alike. There are probably 5,000 unique products that go into a house, which have to be bought and installed. There are finish nails, common nails, box nails, and sinkers of many different sizes and materials; 2x4x8s and 2x4x12s and 2x12x16s; a kitchen range, seven different cabinet components, six different kinds of flooring, three different grades of sheathing, eleven different styles of light fixtures, and on and on. You have to know which ones to get, where and how to get them, and what you have to do to them to get them to meet code. You will also have to select and coordinate the schedules of about 20 subcontractors, maybe 18 of whom you have never met before, and supervise them and evaluate their work.

Maybe worst of all, you will have to envision the entire construction project so that all the parts fit together properly. When that custom stovetop made in Europe arrives and turns out to be two inches taller than your counter cabinets, that's your problem, not the subcontractor's. When the walls are covered with wallboard and you realize that you didn't ask the carpenter to put any blocking where you want to install the towel racks and medicine cabinets, that's your problem. When the roof trusses arrive and you realize they're too short because the walls are made out of a thicker wall system than the one shown on the plans, that's also your problem. The subcontractors aren't responsible for thinking all these things through—half the time they don't even know exactly what you're planning for the house.

When you hire a general contractor, all those things are the GC's responsibility. And a professional knows to check the specifications of a new range, chart the positions of all fixtures and make sure all the ones that need blocking will have it, and measure the outside dimensions of the final wall design before ordering roof trusses. And these are just a few examples.

I decided to act as the general contractor on my own house for a variety of reasons. In the end, my house probably cost me about 5% to 10% more than it would have if I had hired a good GC—and believe me, I know some good GCs who would have done the job for me. It took a year to build, more than twice as long as it would have taken a contractor, mostly because construction was very busy at the time and my subcontractors had other jobs that people were screaming at them to complete, so I often waited weeks at a time for some crucial crew to get back to my house. There were also a couple of important flaws in the house that surfaced after it was "done" and we had moved in—I had to have these fixed later at much greater expense than they would have cost if I had known how to do things right in the first place. During all the work, I was so busy that I neglected my real job and definitely fell behind some of my colleagues on the professional ladder. This all happened even though I definitely knew a little more than the average person about construction.

But I served as my own general contractor mainly because I got some other benefits from the experience that made it all worth it. First and foremost, I got a lot of firsthand knowledge about how homebuilding works. My current job is to do research on new construction products, so this knowledge has proven extremely valuable to me and helped me make a living ever since.

But I also got a kick out of the experience. I really enjoy the details of construction, and this immersed me in them big-time. I definitely enjoyed it less than I expected because it went so much worse than I thought, but I still have good memories and stories I value.

I guess if you're also building your own house for these kinds of intangible reasons, I have no argument against it. Get one of the good books about building your own house and start asking contractors lots of questions to learn as much as you can. And read Chapter 10 of this book—I give you a few tips there. But if you're only interested in saving money and maintaining quality, I would definitely not recommend it.

CONSTRUCTION MANAGER

I've heard that you can hire someone else experienced to do the supervisor work. Why can't I do that but still technically be the general manager?

You can. A person like that is sometimes called the **construction manager**. And that would help a lot. In fact, a construction manager is often a professional general contractor who agrees to let you, technically, be the GC on this job and act only as your "eyes in the field."

But then you pay more money and you aren't personally checking the quality of the work. So this doesn't have much advantage over the usual arrangement where you hire the regular general contractor. You might save a little money because you technically will be responsible for the construction, but then you pay for any mistakes, too. Simply put, the more you pay, the more you get.

OK, so it sounds like the key person I need to find for my new ICF house is a good general contractor or architect. Is that right?

Yes, that's exactly right. I call the general contractor the team leader, unless you use an architect, in which case the architect normally acts as team leader. The team leader has overall responsibility for the project and is the single most influential person on how it goes. Hire a good one, listen, and it will likely go well.

FINDING PEOPLE

So how do I find a general contractor or architect? The time-tested way is best. You get names of some local ones, talk with them, and talk with people they have worked for in the past. It's a lot like interviewing someone for a job. You talk to them about your house and about their work style to see whether their ideas seem sound and make sense. You ask for references and talk to as many people they've worked for as possible. I would recommend talking to a minimum of three references before you actually hire someone. If all seems good with your top choice, you are ready to sign up and get started.

What am I looking for in the architect or general contractor?

To my mind the basic questions are these:

- Do I feel comfortable with this person?
- Is he reliable?
- Does he do quality work?
- Does he appear to build the kind of house I'm interested in?
- Will he give good advice on issues when I need it?
- Will he help make things right when there's a problem?

These are all qualities you have to get a feel for through talking to their customers or others they've worked with. But since you're building an ICF house, you have one more critical question you have to answer: How will this person guarantee that the crew building the house will have experience with ICF construction?

Why is experience with ICF construction so critical?

This is the single biggest factor that determines how well built the ICF parts of the house will be and how well connected they will be to the other parts, meaning interior walls, floors, the roof, interior and exterior finishes, electrical lines, and HVAC equipment.

This is really no different from any other part of the house. If the crew that builds, say, the kitchen has never worked with cabinets or appliances before, they will make mistakes. They can try to correct these as they see them. But some may escape their notice, or some may be too hard to correct. Some may not even show up until after you've moved in. A crew experienced at doing kitchens will make many fewer mistakes and will probably be able to correct them thoroughly.

This is no different from anything you do that's very complex. If you are doing a large crafts project or a research project or a gardening project of a type you've never done before, you will be slower and make more mistakes than you would make on your third or fourth project. Practice makes perfect, especially with something complex, where extensive planning and understanding the end results of your actions are involved. So you really don't want the workers getting their first experience with ICFs on your house. Things go much, much more smoothly, and the results tend to be better if they have done a few ICF houses before.

How do I make sure I have experienced ICF people working on my house?

The key is to have an experienced person supervising the ICF work. It's nice if the laborers on the crew have ICF experience, but a good supervisor can usually direct inexperienced workers just fine.

There are different ways to ensure that you have an experienced supervisor. The most common is for you to hire a hands-on general contractor who not only has experience with ICFs, but also runs the ICF crew. Many general contractors work extensively at their own job sites. On conventional wood houses, small contractors typically run the carpentry crew that puts up the walls, floors, and roof. They have a few regular workers they hire to staff the crew. When the work gets to the specialized trades, like electricians and plumbers, the GCs generally step back and just supervise, and maybe do a few odd jobs. Now there are also general contractors who work the same way with ICFs. They have a regular group of workers they supervise personally in constructing the ICF walls. This is really the best type of GC to hire—as long as this GC meets the other requirements I already mentioned.

But you may also find a GC who has experience building ICF houses *without* directly running the ICF crew—or any other crew, for that matter. When a GC gets a little larger, he becomes more of a straight manager, and less of a worker. When a GC reaches around 15 to 20 houses built per year, it's impossible for him to be at every job site doing the actual construction. So a general contractor managing multiple job sites concentrates on finding good crews to work for them and supervising their work, or he may hire a project manager to be on the job sites supervising the crews. In a case like this, you should still opt for a GC who has experience building ICF houses. You want a GC who has some regular crews who have worked on a few ICF houses, so they know what they're doing. Again, this type of general contractor is a good one to get, as long as the other requirements are met.

Is there anything else I should know before I choose a general contractor?

Yes. I recommend that you make sure you've read through Chapter 9. Knowing something about construction, and about how good and not-so-good general contractors operate during the construction process, will help you judge your candidates better.

What if I'm hiring an architect to supervise construction as well as design the house?

Then what you want to look for is an architect who is comfortable working with new technology. And you have to make sure that the architect will get you that experienced GC, too.

An architect who has designed ICF houses before is helpful, but not really necessary. Designing a house with ICFs is almost exactly the same as designing conventional houses. There are a few rules the architect needs to learn and follow to hold costs down, but any experienced ICF contractor can explain these. The key is finding an architect who will take the time to understand the product and who is willing to listen to the contractor who is doing the work.

This is actually a good rule for building a house out of any products. The better coordinated the architect and the general contractor are, the better the results. The contractor can give the architect feedback during the design process that will make construction more efficient. He can also alert the architect to some options that might hold down costs or jazz up the building to make it better quality or more useful to the owners. A good architect knows most of this already, but an experienced contractor will likely have a few fresh insights. If the architect is willing to listen to the contractor, then the project will go that much better.

This kind of communication is *especially* important if the architect has little experience with ICFs and the contractor has a lot. The contractor will know the tricks and options that are peculiar to ICFs, and the architect won't. If the architect you hire is inexperienced with ICFs and does not work cooperatively with the contractor, then you can expect a lot of problems.

Communication during construction is important, too. That's where a lot of things come up that nobody could have foreseen. Or things that the contractor didn't think to bring up when the design was just on paper. At that point the architect and the contractor can put their heads together. The architect knows what the design of the house is supposed to accomplish and how to make all the little decisions along the way to make sure things are done in a way that is consistent with the master plan. The contractor knows how the little things will affect cost and the rest of construction.

What if I can't find a general contractor experienced with ICFs, or the best GC doesn't have ICF experience?

Let me start out by saying that having a GC with ICF experience is *much* preferable. You are much more likely to get the work done efficiently and with quality. However, you can get the ICF experience for the team from the ICF subcontractor, if need be. If you have a good GC who is open to new things, an experienced ICF crew may be enough. The key in that case is to get an ICF subcontractor with a lot of experience who can help the GC. The supervisor of that crew should communicate with the GC (and the architect, if there is one) starting at the design stage.

In fact, even if the GC has ICF experience, you really need the supervisor of the ICF crew to have ICF experience, too. It can be a bit confusing with ICFs because one person can wear more than one hat. You must have someone experienced with ICFs leading the

ICF crew. That can be the general contractor himself, or the general contractor can hire a separate experienced ICF crew. If you have that experienced ICF crew, and the GC also has ICF experience, that's even better. But it may not be critical if the ICF crew is very experienced and can advise the GC. It's even less important for the architect to have ICF experience, but it is a plus. To sum it all up, the list shows the importance of ICF experience for different members of the team:

Importance of ICF Experience

- Architect (if any): ICF experience is a plus
- General contractor: ICF experience is very helpful★
- Supervisor of ICF crew: ICF experience is critical★★
- Workers on ICF crew: ICF experience is helpful

★ It is critical if the GC is also the supervisor of the crew.
★★ The amount of experience needed by supervisor is greater if the GC does not have ICF experience.

How do I find an ICF-experienced general contractor in my area?

There are three sources I would check. The first is the Web site of the Insulating Concrete Form Association, **www.forms.org**. This site has a directory of association members where you can look up the names of contractors in a specific geographic area. Contact the ones closest to you and see if one of them might be suitable. The second source is the independent Web site, **www.ICFWeb.com**. It also has a directory of ICF-related businesses, including contractors. The third is to contact local distributors of the ICF forms and ask them what local GCs they recommend to build a house. You can get the distributor names from these same two Web sites—the distributors are in their own separate category.

Is it important for me to pick a contractor who is a member of the Insulating Concrete Form Association?

Personally, I would tend to favor them. There are certainly good ICF contractors who are not ICFA members, but the ones who are association members have a couple of things going for them. They were willing and able to join the association so that they can stay up-to-date with the growing ICF technology. I have met some real standout ICF contractors—the guys everybody looks to for their expertise and advice—and virtually all of them are members of the ICFA. Having said that, if you've found a contractor who seems to be great and whose customers all speak glowingly about him, I wouldn't avoid hiring him just because he's not a member.

OK, so I get a few names of local general contractors. Then what?

Then try to get names of a few other GCs who are also supposed to be good. Remember, even if the GC isn't too familiar with ICFs, as long as he is open-minded and competent, you can instead rely on an experienced ICF subcontractor. So ask some friends about local GCs who are supposed to be good. You might just find a gem of a contractor who is willing to work with ICFs and will do a good job. Then you talk to the candidates, talk to their references, compare, and pick the one who seems best.

What if I want to use an architect?

The procedure is the same. Search first for architects who are on the ICF Web sites, or who the ICF distributors recommend, then add some more you've heard are especially good. Pick the one that you feel most comfortable with and that has the best record and reputation. But no matter what, it has to be someone who is willing to try new things and who will talk to the contractors. Then the architect will typically recommend a general contractor, in this case one with ICF experience, or at least one willing to work with an experienced ICF crew. You and the architect can use the same sources I recommended a moment ago.

Suppose I have a general contractor without ICF experience. Do I become involved in finding the ICF subcontractor?

That's up to you and the GC. General contractors usually find and pick their own subcontractors. But this is a little different, if the general has never had contact with an ICF subcontractor before. You should have a talk and emphasize the importance of hiring someone with ICF experience. You can show the GC the methods I recommend to find an experienced sub. The GC might then go find some candidates and check them out. Or the two of you might decide that you will help do some of the legwork to find candidates.

But in the end the GC should pick the sub. The GC has to work with the subcontractor day in and day out, and you don't. You will have to trust the general to make ten thousand different decisions along the way in building your house. If for any reason you don't feel you can trust the general contractor to make this decision, you've got a deeper problem. You should probably part company and go find another GC you really can trust.

One clear problem situation arises if you pick a GC without ICF experience, then that GC picks a sub who has no ICF experience to do the ICF work. That's a big red flag. You should make sure you know how much experience the crew selected to do the ICF work has, and if it's not adequate, call in the GC and get a very, very good explanation as to why they should be on the job, or get the ICF crew changed.

Of course, if the GC has ICF experience, no one has to go through this exercise at all. The GC may personally supervise the crew that does the ICF work. Or the GC may have the names of experienced ICF crews he likes to work with.

And what if I'm starting with an architect?

The process is just about the same, with one extra level of people to find. Once you settle on the architect, the two of you can look for a general contractor. The homebuyer is often heavily involved in picking the GC, but you'd better make sure it's someone the architect is happy with.

With the GC in place, if the team still doesn't have ICF experience, you'll need to go through the same procedure I already described to find an experienced subcontractor. Only this time, you'll be doing it with two other people, instead of one.

How do I know if a GC or subcontractor has enough experience?

That depends a bit on whether both the GC and the ICF subcontractor have ICF experience, or if only the subcontractor does. If they both have ICF experience, the ideal is to get people who have each built at least three ICF houses within the last two years. The record consistently shows that ICF contractors gain a lot of efficiency on their second house, and a sizable amount on their third. They continue to improve as they build more houses, but not a lot more. They're pretty well up to speed after three.

This experience also needs to be fairly recent. Now and then you run across a contractor who did a few ICF houses several years ago, then got out of the ICF business for one reason or another. When they come back to ICFs, these people almost always have to relearn it. The products have changed and they've forgotten some of the key things. So on their first couple of new houses they are going through the learning process all over again.

If only the subcontractor has ICF experience, I would look for someone who has done at least ten ICF houses in the last three years. If only the sub has ICF experience, the GC will be depending on the sub for direction. For that reason, the sub needs to have done so many of these houses and worked with so many GCs that he knows exactly what the GC needs to be doing and is not shy about telling him. And these people exist. There are plenty of ICF subs who are accustomed to coaching GCs who are new to ICFs.

So whoever will be running the ICF crew, whether it's the GC himself or the foreman of a separate sub-contracting crew, you want that person to have done some ICFs recently. Ask how many ICF houses they have built—and when—directly when you interview them. And make sure that if the GC does not have ICF experience, the subcontractor has a lot.

WORKING WITH DEVELOPERS

I heard you mention developers before. What if I'm getting my house from a development company that hires the general contractors?
A developer is a different beast altogether. Developers typically buy up large tracts of land, divide them into house lots, get all the roads and utilities (water, sewer, electricity, gas, etc.) laid in the ground, and then arrange to have houses built on them and sold to the public. How the houses get built may vary. Some developers just sell off the lots to private individuals who are free to hire any GC they want. That's just a variation on the custom house arrangement.

Sometimes there are a few restrictions on who you can hire and what kind of house can be built. This is to ensure a certain "style" or level of quality throughout the development. Other developers sell the lots to general contractors. The GCs then build on the lots and sell the resulting houses. Often there are restrictions on what can be built in this case, too. You could consider all these to be somewhere between true custom and semicustom arrangements, depending on how tight the restrictions are and how much choice the GC gives his buyers.

Many developers may also build the houses themselves. They hire the crews and supervise them. They either take the role of the general contractor, or they hire one or more general contractors or project managers to supervise the work according to their directions. In this case the developer usually has some set construction procedures. There may be a few house designs, and the houses may be all built before buyers like you even have a chance to look at them. So it's a new house, but you have no choice in what it's built of. You simply pay the stated price, or maybe have room to haggle a little. In other developments, the buyer gets to pick a lot and specify at least some of the features that will go on it. So the arrangements are speculative, semicustom, or somewhere in between.

So how can I get an ICF house from a developer?
If the developer is just selling off lots, that's easy. You are back to a pure custom arrangement. You buy the lot you want and hire your own general contractor or architect, as usual. You should just make sure that there are no restrictions from the developer or the town that would stop you from building the house you want.

If the developer is selling lots to general contractors, usually the GC will require you to hire him to build the house. You will have to buy the house, lot and all, from him. So find a GC in the development you like who has the right qualifications and is happy to build you an ICF house. If the developer builds the houses, talk to the company's salespeople to see how much flexibility there is. Some developers will work with a new building system. But don't be surprised if the developer is not open to learning about and building with ICFs. In that case, if you want an ICF house you will have to go elsewhere.

ENGINEERS

When do I hire an engineer?
Usually you don't. In fact, usually nobody does. Most houses don't require an engineer. The structural requirements of typical houses are already worked out in a set of tables that your contractor and the building department can read.

But there are some cases in which an engineer will be necessary. If you want a very large house or one with highly unusual design features, it may not be covered by the tables. In that case the local building department may require an engineer to examine the plans and make sure key parts of the design and materials are okay (Fig. 6-4).

Some very conservative building departments might ask for an engineer even if your house is *not* unusual. They may have never seen ICFs before and may be a bit afraid of having an ICF house built in their area. Even if the engineering tables do cover your house, they may require you to hire an engineer to check everything. Their problem is usually that they are so unfamiliar with ICFs that they don't know what to look for when they inspect them. They're afraid that they will miss something and allow a house to be built that has problems later on. So it's in their authority to require an engineer even for things that are already covered with complete tables in the building codes.

Also, there are some cities that require an engineer to examine the plans of *every* single new house in the area and sign off on them; Phoenix, Arizona, is a good example. In these cities you can't get away without an engineer no matter what kind of house you build. But it's usually not much of a problem. In places like this the general contractors, architects, and engineers have the process pretty streamlined.

Why shouldn't I have an engineer look at my plans?

The only downside is time and cost. You pay the engineer anywhere from a few hundred to a few thousand dollars. It may also add a couple of weeks or a month to the time it takes to get your house design finalized and submitted to the building department. If the house is simple enough that it's covered by the engineering tables, most people don't choose to pay and wait for engineering. However, you could always demand and hire an engineer if you want one and you're willing to pay.

If the building department is requiring an engineer and I don't want to pay for one, what can I do?

Your first resort is to find out why they want the engineer. If you have wildly unusual features in the design, like beams of concrete floating in space, you and your GC or architect should talk over whether you really need them. If you can do without it, you can probably redesign the house to make it more conventional and get approval for the plans without an engineer.

6-4. Engineers reviewing plans. (Portland Cement Association)

What if I have a pretty standard house and the building department wants to require that I get an engineer?

That's the sort of thing that you can usually talk to them about. They should only be requiring this if they feel they do not have enough experience or information to inspect the house correctly themselves. So they want the engineer to look things over carefully to help them. If they can be given more information and gain confidence with the ICFs and the design, they may drop the requirement of an engineer.

This is the job of your general contractor or architect—whoever is running the show. And it's not hard to do. The GC or architect can show the building officials where ICFs are covered in the building codes. The most ICF-experienced person on the team can explain the system to them and possibly direct them to some other houses nearby that have been built with ICFs. Another useful method is to find a building inspector in another town (the closer the better) who has inspected an ICF house before. Let your official call that inspector and chat about it. The inspector in the other town will likely say that everything went fine, and tell your official what he should look for in the inspection.

But this is the job of your GC or architect. You can give them these suggestions, but they should be able to handle it. They've probably been through this kind of discussion a dozen times before.

If I need to hire an engineer for some reason, how do I find a good one?

Your GC or architect may feel qualified to find someone. If not, you may need to take the lead on this, and even if the team leader will find the engineer, there might be some benefit to your giving advice on how to do it. So let's go over the basic guidelines.

Almost any **structural engineer** can check the design of an ICF house. Structural engineers are the engineers who design buildings. They are all trained in the basics of reinforced concrete, and ICFs are nothing more than reinforced concrete with foam over it.

As with any profession, some engineers are more capable and efficient than others. Some also work better with other people. So your team will want to follow the same rules they would for anyone else—talk to a couple different engineers, talk to some of the engineer's customers, and so on. Of course, most general contractors and architects already know engineers that they have worked with before and are

comfortable with. So they might just go to one of them. That can be fine. However, it might be better for them to find someone with ICF experience.

How important is ICF experience for my engineer?

That's really a matter of time and cost. As I said, just about any structural engineer can do the job. A house is not hard to design, as structures go. But an engineer who has never worked with ICFs before will have to go through the books on them and learn the details. And when it comes to the actual design work, an engineer who's not familiar with ICFs will usually work more slowly. So you'll likely get charged more and have to wait a little longer.

An engineer who has done considerable ICF work will typically work very fast. The difference can easily be a savings of a thousand dollars and a week off your schedule.

How do we find an engineer with ICF experience?

The same way you find a GC or subcontractor or architect. Look on the ICF Web sites under "Engineers" or "Professionals." Ask others in your area who sell ICFs or are familiar with ICFs. They probably know an experienced engineer or two.

Does my engineer have to be local, too?

Not necessarily. Many times people send their building plans to an engineer hundreds of miles away. The engineer can go over them, analyze the design, and make corrections without ever visiting your town.

However, if the local building department is requiring that your plans be analyzed, they will probably also require that the engineer be registered to practice in your state. That means the engineer must have taken and passed the state's licensing exam to demonstrate understanding of the building requirements and correct engineering practices in the state. If you live, say, in Idaho, and you find a good engineer in, say, Texas, it is likely that that engineer is not registered in Idaho and you will have to look further. But you should always ask engineers about their states of registration. Some are registered in many states, so even a few faraway ones may be fine to work for you.

OTHER SUBCONTRACTORS

What about all the other subcontractors? I know it's good to find the right person to do the heating and cooling system.

Yes, for best results a few key subcontractors should be chosen wisely. That includes the HVAC contractor, as we discussed in previous chapters. A good one who can size the equipment correctly for an ICF house might be able to save you a thousand dollars or more and give you a system that runs more efficiently.

There's actually some help available for the HVAC subcontractor. The Portland Cement Association has come up with software to help size the HVAC equipment for a home with concrete walls, including ICFs. It's not too expensive and it's extremely easy to use. It's available on the Portland Cement Web site, **www.concretehomes.com**. Any reasonably competent and flexible subcontractor should be able to use it. So if you or the general contractor has experience with an HVAC sub who has done good work and is willing, you might just use this person and get him the software.

What other subcontractors should be specially chosen?

Working with ICFs is different for electricians because they cut channels (also called **chases**) in the foam to put their wires in (Fig. 6-5). This is different from the usual procedure in a frame house of drilling holes through wooden studs. Some adapt just fine to cutting chases—it's really no extra work. Others balk and think it could be trouble and want to charge extra. So it makes sense to hire someone who is open-minded. The other option is to take a half an hour and show the electrician how to work with foam. Your general contractor or your ICF subcontractor—whichever one has the ICF experience—has probably done this before and should be able to handle it.

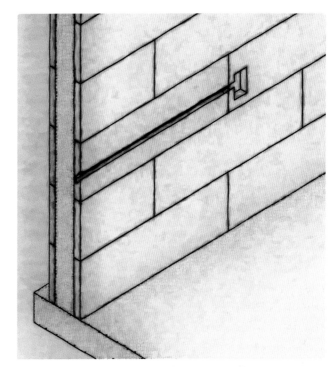

6-5. A chase cut in an ICF wall for an electrical outlet.

Sometimes the ICF crew also builds the wood framing—the interior walls, floors, and roof (Fig. 6-6). If they don't, the GC will probably be bringing in a separate carpentry crew to do that work. Separate carpenters may be a little uncertain about how to connect their framing to the concrete. But again, the experienced person on your team can usually show them pretty easily. These kinds of details are also found in most of the ICF manuals, which the GC and ICF sub should have by the time the carpenters come into the picture.

Occasionally, the folks who install your wallboard or exterior finish (siding, stucco, brick, or whatever) will have a few questions. Attaching things to the ICFs doesn't look quite like attaching them to wooden studs. But it's not much different, and, again, your contractor who knows ICFs, along with the manuals, should be able to cover this.

6-6. Wood-frame interior walls inside ICF walls. (Arxx Building Products)

Should I be involved in finding or training these other contractors?

Not usually. The selection and supervision of these other subcontractors is definitely something that should be the responsibility of the GC. As usual, you can give some tips, but the GC is probably the better judge of subs and also has to decide who he can work with best. But a good HVAC contractor who will size the system correctly and include the right ventilation is extremely important. It is worth checking to make sure that this subcontractor is chosen with care.

Is there anything else I need to do to pick the right people for the job?

That's about it. It's time to get started designing and planning your home.

Planning, Even If You're Impulsive

AN OLD DUTCH PROVERB says, "A good beginning is half the job." Our parents told us this, too, and though we're sick of hearing it, it's true. Some careful planning at the beginning of a major project goes a long way toward making sure it

A house plan.

7-1a & 7-1b. An ICF house under construction (left) and finished (right). (Arxx Building Products)

runs smoothly down the road. And that means lower costs, higher-quality results, and better decisions when unexpected things occur. Building an ICF house is no exception. Homebuilding is a complicated venture, and using a new product like ICFs adds a few more twists (Fig. 7-1). It's very important to do some planning upfront. You won't regret it.

What kind of planning should I do?
You should have your team leader by now. If that's a general contractor, the GC should have an experienced ICF crew or ICF subcontractor lined up. If it's an architect, the architect should have the GC selected, and the GC should have the ICF subcontractor or crew selected. The planning begins when you meet with these people and talk to them about what you want in your house. This leads to a design for the house that should be as detailed as they can reasonably make it at this point. In addition, you should have a good understanding with your general contractor or architect about who is supposed to do what, and who tells what to whom when.

PLANS AND ADJUSTMENTS

What do you mean that the design should be "as detailed as you can reasonably make it at this point"? Don't we set it at the beginning and stick with it?
If you could, that would be great. The fewer changes made during construction, the better. That keeps things moving and holds costs down. It also prevents frayed nerves and flaring tempers. But very rarely is everything decided at the beginning.

Why is it hard to set the plans and then stick with them?
There are a lot of reasons for this. For one thing, it's impossible to foresee everything. It's hard to explain this to people who haven't been through the process, but dozens of surprises pop up during construction that affect how the house has to be built. You couldn't possibly anticipate all these issues in advance.

For example, the manufacturer might change the dimensions of the kitchen cabinets without showing this in its literature. This means that a wall may have to be moved or lengthened, and that will require other things to be adjusted. Or maybe the crew digging out the ground for your foundation hits solid rock. You'll have the choice of paying the high price of blasting out the rock, or leaving a solid rock in one section of the basement and not using that part, or changing the design of the entire house to fit around the rock.

Or perhaps the contractors will figure out that with the way the plans show the pipes and the vents, they will run into each other. So now the pipes have to be run through a different wall, and that will have to be enlarged. Or possibly, the price on the oval-shaped windows will turn out to be much more than you expected, so you will decide to eliminate them and go with standard rectangles. And so on and so forth.

OK, so surprises can occur and force us to adjust. But if I stick to my guns as best as I can, we can keep this to a minimum, right?
Yes, but you may not want to "stick to your guns" on everything. As the building goes up, you will probably think of some adjustments to make that you would really prefer to have. And that can even be a good thing, but it will mean that designs and plans are altered.

As the walls go up, you might see that it would be nice for the window overlooking the woods to be larger. Or you'll see an attractive new tile pattern that isn't as expensive as the others you looked at, so you'll decide to use that one in the kitchen instead of the vinyl flooring you picked out before. Or maybe during construction the general contractor will point out that adding a little porch off the master bedroom would only cost a few hundred dollars more, and you'll want to go with it.

But won't all these things cost more money?
Absolutely. Typically, you sign a contract with your general contractor that specifies how much you pay, what the design of the house is, and what materials it will be built of. Certain unforeseen events (like bad weather or subcontractor errors) may be somebody else's problem—the GC often has to bear the extra costs of things like this, which is why GCs are so careful when they prepare their bids. But if you choose

to change the design or materials after that agreement is reached, you pay. Usually, you ask your general contractor or architect how much such-and-such a change will add to the price. You get back a number, then make the decision as to whether you want it or not.

How big a cost increase can I expect to result from changes I make?
In practice, most people buying a custom house end up paying 5% to 10% more for it than the original price they got from the general contractor. I'm not trying to convince you to make changes. If you can come up with a really excellent design initially and stick with it, you will probably save time, money, and aggravation. But that's rarely the case, so you need to be prepared to flexible.

With this level of uncertainty, how do I design at all?
As best you can. Come up with the best design you and your team are able to. The more time and thought you can spend on it, the better things will go down the line.

So what does all this planning talk have to do with ICFs?
For the most part, you design a house with ICFs the same way you do any other house. It doesn't make the process significantly easier or harder. But the one thing you want to try to lock in during design is exactly which parts of the house will be built out of ICFs. Chapter 3 goes over the options: ICF exterior foundation walls, above-grade exterior walls, interior walls, floor decks, roof (Fig. 7-2). Changing these things midstream can be extremely difficult. Some of these decisions will raise a few other questions you need to resolve early on. The big one is what roof covering you will put on, if you choose to have a concrete roof. Depending on what the covering will be, the crew that builds the roof may have to plan ahead and install special parts to make it easy to attach the roof covering later.

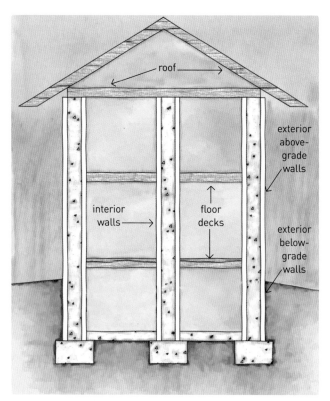

7-2. Parts of a house that can be built with ICFs.

How do I make these decisions about what to build out of ICFs?

The same way you make all the other major design decisions. You consider the options, think about their costs and their pluses and minuses. Then go with the one that seems to offer the best deal for you, all things considered.

For what you can build out of ICFs, go back to Chapter 3. Which things do you really want built out of ICFs? Why? What are the positives and negatives? For anything that makes it past your first cut, talk with your GC or architect. What do they estimate it will add to the overall cost? What will it do to the schedule? You make your decision by putting all these things side by side. And there's one more important criterion—whether there are suitable people available to do the work.

AVAILABILITY OF CREW

What do you mean "whether there are suitable people available"?

That's not much of an issue for ICF walls. Any good ICF crew should be able to build any standard wall—exterior, interior, below-grade, above-grade. But ICF floors and roofs haven't been around as long, so fewer crews have experience with them. In some areas of the country you might have to accept a higher price and a less experienced crew to build them.

But should I let the availability of crews make my decision for me?

Hopefully you won't have to do that. But where the costs will be much higher and the work might be less competent, you have to be realistic and take that into account.

To me, the determining factor is how confident you and your team are with the plans. If you're considering an ICF floor deck, but the general contractor has doubts about it and about the crew's ability to build it, I would decide to go with a traditional floor instead.

It hurts to avoid using a certain construction product if it would be better suited to your needs. But it will hurt even more to force something onto your team that they don't feel comfortable with and then later find that it is not installed to high standards. Pioneers may discover exciting new territory, but they might also fall over cliffs.

What about the other materials and systems available for interior walls and floors and roofs? Things like steel framing and other concrete deck systems?

The same rules go for them. If they seem to fit what you want—pluses and minuses and all—look into them with your general contractor or architect. Again, I cover these in Chapter 3.

SOURCES OF PLANS

How do I come up with plans for an ICF house?
It's basically the same way you come up with plans for a conventional house, but with a few twists. Normally you either use or adapt some standard house plans or someone designs the plans from scratch on a clean sheet of paper. Standard plans are available in "plan books" on the shelf of your local home center. If you buy half a dozen house plan books, you'll have hundreds of plans to choose from. You can either send away for the full set of plans for your favorite house, which cost a few hundred dollars, or you can ask your general contractor to figure out how to build the house just by looking at the book. You can even ask the GC to make a few changes—move a wall here, enlarge the floor plan there, shift around the cabinets, and so on.

Some GCs will even provide you with a few sets of plans. Usually these are for designs that are popular in the local area and that they are comfortable building. Some contractors are comfortable developing a full set of plans from scratch or significantly modifying a stock plan from a book. These are often called **design-build contractors**.

How do we come up with plans if I have an architect?
Then you're usually using the clean-sheet approach. That's why you hire an architect—to come up with something different and unique and very precisely suited to your specific needs. Depending on how the architect likes to work, you may start by picking out some plans you like to use as examples. But pretty quickly you'll be looking at original drawings and suggesting changes to them.

What's different about ICF plans?
Not very much. The biggest difference is that the walls are thicker. That means that *if* you use standard plans you will need to modify them to take into account the thicker walls. Ninety-five percent of the time that's a piece of cake. The general contractor just leaves the interior the same, and draws the walls thicker on the outside. The house "grows" outward by a few inches (Fig. 7-3).

If you use standard plans and put some ICF walls on the interior, they will be a few inches wider and take up some floor space. In that case you might need to

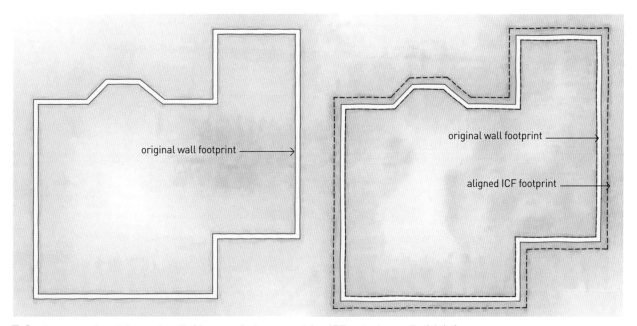

original wall footprint

original wall footprint

aligned ICF footprint

7-3. A conventional floor plan (left) extended outward for ICF exterior walls (right).

7-4. Curved ICF wall under construction. (Formtek, Inc.)

shift some things around, or it may not really make much difference.

If the house is designed from scratch, the designer simply takes the wall thickness into account. The architect should get the exact dimensions of the ICF that will be used from the ICF contractor.

Aren't there other things to take into account?
Yes, and we've mentioned most of them before. For instance, curved walls may be easier to form out of ICFs (Fig. 7-4). Overhangs—where the second-story walls don't line up with the first-story walls—can be harder to make out of ICFs. You will probably take these out of the design, or build them out of frame instead of ICFs (Fig. 7-5). All these design features may require you to make a few other decisions or changes in your house plans.

How detailed should the plans be?
If you're working with a general contractor, the plans are supposed to be very detailed before you sign a

contract. And most of the detail is not on the drawing. The majority of the detail is in the written specifications. Those are usually pages and pages long. They tell what all the parts of the house will be built of. Then if you ask for changes along the way, the GC checks and tells you how much you would have to pay to make the changes. This is the traditional way of getting everyone's agreement on the plan and the cost, and then handling changes.

LEVEL OF DETAIL IN CONTRACTS

How do I know when the contracts are detailed enough?
Look at contracts other people have signed, and talk to friends who have been through this. Unfortunately, there's no rule of thumb. Some general contractors typically write out very detailed specifications and others provide much briefer descriptions. But if the

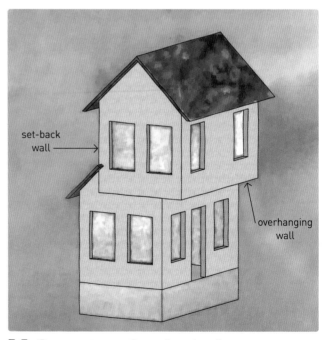

7-5. Common types of nonaligned walls.

GC's references are good, either way can be okay. Just make sure you get, in writing, anything that's really important to you.

But how can I know exactly what kitchen cabinets (or other materials) I'll want upfront?

You don't always have to choose all the specific finish materials you want until later in the process. It's hard for people to pick things like cabinets, flooring, paint colors, and so on at the very beginning, so there are some provisions for making these decisions later on.

In the case of, say, paint, the contract usually just specifies the grade or brand of paint you can choose from. Then you choose the colors later on, before the painters are due to arrive. If you want a different type, or you want to switch to wallpaper, you ask the GC what you would have to pay to switch it, and then make a decision.

For things like cabinets and the exact floor tile you want in a certain room, a common practice is for the contract to include an **allowance**. An allowance is an amount of money—maybe $2,000 for tile, $18,000 for the kitchen cabinets, and so on. When it comes time to select these things, you pick the ones you like. If you pick ones that cost less than their allowances, you get the savings shaved off the house price. If you pick more expensive ones, you pay the difference.

ALLOWANCES

Then how do I know if the allowances in the contract are enough?

It's a good idea to shop around a little—just enough to see if you can get the kind of things you like for the allowance amounts. The GC will usually give you a store or two to go to for these products. You can look around and see how much flooring, cabinets, and the like cost.

Do I have to get my products from the store the GC recommends?

That depends on the GC. Some will give you a few stores to choose from, and some will buy products from anywhere that's nearby. You need to ask. But general contractors establish accounts with certain home supply stores and can usually get discounted prices there. If you want to buy at a specialty store or a store where the GC does not have an account instead, you may end up paying full price.

What goes in writing with an architect?

When you work with an architect, things usually work a bit differently. Upfront you agree on the architect's fee and payment schedule, and sign a contract that spells out all the specifics. Often the fee is a percentage of the total amount you spend on the house, so the bigger the project gets, the bigger the fee ends up being.

The architect works with you on pretty much everything, from the general design down to the materials. At the same time, the architect is working with the general contractor on the contract for building the house. The architect tells you what kind of prices the GC is giving back and helps the two of you adjust the design. If you want changes during construction, the architect works through that with you, as well. So the architect really is your liaison to the general contractor.

Is that all there is to talk about concerning design?

That's about all we can say about the overall design at this point. The design of a house never goes exactly the same way for two different people. It's a matter of thinking hard, working with your team leader, and being reasonable. Remember not to go for a plan that would stretch your budget too far—you'll probably have to kick in another 5% to 10% down the road, so you don't want to start at the limit of what you can afford. When you get down to specifics, there are a few other things you might want to consider with ICFs, discussed below.

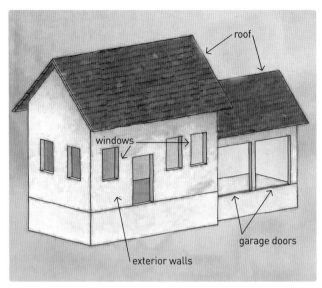

7-6. The wind-critical parts of a house.

OTHER SPECIFICS

What are the other specifics to consider with ICFs?
For the most part, these are other strength or energy-efficiency features. Another very important one is ventilation.

What are the other strength issues to consider?
Many people buying an ICF house are doing so partly because this type of dwelling offers greater resistance to things like wind, flood, vibration, and settling over time. If that is part of your motivation, you will probably want to consider using high-strength materials for other components of the house as well.

I'm definitely interested in high wind resistance because there are hurricanes in my area. What other wind-resistance features should I consider besides the ICF walls?
I've heard some careful analysis of this from an experienced insurance adjuster. The walls are definitely a weak spot in a hurricane or tornado. But if you really want to be safe, you don't quit with ICF walls (Fig. 7-6). The other major design features recommended are: a beefed-up roof, beefed-up windows, and single garage doors.

Why do I need a beefed-up roof?
The really serious wind damage occurs when the wind rips off the roof. After that happens, you run into two other problems. One is that the walls lose the support that the roof gives them, and they can collapse. The ICF walls usually solve this problem because they are much stronger than frame walls. If the roof blows off, the ICF walls usually stay intact. But the other problem isn't helped even by ICF walls: With the roof gone, all the wind and rain and debris can get into the house freely from above. The interior can be trashed, and anyone inside risks injury. If a stouter roof is used, it cuts the chances of this happening.

So what choices do I have for a beefed-up roof?
There are really four.
- The top of the line is an ICF roof, or some other form of reinforced concrete roof (Fig. 7-7). This is very strong. However, it can be expensive, especially if it will be a pitched (sloped) roof, which most house roofs are.
- The second choice is the **safe ceiling**. This is a flat concrete roof put over the house, with a

7-7. Pouring concrete on an ICF roof. (Lite-Form Technologies)

conventional frame roof installed over that. It doesn't protect the contents of the attic. How-ever, it protects the rest of the interior very well, and it can be less expensive than instal-ling a pitched concrete roof.

- The third choice is an SIP roof, which we discussed before (see page 54). If that is connected correctly, that can be very strong.
- The fourth option is to build a conventional frame roof, but to build it stronger than usual.

Do I have to do anything special with the concrete roof to get high wind resistance?
Not really. That's one of the advantages of an ICF roof or any of the other reinforced concrete roofs. Higher strength is pretty much standard. And they are con-nected to the walls extremely well because there is rebar running from the walls into the roof. If you need extra-high strength, to withstand a tornado, for instance, that may require a thicker layer of concrete and more rebar. Someone should consult the company that supplies the roof system to check on this. If you are really designing for a tornado, you probably will have an engineer, and the engineer will check on this. If you don't have an engineer, the GC will probably be the one to look into it.

So how do I get the SIP roof to be strong enough?
The SIP panels themselves are quite strong. That is the reason they are a good option for a beefed-up roof. The other thing that needs to be looked into is how they are connected to the walls and to one another. To resist high winds, those connections will need to be stronger than usual. It will typically take extra screws and steel straps to do the job. You should have a contractor installing them who has worked with SIPs before, and, if necessary, that contractor can talk to the SIP manufacturer to make sure things are done right.

How do I build a frame roof stronger than usual?
The major weak points of a conventional frame roof are the connection of the roof members to the walls,

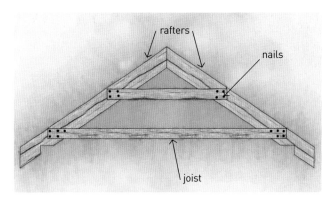

7-8. Roof rafters and joists.

the connection of the roof members to each other, and the connection of the plywood sheathing to the roof framing.

What the heck is a "roof member"?
That's just a fancy name for the big pieces of wood the structure of the roof is built out of. In traditional construction, the main roof members are **rafters** and joists (Fig. 7-8). The rafters are the pieces of lumber that go from the top of the wall up to the top of the roof, where all the rafters meet at a point. The joists are the pieces of lumber that go horizontally across the house from one wall to the other.

In modern construction most houses use **roof trusses** (Fig. 7-9). These are prebuilt large lumber triangles. They have two rafters and one joist, all connected to each other, in a triangle shape. (However, in a truss these pieces are not technically called rafters and

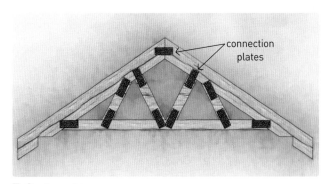

7-9. A roof truss.

joists.) They also have a series of shorter pieces criss-crossing between the main pieces to help stiffen the whole thing.

So how do I make sure the roof framing members are connected well to the walls?
The key is for the contractor to use hurricane straps, which I mentioned before. These are special steel straps or plates that the ICF crew embeds into the concrete when they fill the walls. One end is embedded, and is very difficult to pull out. The other is designed to be screwed into the roof member. It is very tough for the wind to pull these things out of the wall or break them away from the rafter or truss.

Do I have to ask for hurricane straps?
That's a good idea if you want extra wind protection. In high-wind areas, like Florida, installing them is pretty much standard practice. In other places the contractor probably won't use them unless you ask for them. They add a little more work and a little more money, so they're not standard in most areas.

What do we have to do to make sure the different roof members are well connected to each other?
If you are having a roof built of rafters and joists, just tell the GC that you want a stronger roof. He should be putting in larger pieces of wood and using an extra nail or two at each connection.

If you are having trusses installed, the contractor should order trusses that are heavier duty than the minimum required. Trusses are prebuilt at a factory, and often they are engineered to take every extra cent out of the cost. That means that they use the fewest pieces of lumber, the smallest pieces of lumber, and the lightest connections that will meet the minimum local requirements. You want to step up a notch or two from this. Order heavier plywood sheathing as well and use extra fasteners.

Why do I care about how well the plywood sheathing is attached to the roof?
Because that's one common way the wind gets in. It blows under the roof at, say, a corner. It blows long and

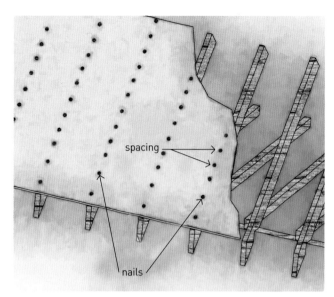

7-10. A careful nailing pattern on roof sheathing.

hard enough to pull up some of the nails in the sheet of sheathing there. Eventually, it peels back the whole sheet. Then it has a free path into the attic. It might blow in and pop off the whole roof in one piece, or it might pull off the other sheets, one by one. The effects are about the same either way.

How does the contractor secure the sheathing down better?
By putting in more and larger nails. Instead of putting one nail along the edges of the plywood say, every 8 inches, ask for them to be put in every 6 inches, and as close as 4 inches around the perimeter of the roof and along the top (Fig. 7-10). This makes a huge difference. Using special nails that resist pulling out (such as ring-shank nails) is also sometimes recommended in high-wind areas. Staples should be avoided. But this is the kind of thing that can easily be overlooked if someone isn't on top of the crew. It's not their usual practice, so someone has to remind them about it and check on it.

It sounds like to get a beefed-up frame roof I would have to go out and be a construction supervisor.
You shouldn't have to. You should be discussing all this with the GC upfront in the planning phase. It's the

GC's job to make sure it happens. You shouldn't be picking out the roofing members and deciding how closely to space the nails. You should be telling the GC what kind of wind resistance you want, and he should be able to figure out what pieces to use and how to put them together.

Why are the windows so important?

If the wind or debris can break the windows, it can get into the house. That causes the same sort of problems that losing roof sheathing does. The wind can blow in through the windows and push the roof off. Or it can ruin the interior and hurt the occupants.

What about beefed-up windows and how do I get them?

There are a couple of choices here, too. One is to simply buy windows that are manufactured with special glass and frames to be stronger. Most major window manufacturers now offer a line of these "storm-resistant" windows. They're more expensive, of course, but if you really want high wind resistance, you'll pay for them.

The other approach is to install special shutters that you can pull over your windows before a storm arrives. These are becoming more common in Florida, but they are not as readily available or familiar in other places. Your architect or GC might know if they are an option in your area.

Why do I care about having single garage doors?

Because double garage doors are pretty easy to blow in. And once the wind gets into the garage, it may get into the house and blow the roof off again. Two single doors are better because they have that support section of wall between them.

You also brought up energy-efficiency features. What other things are there to consider related to energy at the planning stage?

That is an issue similar to wind. If part of your motivation for using ICFs is to have an energy-efficient home, you may also want to consider making other parts of the house energy efficient.

The other critical parts we already discussed in Chapter 4. For the envelope, the remaining weak points are the roof and the windows and doors. You can bring the roof up to a high level of efficiency by adding extra insulation or by switching to an SIP or ICF roof. For the windows you should look for low-e double-pane glass with argon or similar fill between the panes. If you are in a hot climate, you want sun-reflecting windows or an added reflective film, especially on the windows that face south and west.

You should choose a design that runs all the ductwork for the HVAC system inside the insulated shell of the house as well. For your HVAC equipment, you should look for a high-efficiency furnace and high-SEER heat pump or AC unit. You should also avoid products that may allow a lot of air to leak into the house, like sliding glass doors and recessed lights that are not fully sealed. Chapter 4 goes into more detail on all of this, but you should discuss it upfront with your team. It can be much harder to change these things later.

What about flood resistance? If I want to build a house that stands up better to flood waters, what should I be doing besides using ICFs?

As discussed in Chapter 2, surviving floods reasonably well depends on structural strength, proper elevation of the house, and use of water-resistant materials. For strength, you do the same kinds of things you do for wind. For one thing, floods are often accompanied by high winds, so you need the wind resistance anyway. In addition, flowing water puts similar sorts of side forces on the house. Building with ICFs is a good start. Try to follow the other recommended steps for wind resistance as well.

How to elevate the house depends on how deep floodwaters can get. If they might get up a foot or 3 feet above the ground, you can simply make the basement or stem wall foundation a little higher than that. If you are in one of those coastal areas where a powerful storm surge of 5 to 10 feet can push ashore, you should seriously consider putting the house on concrete piers that raise the first floor above the projected flood level.

Choosing water-resistant materials for things other than the walls can be tough. Clearly, concrete floors and a concrete roof make sense if you can afford them. For siding and trim, try to stay away from wood products and favor things like vinyl, fiber-cement, stucco, brick, and so on. For the interior, tile and vinyl are better than most carpets, synthetic fibers are often better than natural ones, and so on. If you can afford one of the new water-resistant wallboard products to finish the inside of the walls, that is great. But as you can see, this can get pretty restrictive pretty fast, so you will have to put the brakes on yourself at some point and admit that some things will be ruined if water gets in the house.

You also mentioned ventilation. How should I take account of that in planning?

As discussed in Chapter 5, an ICF house tends to have markedly lower air infiltration than ordinary wood-frame houses. If you follow the other energy-efficiency recommendations in this book, your air infiltration will be even lower. You should be talking with your team about whether it is advisable to bring in some outside air in a controlled way—that is, by installing mechanical ventilation. This may be done with some exhaust fans or with something like a heat recovery ventilator that exchanges some of the inside air for outside air without losing all the heat (or cooling) of the inside air.

Some specialists don't recommend increasing ventilation. Instead they favor precise control of the air and air filtration. But in either case, you need an expert you can trust to give you the specific measures to follow. Chapter 5 goes into more detail on this. But this is something you should be considering, and it should be done now, at the beginning of your project.

What about your advice to get an understanding about who is supposed to do what, and who tells what to whom? Why isn't this all standardized?

In a way it is. The GC is supposed to work from the plans, supervise the crews, and consult you when a question arises. If there is an architect, the architect is supposed to work with the GC day-to-day, and only consult you when there is a major issue or a decision that you might want to be involved in. But different people are different, and it is usually better to talk honestly about how things will work at the beginning. What are your expectations for the project? When do you want to be consulted? How can you be reached at odd times? When will you be checking in on things, and why?

Should I be checking in on things a lot?

That depends. If you have some very competent hands running the show—people who have received great reviews from their previous customers—you may choose to let them do their jobs on their own and talk to them only when they ask you a question. And you certainly do *not* want to be breathing down their necks. No one likes others looking over their shoulders while they work, and not many people work well under these circumstances.

Having said that, I'm a fan of learning something about construction, and coming out to the job site once in a while and asking questions. I'll say a lot more about this later on, but it boils down to knowing what to look for and doing an occasional mini-inspection. There are some things that your town building inspector will *not* be looking for that you might want to check out.

What would I want to inspect for myself?

Some things that are obvious are checking that things are actually built the way the contract says and the way the GC or architect told you they would be built. If not, why not? Is there anything that looks really odd or wrong? If so, is there an explanation?

Of special interest for readers of this book are a few specific things having to do with insulating concrete forms. There are a few telltale signs of a good job that you can check for. And I think it's a good idea for you to check for them. I'll go into detail on this in Chapter 9.

It's also good to tell the general contractor *upfront* that these things are important to you, and that you'll be checking on them. That way the GC knows some key places where he should devote his care and attention *before* they're done. That's when he can actually make sure they're done correctly.

What if I don't want to do inspections, or I don't feel qualified?

You don't necessarily have to. It's just an option that can be useful. If you prefer, you can usually hire a professional to do them for you. Chapter 9 talks more about the options, so it might make sense to read it before you make a final decision about this. But whatever you choose to do, you should inform the GC upfront.

How picky and demanding should I get in this kind of situation?

Not very. If you have to get into arguments with your GC or architect, you have probably picked the wrong one for you. I'm definitely *not* suggesting that you plan to go to the job site as some kind of cop or enforcer. When I was young, I worked on wood-framing crews, mostly during summers and vacations. I always hated it when the customer came out trying to find little things that were wrong. Typically, the customer didn't know the really important things to look for, so he complained about a lot of trivial matters like bent nails here and there. Or worse, he had it in his head that a certain job was supposed to be done a certain way, and he was either dead wrong or was concerned about something that could be done in more than one way with no particular ill effects. These are the people who suffer from the "a little knowledge can be a dangerous thing" problem. Their complaining causes a lot of extra work and aggravation, and it doesn't get the house

built any better. So too much checking up can create problems, but a reasonable amount can be helpful. Though it can sometimes be uncomfortable, the general contractor will tend to do a better job if someone is checking up.

What if I'm using an architect?

Then it's usually the architect's job to inspect the work. So you might offend the architect if you're snooping around a lot. But it might not be a bad idea to show up now and again, take an interest in the details, and ask questions.

Why do you mention all this checking-up stuff in the planning chapter?

Because I think it's best to tell your team upfront that you will be doing this. You don't have to sound as if you don't trust them. Just say that you are extremely interested in the house, you've learned a lot about ICF construction, and you are curious to see it in progress. You expect to get to the job site when your schedule allows, and hope that you can look around and ask questions when you do. And be sure that you mention specific things in the ICF construction that are important to you (Fig. 7-11).

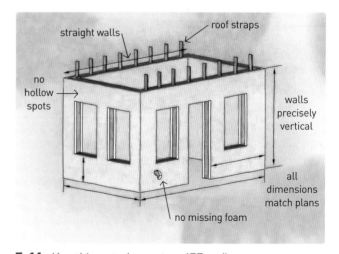

7-11. Key things to inspect on ICF walls.

Table 7-1

Construction Planning Organizer			
Option: House Has:	**Positives**	**Negatives**	**Costs/Savings**
Some ICF interior walls			
ICF floor deck			
Some other type of concrete floor deck			
Steel-framed floor deck and interior walls			
ICF roof*			
Some other type of concrete roof*			
Concrete safe ceiling			
Steel-framed roof			
Structural insulated panel (SIP) roof			
Beefed-up frame roof attached with hurricane straps			
Upper-story overhangs and setbacks			
Wind-resistant windows or shutters			
Concrete pier foundation			
Extra roof insulation			
Energy-efficient windows			
Sun-reflecting windows or added film			
Ductwork run within the insulated areas			
High-efficiency furnace			
High-efficiency air-conditioning			
Airtight sliding doors			
Airtight recessed light fixtures			
Mechanical ventilation			

*Plan ahead for the roof covering.

WARNING: A job site can be a dangerous place. If you intend to go to your site to look over the work, or for any other reason, take every precaution. Consult the general contractor on this. It might be very reasonable for him to limit the times you come to the site, to want to know in advance that you are coming to fix up any risky conditions, or to require that someone accompany you.

You've given me so many things to consider during planning that my head is starting to swim. How can I keep track of it all?

There are really only two major kinds of things I've given you to pin down during planning: how the house is built, and who does what.

Let's recap it all here. First of all, you can make yourself a chart of the major design and construction options listed in this book, like the one in Table 7-1. For each option, ask yourself what the pluses and minuses of that option are. Then, with your construction team, get an estimate of what the costs of doing things this way will be. Finally, list your estimate for any savings it might yield. When you're done, you can weigh the facts and decide which features you want to include in your house and which you don't.

Of course, you can extend Table 7-1 to include all the other decisions you need to make on the house, even if they have nothing to do with ICFs. As for who does what, here is a list of the things I advise you to get straight with your team. You can carry it with you and check off each item when it's done:

- Who will there be on the team that has substantial ICF expertise?
- How and how often will the team members talk with one another to stay coordinated?
- How will the person with extensive ICF expertise be involved in these discussions?
- Will the buyer inspect the job site or have someone else inspect it, and when and how will this happen?

What about the things I'm supposed to inspect? You said that if I'm going to inspect the ICF work I should tell the contractor upfront what I'm going to be looking for.

That's right, and I tell you in Chapter 9 what I advise you to inspect. Here's a handy list of those items, so you can bring them up with the GC now. I hope you will read Chapter 9 before you have that discussion, so you will know better why you'll be looking at each of these things. The things I suggest you look for are:

- The formwork matches the house plans.
- No foam is missing anywhere (that is, there's no exposed concrete).
- The walls are straight and vertical everywhere.
- There are no hollow spots inside the walls (no missing concrete).
- The steel straps for the roof (if you're using them) are in place correctly.

The initial plan of a very young homebuyer.

Is there any more to know about planning?
Yes, a ton. Unfortunately, I can't be specific about it. It's different in every case. Get a GC or architect you can talk to, and then talk. Try to think things through together as best you can. Talk to other people who have been through all this before. And heck, if you have the time, read some other books about building your house. They usually have lots of good things to say about homebuilding in general. In this book we just key in on the ICFs and related items.

Down the road, you will definitely appreciate the time you have spent upfront planning the design and construction of your house. Like the rest of us, you should find that "a good beginning is half the job."

CHAPTER 8

Special Programs, Incentives, and Subsidies

THERE ARE AGENCIES and companies that give price breaks or other benefits to the owners or builders of ICF houses. Some of these can reduce your overall costs. Others may simply give you assurance that you are getting a quality building.

A roof goes up.

8-1. ICF house with a modern design. (Quad-Lock Building Systems, Ltd.)

Why would anyone give you extra perks for building with ICFs?

Because when you build a durable, energy-efficient home, that benefits people other than just yourself. Certain organizations that get some of those benefits offer you money or help as a way of encouraging people to build more of these houses.

What exactly are the price breaks or other benefits I can get?

The list of benefits available to you changes over time, so it is impossible to answer this question exactly. But currently the main ones that may be available are:

- Assurance that your house has high resistance to natural disasters.
- Lower insurance rates because your house has higher resistance to disasters.
- Assurance that your house is highly energy efficient.
- Better mortgage terms because your house is energy efficient.
- Direct grants or subsidies because your house is energy efficient.
- Federal tax credits because your house is energy efficient.

You cannot be certain of getting these benefits. Many of them are awarded only in some areas or for certain types of homes. But all of them have been awarded to at least some new house projects. You also need to be aware that not all of these are awarded to the homeowner. Some are given to the general contractor. The GC may have to do the work of applying for them, and it will be up to the GC (and perhaps you) to decide whether the award gets passed along to you, the homeowner. This may all sound complicated, but it is much easier to understand when we talk about one specific type of benefit.

INSURANCE RATE

OK, tell me about reductions in my insurance rate. How do those work?

To make this clear we need to start with some background information. Insurance companies collect regular, small payments, called premiums, from a large number of homeowners like you. If your house suffers damage, the insurance company pays for it in order to compensate you. Insurers can do this because only a fraction of the houses they insure get damaged, and they can use the premiums from the whole pool of houses to pay for the damaged ones.

If the houses they cover are less likely to get damaged, or the damage is likely to be smaller, they can afford to collect smaller premiums. This is why premiums tend to be less costly in low-wind areas and on smaller houses, to name two examples. ICF houses are more resistant to damage from various types of disasters. So, logically, insurance companies should charge you less for your homeowner's insurance.

You say they "should" charge me less. Isn't it a sure thing?

You can almost always get a reduction in your homeowner's insurance policy. However, you may need to do a little shopping around to get it. Different insurance companies have different policies on what type of homes they will give a break to, and how much of a break they give. For that matter, they charge different premiums to start with, even before any break. To find the best deal, you have to ask a few companies and see what they will give you. There really is not a simpler way to go about it.

What do I tell them? Do I ask what their rate is for an ICF house?

Most of them won't know what that is. Things may change in the future, but most insurance agents as of 2007 are still not familiar with ICFs.

Most insurance companies have two "classes of construction" for houses. These are categories they put houses into, according to how they are built. One is for wood-frame houses and the other is for concrete-block houses. Concrete block is the most common form of house in Florida, and was once also fairly common in other parts of the country, so it has its own construction class.

Nearly every insurance company charges somewhat lower premiums for houses in the concrete block class. This is because experience over the years has shown that they suffer less damage from things like wind and fire.

Most insurance agents will put an ICF house into the block class, and that will give you lower premiums. But check on this. They may not even check to see what your house is built of if you don't call it to their attention. Wood frame is so common outside of Florida that they just assume everything is built with wood. Or they may realize it's not wood, but not know enough about ICFs to understand that they, like concrete block, produce concrete walls. The size of the savings will vary widely from situation to situation, but I have heard of cases where it was a few hundred dollars a year.

THE "FORTIFIED" PROGRAM

You also mentioned "assurance that your house is resistant to disasters." What exactly does that mean?

There's an organization called the Institute for Business and Home Safety (IBHS) that has set up a program called *Fortified . . . for safer living®*. The program has recommended techniques for making a home more resistant to natural disasters. You can have your house built according to their recommendations and have an independent inspector, trained by IBHS, check it. If the inspector verifies that the house does incorporate the recommended techniques, the house is registered as a "Fortified" house with IBHS. You have the assurance that the house was built to high standards of disaster resistance, and you can show the registration to buyers to prove it if you ever sell the house.

What does the process of getting Fortified registration cost?

Currently, the fee for the inspector is $1,000.

What does the cost of the recommended building techniques add to the cost of the house?

IBHS estimates that it adds 3% to 10% to the cost of a moderately priced house. However, if you are building with ICF walls, their strength will improve the disaster resistance of the house, so you are already partway there.

What types of disasters does the Fortified program have requirements for?

That depends on the location of the house. The Fortified program uses maps that show where different types of disaster are most common (Fig. 8-2). A particular house must meet the requirements for all disasters common to its local area.

How do I get in touch with the IBHS?

Through its Web site or by calling. The Web address is **www.ibhs.org**. The main phone number is 813–286–3400.

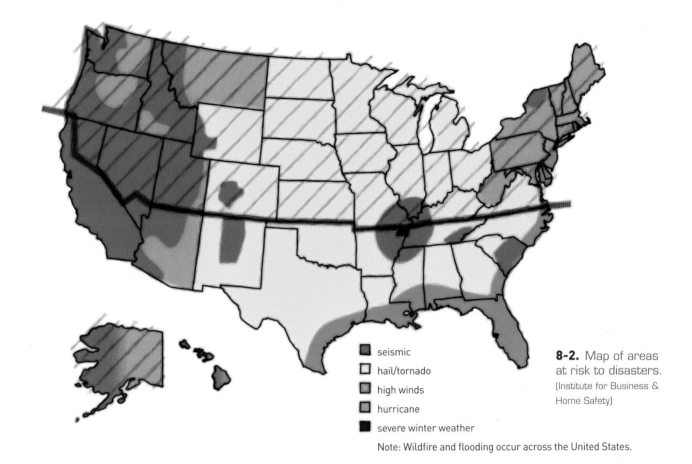

8-2. Map of areas at risk to disasters. (Institute for Business & Home Safety)

- seismic
- hail/tornado
- high winds
- hurricane
- severe winter weather

Note: Wildfire and flooding occur across the United States.

Does the Fortified program have anything to do with insurance rates?

Some insurers will give you a reduced premium on your homeowner's insurance if you show them that your home is registered with the program. But that's up to the insurance company. It's not a part of the program. You can check with your insurer about it.

Doesn't the local building department make sure that the house is built with the right things to resist natural disasters?

Yes, it does. Many rules of the local building codes are designed to ensure that a house will stand up to the types of disasters that are most common in the area. However, the standards of the Fortified program are even more stringent. For example, local codes might be designed to ensure that new homes can successfully resist winds of up to 100 miles per hour. But the

recommendations of the Fortified program might require measures that will allow the house to resist 130 mph winds. It's really for people who want a level of assurance beyond what the minimum code requires.

ENERGY-EFFICIENCY CREDITS

Tell me about the energy-efficiency benefits I can get.

When you build an energy-efficient home, like an ICF home, you pay lower energy bills for heating and cooling. The savings can amount to hundreds of dollars a year, even thousands, depending on the size of the home, the climate, and fuel prices.

Of course, the energy savings are directly beneficial to you. There are even ways to get assurance that your new home will be energy efficient, if that is of interest to you. The energy savings may also make the house more attractive to potential buyers when you resell. And it can sometimes also get you more favorable mortgage terms from your lender.

On top of all that, general contractors who build energy-efficient houses can currently get tax credits of $2,000 per house. You don't get this—they do. But some of them may give you a price break because they get some financial benefit when they build you an ICF house.

How can I get assurance that my house will be energy efficient? Is this something like the inspections for disaster resistance of the Fortified program?

It does have some similarities to the Fortified program, but the people involved are all different. There are many independent energy consultants who will examine your house plans or your constructed house to advise you on how energy efficient it will be. If you think you might want to hire one of these consultants, I explain how to locate these people in Chapter 4, which covers energy efficiency in detail. You pay them a fee, just as you would pay for any service.

In addition, there is a formal program that puts a stamp of approval on energy-efficient homes, much as the Fortified program puts one on disaster-resistant homes. That is the **Energy Star** program of the U.S. Environmental Protection Agency (EPA). Under the Energy Star program, you can hire a specially trained inspector to estimate the energy efficiency of your house, and if it exceeds building code requirements by a certain amount, it can be labeled an Energy Star home. That shows you—and anyone you may want to sell the house to in the future—that the efficiency of the house has been independently verified.

Where did this Energy Star program come from?

Energy Star is actually a government program with a couple of different parts. One part rates appliances, like air conditioners, for their energy efficiency. The other, run by the U.S. Environmental Protection Agency, provides energy efficiency ratings for houses.

The house rating program is really designed for the builders. The home builder is expected to sign up with Energy Star, arrange for the inspections, and pay the fees. At the end of the process, the builder may use the Energy Star name to help sell the houses. But you, the homebuyer, can ask that your house be built as an Energy Star house. You can keep looking until you find a general contractor who regularly builds Energy Star homes. Or you can tell your general contractor that you want the Energy Star certification, are willing to pay the extra cost, and ask that he sign up with the program. But expect that he will want something to cover his time and effort, too. This is a well-established way to get independent verification that your house is truly energy efficient (see sidebar titled "Meeting Energy Star Standards").

Who does the inspections for Energy Star?

The program actually encouraged various energy experts to start up their own businesses doing Energy Star inspections. Many of these are the same people you will find if you go looking for the energy experts I talk about in Chapter 4. If you tell them you want to get your house approved for Energy Star, they follow the Energy Star rules for inspection and provide the results to the program's offices in Washington. If you just want to make sure that your house is energy efficient and you don't care about getting official recognition from the Energy Star program, you can also have an energy expert do the inspection however she sees fit and deliver the results just to you.

There is an official name for the energy experts who are certified to do Energy Star inspections. They are called **Home Energy Rating Services (HERS)**. Of course, they have their own separate company names, but the Energy Star program classifies them all under this general heading.

How do I find a Home Energy Rating Service?

Nowadays most of the inspectors are members of the **Residential Energy Services Network**, which is also called RESNET. This is an organization of professional energy raters. The network's Web site is

8-3. Blower door in operation. (The Energy Conservatory)

www.natresnet.org. You can contact RESNET to find a rater in your area. But there are also some who are not members of RESNET. Look for them in your local business listings under headings like "Home Energy Services."

What do the Energy Star inspections involve?
The HERS rater examines the plans of the house during the design phase. The rater tells you whether the house will meet the Energy Star requirements if it's built as designed. If it won't meet the requirements, the rater tells you ways you can change it so it will.

During construction there are inspections to ensure that the work is done according to the plans. After the house is completed, the rater tests the house with a **blower door test**. In a blower door test, the testers mount a big fan (called a blower) in one of the outside doorways of the house. They turn it on and measure how fast it can move air out of the house. The slower

the air moves, the more airtight the house is (Fig. 8-3). This test helps them confirm that the airtightness of the house meets Energy Star requirements. If the house has ducts that run outside the insulation envelope, the rater may also test the ductwork to make sure it does not have significant leaks. If everything is acceptable, the house gets the Energy Star seal.

CANADIAN ENERGY-EFFICIENCY CERTIFICATION

What do I do about energy-efficiency certification if I live in Canada?
Canada has a program for homes that has been in operation even longer than Energy Star. It's called **R2000**. Like Energy Star, it uses experts to inspect home plans and construction to determine whether a house meets high energy-efficiency standards. The house also needs to meet some additional requirements meant to ensure high performance on other measures, such as indoor air quality. The contractors involved are required to have some training in the recommended methods of construction. You can find more information on the program at **www.r2000.chba.ca**.

ENERGY-EFFICIENT MORTGAGES

How can I get better terms on my mortgage just from having an energy-efficient home?
To understand that, you first have to understand how lenders set their terms for home mortgages. One of their greatest concerns is that some people will buy a house with the help of one of their mortgages, and then not be able to make their monthly payments. If the borrowers default on their payments, the lender may be entitled to take ownership of the house and resell it to get its money back. However, because of the time and costs involved in reselling a house, the lender may still lose money. One way lenders try to guard against these defaults on mortgage payments is by

To be awarded the Energy Star certification, a home must be at least 15% to 20% more efficient than houses that meet strict energy guidelines. The savings can come from a lot of sources, because Energy Star takes into account not only the energy used for heating and cooling, but also water heating, major appliances, and lighting. Most people building ICF houses usually get most or all of the required savings in their heating and cooling energy, but savings can come from increasing efficiency in these other areas as well.

To determine the amount of savings in a particular house, the raters compare its projected energy consumption to the energy the house would have used if it had been constructed according to a building code called the International Energy Conservation Code (IECC). The IECC is the most widely used building code in the United States for the energy-efficiency features of a house. Many communities enforce energy rules that are somewhat different from those of the IECC, but it is probably a good representation of what a fairly well-constructed U.S. house would look like.

Energy Star uses a rating system that measures the energy efficiency on a point scale (Fig. 8-4). It is set so that a house that exactly meets the requirements of the IECC gets a score of 100. If, according to the inspector's evaluation, a particular house will have a 5% lower energy bill, the house receives a score of 95. A rating of 90 means the house is estimated to be 10% more efficient, and so on.

The Energy Star program requires that a house built in a northern climate receive a rating of no more than 80 for certification. In other words, by the evaluation of the rater, the house will have at least a 20% lower energy bill than it would have had if it only met the requirements of the IECC. In southern climates, the house must receive a rating of no more than 85. This means it must have at least a 15% lower energy consumption.

Most currently standing houses were built in earlier times when energy standards were much lower. Of those built recently, many still are not built to the IECC standard. Many new houses rate somewhere in the 100 to 120 range. To put this in perspective, a house with a score of 105 is estimated to have a 5% higher energy bill than it would if it exactly complied with the IECC. A house scoring 120 would have a 20% higher bill. Many old houses would probably get scores of close to 200 if anyone bothered to rate them. That means they will have fuel bills nearly double what they would have if they met IECC requirements.

I therefore consider a score of 80 to 85, indicating that a house that is 15% to 20% more efficient than IECC requirements, to be quite energy efficient. Having said this, it is also possible to exceed the Energy Star requirement. Many ICF houses have received scores of 50 or less. This means that their projected fuel bills were at least 50% lower than they would have been if they had been built exactly to IECC standards. They use half as much fuel as an energy-efficient home! The secret, of course, was that the house had ICF walls, plus good components in the other key areas (roof, windows, heating and cooling equipment, and so on).

limiting how much they will lend to a person. Most have strict formulas for determining the maximum mortgage size based on the borrower's income. A common rule they use is not to lend a person an amount that would result in a mortgage payment of more than 30% of the individual's income. So an individual who saves money on his fuel bills might be able to borrow additional money if the bank views these savings as similar to additional income.

That's all well and good, but does this really happen? Do lenders really offer better terms to someone who is building an energy-efficient home?

Yes, some do. Technically they're called **energy efficiency mortgages**, or **EEMs** (see the sidebar titled "Energy-Efficient Mortgage Calculations"). This benefit is something like receiving lower insurance rates for a disaster resistant home. Only some com-panies offer it, and the exact terms vary from one to the next. You have to shop around to find out who will give you a break. In

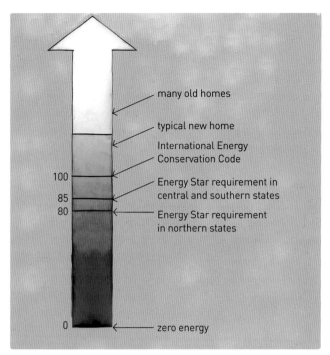

8-4. The Energy Star scale for the energy efficiency of houses.

Labels on figure:
- many old homes
- typical new home
- International Energy Conservation Code
- Energy Star requirement in central and southern states
- Energy Star requirement in northern states
- zero energy
- 100
- 85
- 80
- 0

addition, you have to demonstrate the energy efficiency of the home.

How would I prove the energy efficiency of my home if I haven't built it yet?

Different lenders have different requirements, so you have to ask. However, most will accept the report of a Home Energy Rating Service (HERS) or an Energy Star rating.

Does that mean that for an estimate of energy consumption I just go to the same people I get an Energy Star rating from?

Pretty much. Some lenders require an Energy Star certification. However, some may accept or require something else. For example, a lender might accept a report from a HERS showing that the house achieves an Energy Star score of 80, even if you do not register the results with the Energy Star program. Still others might accept a score from a HERS of 90, or some other form of evaluation from a different type of energy-efficiency expert.

It makes the most sense to shop around for your mortgage and see what the lenders require. It's hard to tell in advance. If you want Energy Star certification for your own personal benefit, by all means go and get it. Most lenders who offer energy-efficient mortgages accept Energy Star, so it will probably serve that purpose, too. Regardless of the lender, you will probably end up going to a HERS for proof that your house meets the energy requirements. These Home Energy Rating Services are set up to do this type of work efficiently.

Is it easy to find a lender that offers energy-efficiency mortgages?

No, it definitely is not. In fact, that is the hardest part about the whole process. By comparison, getting your efficiency rating is straightforward. It is difficult to find lenders that offer energy-efficiency mortgages. Worse still, many people who work for the lenders that *do* offer EEMs don't even realize they offer them. If you ask them about EEMs, they are likely to say they don't have one.

How can this be? Energy-efficiency mortgages seem to make so much sense. Why doesn't every lender offer them to the public?

Because up until now there have not been many customers for them. It takes work and money to create a new type of mortgage. It sounds simple to us, but the truth is that a lot of thought and effort goes into figuring out the application process, what the terms will be, what sort of inspection the company should accept, getting all the information out to the company's many offices, and so on. If the lender will only get a few new customers here and there, it's not worth the effort or the money. Many mortgage companies are doing just fine without offering EEMs, so they don't bother.

As a result, you may have to make some calls and hunt for a while until you find one.

This will likely change in the future. Right now more and more people are building highly energy-efficient homes. Many of them are asking lenders about EEMs. The word may get back to the lenders'

Banks and mortgage companies look at a person's income to determine how much he or she can borrow. For example, someone earning $4,000 a month might be allowed to take out a mortgage that results in a total monthly payment for principal, interest, and taxes of $1,200 (30% of $4,000), but no more. At current interest rates, this might limit a person with this income to borrowing around $150,000 for the purchase of a home. The lender reasons that if the payment is kept to no more than 30% of the borrower's income, the borrower will likely be able to pay without risking default.

Now consider how the energy efficiency of the home affects the lender's reasoning. If the borrower's new home will have a utility bill that is lower by, say, $100 a month, this borrower will have that much more free cash each month. That suggests that even if the monthly mortgage payment were higher by $100, this borrower would be no more likely to default than the average borrower.

In this case the lender may feel free to provide the borrower with a larger mortgage—one that results in payments of as much as $100 more per month. Depending on interest and tax rates, this could allow our borrower with the $4,000-per-month income to receive a mortgage of around $170,000. That would allow the borrower to buy a significantly larger or better home—one that costs an extra $20,000.

Using the same sort of logic, other mortgage lenders might offer buyers of energy-efficient homes other benefits, such as lower interest rates or lower upfront mortgage fees. All these are referred to as energy-efficiency mortgages, or EEMs.

headquarters and motivate them to create these mortgages. So with some luck, by the time this book is in print you'll have an easier time finding an EEM.

But you also said that the workers at some mortgage lenders that offer an EEM don't even realize they have one. How can that be?

It sounds crazy, but it's true. Some large mortgage companies have created EEM programs. They have established the rules for the mortgages, determined the rates they will offer, and created the forms borrowers must fill out to apply. The information is even entered into the company's database. However, the local lending agents aren't always aware that their company offers these mortgages. So when you enter an office and ask about it, the agent might say they don't have any such thing. The agent is not trying to lie—as far as the agent knows, they really don't.

But how can it be that the company offers an energy-efficiency mortgage and their agents don't know about it?

Banks and mortgage companies offer many types of mortgages. Some of the companies have hundreds of different kinds. The company trains its agents on the ins and outs of the most popular ones. But few EEMs have been sold up to now. As a result, many of the mortgage companies that have them do not bother to train their agents about them, or they mention them so quickly as part of their larger training programs that the agents forget about them.

In some mortgage companies there are a few local agents here and there who sell many EEMs, while most of their fellow agents are totally unaware that such a mortgage even exists. Somewhere along the line, these few agents found out that the company offered them, found some people who wanted them, and then got a regular business going by marketing them to homebuyers in the area.

How can I find someone who offers an energy-efficiency mortgage if the people who offer them don't even know about it?

One option is to call a few different banks and mortgage companies and ask about this. And be persistent. Don't take "I don't know" for an answer. Ask to be referred to someone who does know.

Of course, that can be a lot of work. One alternative is to ask your ICF contractor. Many of them have run across this problem before and have learned who to go to for the better mortgages. Another good source is the ICF company that supplies the ICF forms. Several of the manufacturers keep records on which lenders offer EEMs. One other option is to call the Fannie Mae Resource Center (1-800-7FANNIE). The people there can send you or direct you to information Fannie Mae has on the subject, such as printed fact sheets, lists of participating mortgage brokers, and any related information they might have on the Web at the moment.

Click on "Mortgage Broker Center," and then on "Products." EEMs are listed as one of the products, and this page has links to specific lenders.

MORTGAGE HELP FROM FANNIE, FREDDIE, AND THE FHA

Years ago, the U.S. government established several financial organizations to help ensure that there would be plenty of mortgages available to people so they could buy their own homes. Three of these organizations are big, well known, and have a role in a large percentage of the home mortgages issued today. These organizations also have special programs to deal with energy-efficient mortgages (EEMs). They are the **Federal Housing Administration** (**FHA**), the **Federal National Mortgage Association** (nicknamed Fannie Mae), and the **Federal Mortgage Acceptance Corporation** (Freddie Mac). None of these organizations offers mortgages directly to homebuyers, but they may indirectly help you get a mortgage in various ways. Here's how.

The FHA *insures* mortgages that are offered by the lenders. In other words, a lender who gives a person a mortgage may pay some money to the FHA for insurance on the mortgage. That means that if the borrower fails to pay, the FHA has to pay to make up the shortfall. This is good for the lender because it reduces the chances that the lender will have to take a loss. It is also good for the borrower because it makes lenders less fearful of losing money on a mortgage;

therefore, they tend to make loans to some people they might otherwise turn down.

Fannie Mae and Freddie Mac both *buy* mortgages. A lender may provide a mortgage to a particular borrower, then bill the borrower regularly and collect the payments. If payments fail to come in, the lender takes action to try to collect. But the lender may also *sell* the mortgage to Fannie Mae or Freddie Mac. Under this arrangement, Fannie Mae or Freddie Mac pays the lender a large lump sum. After that, Fannie Mae or Freddie Mac sends out the bills to the homeowner, collects the monthly payment from the homeowner, and takes action if the homeowner does not pay. This helps the mortgage lender by giving it the option to have its loans repaid early and still make a profit. It helps the borrower (the homeowner) by making mortgage lending attractive to more companies, so more of them offer mortgages and we all have more mortgage loans available.

Each of these agencies in its own way helps borrowers and makes home ownership possible for more people. However, these organizations will not insure or buy just *any* mortgage. If a lender grants a mortgage to someone who clearly cannot pay, the FHA cannot insure it. The FHA would likely lose money on it, and if that happened on many mortgages the FHA's expenses would be greater than the payments it collects from the lenders. It would quickly go out of business. Likewise, if Fannie Mae and Freddie Mac bought loans that were likely to go unpaid, they would fail as well.

To guard against unacceptable losses, each of these agencies has standards for the mortgages it will insure or buy. These are rules meant to guarantee that the mortgages are reasonably likely to be paid by the borrowers. The rules are similar to the rules that the lenders always apply—the borrower must have a certain level of income that is adequate to pay the premiums, and so on. The rules are carefully spelled out in advance so the lenders know when they provide a mortgage whether it will meet the standards of the FHA, Fannie Mae, or Freddie Mac. Many lenders organize their whole business around this arrangement.

They provide only mortgages that can be insured by the FHA (or bought by Fannie Mae or Freddie Mac), and then quickly turn around and insure or sell them.

These federal agencies will also insure or buy some energy-efficiency mortgages. They have special rules that spell out which features an EEM must have for them to accept it. These are similar to the rules for other EEMs. The result is that you may find that your lender will give you an energy-efficiency mortgage, but only if it passes the requirements of these government agencies. You may find yourself filling out extra forms from the FHA or Fannie Mae or Freddie Mac in addition to the usual ones.

These agencies also give us all another source of expertise on EEMs. Some of the people who work at these organizations know about EEMs and can answer questions about them as well as help lenders and borrowers link up. The clearest example of this is the Fannie Mae Resource Center (1-800-7FANNIE), but you can also sometimes get help finding an EEM by talking to the regional FHA, Fannie Mae, or Freddie Mac office.

TAX CREDITS

I have heard that the U.S. government also gives tax credits for building an energy-efficient house.
That's correct, and that's another benefit your house might qualify for. This is a brand new program that was included in the Energy Act of 2006. It provides tax credits for the general contractor who builds an energy-efficient home. According to the law, the GC gets up to $2,000 for each one he builds.

Wow! Exactly how does this tax credit to builders of energy-efficient homes work?
The general contractor building the house pays a HERS to put the house through an energy evaluation a lot like the one done for Energy Star. The main differences are that, in this case, only the energy used for heating and cooling is counted, and the rating has to be no greater than 50. In other words, the house has

to have an estimated consumption of heating/cooling energy that is no more than half of what it would have consumed if it were just built to the requirements of the International Energy Conservation Code.

These records all have to be kept according to specific rules. At the end of the year, when he files his tax return, the GC can claim a credit of $2,000 for each house he built that met the requirements. So his tax bill is cut by this amount.

But if the builder gets the energy-efficiency credit, how does that help me?
It might help you indirectly. As builders realize that they can get tax credits for building energy-efficient houses, they should start doing the mental math. If they build you one, they get up to $2,000 of savings at tax time. So they should be willing to build the house for you for a little less.

So this tax credit for the builder might mean I get charged up to $2,000 less for my house?
Probably not quite that much. Remember, the builder still has to pay for the testing and do extra work filling out forms and such. But I wouldn't be surprised if this started cutting the cost of an energy-efficient home at least by half the amount of the tax credit—that's $1,000. This would be a nice way to help cut the cost of the energy-efficiency features. And don't forget that you also end up with a house that is not only efficient, but its efficiency is actually verified by an independent party. And you should be able to show that proof to other people.

Where do I get more information about the federal tax credit for energy-efficient homes?
You can check to see if your general contractor is familiar with it; he will have to become familiar with it anyway if he is going to apply for it. The local HERS are quickly coming up to speed on it. Odds are that if you ask a HERS in your area, the staff will know all the details. You can also get basic information on the RESNET Web site (**www.resnet.us**). That site has a directory where you can find the HERS near you, too.

Table 8-2

Special Program Locator Planning	
Program Type	**Where to Find It**
Assurance of disaster resistance	Institute for Business and Home Safety
Reduced insurance rates	Local insurance agents
	National offices of insurance companies
Assurance of energy efficiency	Home Energy Rating Services (HERS)
	Residential Energy Services Network (RESNET)
	Energy Star program
	R2000 program (Canada)
Energy efficiency mortgages	Mortgage lenders
	Federal National Mortgage Association (Fannie Mae)
Federal energy-efficiency tax credit	Your builder
	HERS and RESNET
Energy efficiency awards	Local utility companies
	State energy office

Are there any credits or payments for energy-efficient construction offered by state and local governments?

Some state and local organizations do give awards for energy-efficient home construction. But what the requirements are, who gives the cash, and who gets it, all vary so much that it is difficult for me to provide specifics.

Some states and some electrical utility companies now provide cash awards, or rebates, for the construction of energy-efficient homes or for the use of energy-efficient products. There is usually an application process and some verification that the building was really constructed according to the program requirements. The money may go to the homeowner, or it may go to the contractor doing the work. If it goes to the contractor, it may still be of value to you because the contractor may reduce the price he charges you for the house.

Availability of these programs is spotty. The terms are also different in almost every case. Your best bet is to ask around about them. Your contractor or architect might be familiar with them. Also, your contractor's ICF supplier may know of some in your area.

This is getting confusing. With all these special programs for well-built houses, it seems like a chore to find out which ones are available and how to qualify.

It *is* a bit of a chore. That's why more people are not taking advantage of them. If you're organized, you can decrease the amount of work you have to do to check out your options (see Table 8-2). First ask yourself which of the possible benefits you really want. Then contact the organizations that offer these programs, or ask your builder.

In addition, carry around a list of the programs you are interested in and *ask everyone who might have more information.* Ask your general contractor or architect or the ICF subcontractor—whichever of these has experience with ICFs. Also, have these people ask the ICF suppliers they have dealt with, or get in touch with the suppliers and ask them yourself. These people are good bets to have some inside information because many of them have been tracking down these same programs for years.

With your applications, paperwork, and initial plan reviews all done, you should finally be looking forward to forging ahead with building your house.

CHAPTER 9

Construction, and How
to Keep Your Hair During It

ONCE THE PLANS are all in and the permits are filed and accepted, your contractor can begin construction. This is where the details of the house are finalized. That includes critical issues such as the quality of the construction and

Stacking
foundation walls.

how plans are modified when unexpected situations arise. Although it will probably not be your job to manage the project, you need to be available. If you are working directly with a general contractor, it is wise to meet and talk with the GC directly. I even suggest you inspect the job site at certain critical points. If you hire an architect to manage the project (a service most of them will offer in addition to designing it), you will probably have periodic meetings with the architect to go over similar issues. Plan on all of this, and make time for it.

Why should I have to be involved during construction? There are plans, I got a price quote and a schedule. These are grown-ups. Why can't they just do their job?

That's like your boss giving you a six-month assignment and telling you not to come back to him until it's done. It's fine if nothing new or unexpected comes up, but if something irregular does occur you really need to discuss it with the person in charge. Since in construction there are very often unanticipated problems and changes that must be made it's important to be available to make decisions. There's no way the GC or architect could know exactly what you will want to do in every situation that comes up.

One concern I've had about construction is that contractors try to cheat you. How do I avoid this? In my opinion, the problem is that most people don't understand how to work with a contractor. I have been a contractor and I have also hired contractors, so I have seen things from both sides. There are plenty of contractors who are conscientious and there are some who will cut corners or overcharge, but most people don't know how to tell the difference. They think they do, but in fact they often choose the poorer ones and get into arguments with the honest ones.

The disadvantage that most homebuyers have is that they don't understand much about how a contractor works. As a result, it's very hard to evaluate whether or not the contractor is doing a good job.

OK, then what do I need to know about the work of a contractor?

It's complicated, but I think I can get across a few key lessons with an example. Read the following story. I've made it up, but it is based on events that have all occurred before. In fact, they're fairly typical kinds of things that go on every day in homebuilding.

A STORY OF TWO CONTRACTORS

IN A MEDIUM-SIZED TOWN there are over a dozen general contractors, including Allen and Bob. They have heard of each other, but have no other connection. Each one has decided to bid to build a different house in the area. A bid is a contractor's proposal for building the house. The buyer provides the plans, then the builder returns a detailed description of how he will build it and for what price. Many buyers get bids from more than one contractor, then choose among them. Allen plans to bid on a pretty typical three-bedroom house to be constructed in one of the new developments west of town. Bob intends to bid on a very similar house in a new development east of town.

Allen Wins a Bid

Allen considers the plans for the house he is bidding on. He asks all of his subcontractors how much they will charge for their parts of the work—the walls and roof, the plumbing, the electrical, the flooring, and so on. He also considers his many other expenses, such as his builder's insurance, fees to the building department, the cost of the equipment he will have to provide, the costs of the materials, and the various odds and ends that are bound to come up. He totals these and then adds on the pay for his own time. Some contractors include this as a markup on the materials and the other subcontractors' fees, and some list this as *profit*. But Allen prefers to list it as "general contractor's salary." All of his costs added together are $160,000, and the amount for his salary is $40,000. Allen's total for everything is $200,000.

Allen provides the homebuyer with an itemized list of everything he will put into the new house and how everything will be built. It goes on for a dozen pages. He includes the price of $200,000 and gives the buyer some explanation as to why it will cost that much. The buyer has some detailed questions, so Allen explains why he recommends building the house the way he described in the list. The buyer wants to save some money, and has some suggestions. Allen advises against some of the buyer's ideas because he does not feel the buyer will be happy with the results—skimping on lumber might lead to floors that bounce; using the least expensive roofing shingles will probably require new roofing only a few years later. But Allen does make some suggestions that can save a little money. For example, the bathrooms can have vinyl flooring installed instead of ceramic tile. Then the owners can put tile in later, when they have more money. With the changes, Allen recalculates the total bill at $190,000.

A few days later the buyer says that another contractor gave him a quote of $175,000, and asks why he should pay Allen more. Allen asks to look at the other quote. It fits on one page without much detail, so he can't be very specific in his comments. But he knows the other contractor and feels that his own work is better. At home that night he thinks hard about the job. He needs the work, but if he loses it he might be able to get something else. If he were to match the $175,000 quote he would make only $15,000 for almost half a year of work. He simply can't get by on that.

Allen decides he can't take less than $185,000. With that he makes $25,000 for himself. It's a slim salary, but acceptable. He knows he could tell the buyer that the other contractor does poorer work than he does, but he always avoids criticizing other contractors. Most buyers just assume he's making things up to get the job. Besides, if word gets back to the other guy that Allen said something critical , the other guy will probably start slandering Allen right back. He doesn't want to take that kind of a hit to his reputation.

The next day he tells the buyer that he can come down to $185,000, but no lower. He says he will do a

good job, but if the buyer wants to go with the other contractor, he understands.

But the buyer says he appreciates Allen's honesty and has heard good things about him, so he gives Allen the job.

Bob Wins a Bid

Bob thinks about bidding on the other house, which is across town. Bob has been busy and never has patience for a lot of detailed work. He talks with a couple of his subcontractors about the house and gets a rough idea of what they will charge. He figures that if he goes with the cheapest ones he can build the house for $160,000. He'd like to bid $190,000 and use $30,000 to pay himself. But he has heard that there are other bidders and he needs the work. So he bids $175,000 just to be sure. He really can't get by on the $15,000 margin. But losing the job and getting no pay would be even worse. He hopes that he can find some ways to save some more money or charge extra money later on.

Bob's homebuyer sees the $175,000 price tag and picks Bob to build his house. Another contractor seemed better prepared and had some satisfied customers, but he bid $190,000, and the buyer didn't want to pay more than he had to.

Allen Begins Building

Allen starts building his house, and work goes more or less routinely. A long period of rain sets work back two weeks. During this time the buyer calls every couple of days to ask when things will get moving again. Allen patiently explains that he needs to excavate the site and the equipment can't work until the ground is firmer, but he hopes to catch up later by working ahead on some other things. He tells the other subcontractors to work as far ahead on their other jobs as they can so they will be ready to devote their full attention to his house when it's ready for them.

Soon the rain breaks, and Allen's crews get in to excavate, build the foundation, and build the walls for the house, too. When the walls are up, the buyer walks through and decides that he would like to eliminate one of the windows. It really isn't necessary, and he might save some money. Allen tells him that this will actually cost him some money. Allen ordered the windows a week ago, according to the plans that the buyer gave him, and they are not returnable because they are custom-made. On top of that, his workers will have to rebuild the wall to fill in the opening for the window. Allen will have to pay them more, as well as do more work himself.

The buyer becomes angry. He does not see why he should pay more money for "less house." Allen apologizes, but explains that the change at this point will actually involve more materials and labor. The buyer leaves, still angry, promising to check with other people about whether changes like this should really cost more. Allen offers to give him the receipt for the windows and let him call the window supplier if he wants.

The next day Allen can't reach the buyer. He can't tell his workers to put in the windows since he doesn't know what the buyer wants to do. So he has them work on some other small things. The end result is that work falls a little more behind schedule.

A day after that, the buyer returns Allen's calls and asks about simply moving the window. Allen explains that this can be done for $600 to cover the extra labor and materials. The buyer doesn't like this, but Allen says that those are the costs and he really can't charge less. The buyer gives him the go-ahead, but with some anger in his voice. Allen comes to the site Sunday afternoon with two of his workers to make the change without losing more time.

Bob Begins Building

Meanwhile, Bob hears that he gets the job he bid on. He calls the excavator he likes to tell him to get the site ready. But he hasn't checked with this contractor in advance, and the excavator turns out to be busy. Bob calls some others, but the only ones who can work right away are more expensive. Bob tells the buyer that the ground conditions are not right to start work. He will have to get started in a few days. The buyer is not happy about this, but Bob tells him he can easily make the time up later on.

Bob uses the spare time to call the other subcontractors he wants to use and get commitments from them to work on this house. The electrician and the painter both want more money than Bob figured on. If he accepts their bids, he will have to pay $5,000 more than he estimated, and he will take home even less money. He pushes the electrician to cut his fee. They agree to use some less expensive materials and eliminate some outlets and fixtures that are on the plans, but aren't strictly required by the building codes. Bob can't get any concessions out of his painter, but he finds another one who will do the job for $2,000 less. Bob has never heard of this new painter and doesn't know anything about his work, but he agrees to give him the job if he makes sure to be available and doesn't go over budget.

A week later the excavator is still not ready, and the buyer is becoming impatient. He calls Bob every few days. Bob explains that conditions should be good in a day or two, but says that he has to wait for some more approvals from the building department. He doesn't know how the building department could be so slow, but he can't work without their okay.

Work finally gets started on Bob's house. He has a number of delays for various reasons. He ordered materials late, so some of them are not on site when the crews are ready to use them. Some of the crews are not available because Bob got to them late and he didn't want to bring in more expensive ones. Bob gives the buyer various reasons for the delays that he makes up: Deliveries of materials are late, the building department is slow in doing its inspections, and so on.

When the walls are up on Bob's house, the buyer decides that he would like to move one of the living room windows about four feet for a better view of the countryside. Bob says that he can do this for $1,200. The owner is upset about this. Bob says that a whole set of structural pieces are run over a window opening, and moving the window will require him to tear apart a large part of the building structure and relocate it over a new opening. The buyer gives him the go-ahead, but with some anger in his voice. The next day Bob tells the crew that he will give them $300 to move the window, but they need to do a little of the work each day for a week so it looks like it takes longer.

When the old window opening is closed up and the new one is formed, one of Bob's workers comes to him with a concern. They didn't have exactly the right materials available for the top of the opening, so they used something smaller. He is afraid that it might sag sometime in the future. Bob looks at the work, and sees that if he wants to fix it he will have to send someone to the supply store to get more materials. It would cost a hundred dollars for the materials, plus whatever he is paying to the person getting them, and it would delay some of the rest of the work. He tells his crew that the window opening is good enough and instructs them to get on to the next task.

Allen's Buyers Choose Their Fixtures

Back at Allen's house, the buyers are late choosing their plumbing fixtures. As part of the contract, the buyers have an allowance for things like the bathtubs, the sinks, and the kitchen cabinets. This means that a certain amount of money is set aside in the budget for each of these things. The buyers get to go to the local stores where Allen has an account. They pick out the fixtures they want. The store gives Allen a discount for products he puts in his houses. If the total discounted price of the items turns out to be less than the allowance, the buyers get the difference back. If it turns out to be more, they pay the extra amount.

This has all worked according to plan, except that the buyers decided that they wanted to consider a new Italian line of sinks and tubs that they saw in an architecture magazine. Allen told them he'd install them as long as they could be installed the conventional way. But they turn out to be much more expensive than the allowance, and the buyers don't want to pay the difference. So they start looking for other suppliers that might sell something similar for less.

About this time Allen warns the buyers that he needs the plumbing fixtures in a week to stay on schedule. The buyers are busy with a birthday party that weekend, so they fail to do more looking. They do shop around the weekend after that and find

something they can live with. But by that time, Allen's crews have had nothing to do for three days. Without all the fixtures the plumber can't finish up, and everything else that can be done without the plumbing being ready is pretty much completed. Worse, the exact fixtures the buyers want are not all in stock, so they have to be ordered. Allen has paid his crews to work on minor details for three days. Now he sets them loose to work on other jobs because he can't afford to pay them to do small things anymore. A week later the fixtures arrive and he calls everyone back.

Bob's Buyers Choose Their Fixtures

At Bob's house the buyers are also on an allowance, and they are selecting kitchen cabinets. But at the stores he recommended, they have trouble finding cabinets that fit within the allowance. When they saw the allowance of $9,000 on the contract, it sounded like plenty of money, but to buy cabinets for less than that amount, they find that they either have to buy the plainest, most lightweight, and flimsiest ones, or they have to buy fewer than they had planned and leave some of the kitchen wall empty.

The buyers complain to Bob. But Bob says that $9,000 is enough money for most people. He also tells them that it doesn't really matter what's on the contract, because it says that they make up the difference if they want premium cabinets, so sooner or later they pay the full price. The buyers complain that maybe Bob was the lowest bidder on the job only because he didn't put enough money in the allowances. But there is little they can do about it at this point, so they get some decent cabinets and pay Bob the extra money.

Allen's House Gets Its Finishes

After the exterior of Allen's house is buttoned up, his buyers take a great interest in how the interior finishes are done—the woodwork, painting, flooring, and so on. They begin to arrive almost daily and watch the workers for up to an hour each time. Often they interrupt the workers and ask them why they are doing things a particular way.

They stop the carpenter to ask why he isn't putting some sort of molding on top of the baseboards. He says that he was told to install this particular baseboard without any molding. They tell him that that can't be right and order him to stop work. He mutters and tries to find something else he can work on for the rest of the day.

That night the buyers call Allen at home and ask him about it. He gets out his papers and finds where the contract specifies a one-piece, ranch-style baseboard. They say they would never have agreed to that. Allen responds that he doesn't recall that particular item, but he does remember them going through every line with him, one at a time, and then signing the contract. The contract is indeed signed. They discuss the possibility of paying Allen extra to rip out the ranch baseboard and put in a more elaborate style, but they decide it isn't that important and so they stick with the ranch.

On a different day the buyers ask the painter why he is using caulk to fill in the narrow spaces between the baseboards and the wallboard. It seems to them to be a waste of time and money since the paint will just fill in the gap, and they would rather skip the step and get some money back. Allen is on the site this time, and he and the painter explain that the paint is too thin to fill the gap, so the final wall will look bad if they don't put in caulk.

The buyers leave, but don't fully accept this explanation. That night one of them goes back to the house, opens a can of the wall paint, and paints over a section of wall and baseboard. In fact, the paint just runs down the gap without filling it up, and the results look bad. The buyer keeps on painting over this spot, trying to fill the gap with paint. But he goes through a lot of paint without much success. The buyer leaves. The next day the painter finds one of his brushes covered with dried paint. He has to throw it out. He also finds a spot on the wall and baseboard and floor where gobs of paint have built up. He can't simply paint over this because it will not look even. He does his best to scrape away the excess paint and sand everything smooth.

The workers begin to complain to Allen about the buyers looking over their shoulders and meddling in their work. Allen promises to try to be on the site whenever the buyers come, so he can field their questions and try to explain things to their satisfaction.

Bob's House Gets Its Finishes

After the exterior of Bob's house is buttoned up, his buyers also start watching the finish work that's going on. They ask about several things that look odd to them. They are fairly certain they asked for baseboards that are 4 inches tall, but the ones the carpenter is installing look smaller than that. That night they call Bob, but he doesn't answer his phone. They see him at the site a couple of days later and ask him about it. He says that he is certain they asked for 3-inch baseboards, and besides the baseboards are now all in place anyway. But if they want to pay for new, 4-inch baseboard material and pay for the labor to replace the old baseboards, he can do that. They say no.

They also think they see some crooked pieces of trim around the windows and doors. They bring this up with the carpenter doing the work, and he tells them he's just doing what he's told so they should see the boss. When they see Bob, they bring this up. He says that a little bit of warped wood is standard nowadays, and no one will notice after the paint is on. He adds that if they want "select" trim he can get it, but it costs more and he will have to pay the carpenter to redo the work. After looking over the bad parts of the trim, the buyers decide that a few pieces really need to be replaced. They agree to pay Bob $1,500 to have this work redone.

Allen Completes the Job

Allen's workers finish their house about a week and a half after it was originally promised. The bills total $187,000. This is $2,000 over the original quote because of some changes and additions that the buyers wanted.

The buyers seem more or less satisfied with the results, but are a bit annoyed that the work ended late and they had to pay some extra money. They move in, but do not pay Allen the final check for $20,000 that is due to him. He calls every few days, but they are either not home or say they'll have to "check" about that final bill. They finally pay it about two months late, just as Allen is short of money to make the payments on his truck.

Bob Completes the Job

Bob tells his buyers that he is finished. They walk around the house and see some things that look like they're not quite done. Bob becomes annoyed, but sends some workers over to finish them up. The buyers are still concerned about a couple of light fixtures that they are sure they asked for but aren't in the house, and a couple of walls that appear to be painted with only one coat. Bob tells them that everything is done, and they need to pay their final check to him or he will not call for the final inspection by the building department, and without that they can't move in.

The buyers pay Bob and move in, but they are worried that some things may not be quite right. In the end, the house Bob built was completed three months after originally promised, and the buyers paid a total of $197,000. This includes more expensive cabinets, a moved window, installing some better trim, and various other added expenses for changes or improvements to the work.

DISCUSSION

It's terrible how that contractor Bob cheated his buyers! Is this typical?
Luckily, it isn't, but it strikes me how you keyed in on the contractor who *wasn't* forthright with his buyers. It seems to me that it's also sad how poorly Allen's buyers treated him, even while he was giving them good service at a fair price.

Fortunately, contractors with principles as loose as Bob's are the exception, not the rule. Unfortunately, people still hire them because they promise to deliver so much for so little. Many buyers want so badly to

believe that they can get the house of their dreams for 10% less, that they fall for the pitch of a contractor who promises it.

On the flip side, conscientious contractors like Allen often get blamed for things beyond their control. The weather, changes in instructions from the buyers, and any number of chance events can increase costs and delay work. Often good contractors will bear some of these costs themselves just to avoid arguments. But they can only do so much of that before they go broke. If the cost overruns are clearly the result of the buyer's actions (like them asking to change the design of the house in midstream), the buyers are supposed to pay the difference. But buyers often get angry about things even if they are treated fairly. Building a house is a risky undertaking, and buyers don't like the unpleasant surprises that sometimes occur. They prefer to blame them on someone, like the general contractor.

MINIMIZING PROBLEMS

So how can I minimize problems and bad work?
First of all, choose your general contractor the way I recommended in Chapter 6. That is, use references—get names of people the GC has worked for before, and talk to these people about how the project went and how the contractor was to work with. Don't slack off on this—this is one of the most important things you can do in the whole project. Talk to at least three past customers, and have a long chat with them.

The key with interviews like this is to force people to be *specific*. Then you can stare at the facts and see what you make of them, instead of just relying on someone else's first impression. You need to talk to more than one person to get an idea of what is a trend and what is an exception. If all three people say that Mr. X bent over backwards to make sure the work was done correctly, that's probably true. If only one person says that and the others have examples of how he let some shoddy work go uncorrected, you have to be suspicious.

It sounds as if I should look for a contractor who has no complaints against him.

No, actually that's unfair. As the example shows, people can complain about contractors who do a good job. No construction project ever goes perfectly, and buyers sometimes complain about things that actually are done correctly or are just the fault of bad luck, not the contractor. What you should be looking for is a contractor who appears to have been conscientious, produced good work, and treated people fairly. You will never find perfection.

INSPECTIONS

What about inspecting the work as it goes along?

That can be helpful if it's done by someone who knows the details of construction. It tends to be harmful if it's done by someone who has just an average knowledge of construction.

As discussed in the example, people who are not experts in construction can tend to criticize things that are actually done correctly. This can lead to pointless arguments and wasted rework. In addition, close supervision of the workers is annoying. It's like your boss reading over your shoulder and making suggestions while you write a report. On the other hand, inspections can be a constructive thing if they are done in a professional way.

So how are inspections done correctly?

First, tell the contractor in advance that you would like to have inspections done. Do this at the time you ask for the bid so he can take account of it in his plans. Second, have the inspections done by a qualified person—an expert, not yourself or a friend who happens to be available. Third, make the inspections *periodic*. In other words, check over a chunk of work after it is completed, but before it gets covered up. This way you can see it, yet it's not too late to correct mistakes. Actually, any good inspector will do inspections in a periodic way.

Who should I get to do inspections?

If you want professional inspections, you can usually get a home inspector to do them for you. These are the same people who look at an existing house for you before you buy it to make sure it doesn't have any big problems. That is probably 80 percent of the work they get. But if someone is building a new house and wants them to check on the work during construction, most of them will do that, too. It can cost a couple thousand dollars all together, but it can help ensure a quality job.

One word of caution: Most home inspectors are still not familiar with ICFs, so if you hire one, you will have to work with him to make sure he is up to speed on what to look for in the walls.

Do I have to have inspections?

Absolutely not. Inspections are rarely needed for good contractors. It is still good to be interested and ask polite questions and visit the job site every few days. This keeps people on their toes. But a good contractor should do good work for you without being inspected by an expert. Besides, the local building department will do its inspections and spot really big problems.

Regardless, I *do* recommend that you check for some critical things in the quality of the ICF work. ICF walls do not have any more problems than any other parts of construction, in my experience. But they are a new form of construction and many people are less familiar with them. Hopefully, you have taken the correct precautions to get an experienced ICF crew. But to be absolutely certain that you are receiving a quality job, there are a few critical items that someone should check (see "Critical Inspection Points").

Who should check for the quality of the ICF work?

This chapter gives you instructions on how to do it yourself. There are only 4 or 5 things that need to be checked. We can arm you with enough information to inspect them well.

If you happen to be using a home inspector, more than likely the inspector will not be familiar with ICFs. In that case you can give your home inspector the information from this chapter to learn what to look for and how to do it.

The only other option would be to get some other person experienced with ICFs to check the work. But this is difficult. Another ICF contractor is likely to be either a competitor of your ICF contractor, or a friend. In neither case can you count on this person to be objective. You could ask a representative of the company that supplied the ICF forms. But the rep has a business relationship with your installer, and is therefore also not likely to be very objective.

What you need is someone independent, without an ax to grind, which tends to limit it to you yourself or your hired inspector. **BEWARE: A job site can be a hazardous place, and by stepping onto it you are accepting liability.**

Now that you've recommended that I inspect the ICF work, I have one doubt about it. Isn't the building department supposed to be inspecting the house? Why should I have to do it, too?
In nearly all parts of the country, the building department does indeed inspect the construction at several points in the process, and they're usually trustworthy. So in a sense, no, you don't have to do your own inspections.

On the other hand, the building department is supposed to make sure that the construction meets certain *minimum* standards. A lot of things might be of poor quality, but if they are not dangerous they are usually not covered by the building codes, and the local building inspector is not authorized to order that they be corrected. When I built my own house, one inspector who came out told me about several things that he found that were technically acceptable, but that he thought should be done differently for quality's sake. Most building inspectors don't mention these things, and even if they do the buyer rarely hears about them. They are simply outside the realm of the building inspector's official authority.

But because you have an interest in ICFs, I'm assuming that you want to hold the construction of your house to a higher standard. You want to make sure it isn't just

---

> ### Critical Inspection Points
>
> - Does the formwork match the house plans?
> - Is the foam missing anywhere?
> - Are the walls straight everywhere, horizontally and vertically?
> - Are there any hollow spots in the walls?

acceptable, you want to make sure it is *exceptional.* A good way to help guarantee that is to inspect for some finer details than the ones the law requires.

What items in the ICF construction do I need to check?
The four items I consider the most important to verify are shown in the Critical Inspection Points box and in Fig. 9-1.

What's so important about matching the walls with the plans?
Checking that the formwork matches the plans just verifies that the walls are where you want them, the windows are where you want them, and so on. If something is out of place, you need to catch this before the walls are filled with concrete. At this early point, things are much easier to correct than later on, when the concrete is in and hard.

What about missing foam? Why is that important?
You also don't want to find random patches where the foam is missing from the wall surface. All the foam should be in place because it acts as your insulation (Fig. 9-2). During the pouring of the concrete, sometimes the concrete can break through the foam forms. That is called a **blowout**. It's easy for a good crew to repair a blowout in a few minutes by replacing the broken foam so the wall ends up with a layer of foam everywhere, even where the break was. It may have some slightly uneven spots and a few smudges of concrete, but it will be fine. If a blowout is repaired incorrectly, the crew does not bother to replace the

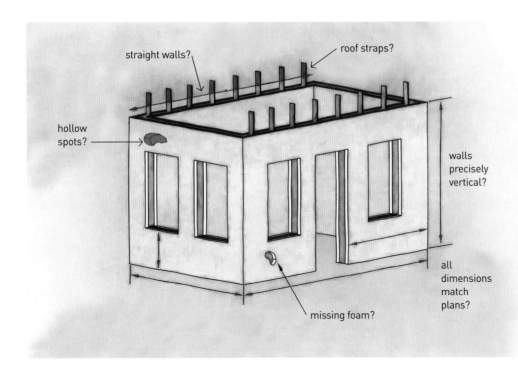

straight walls?

roof straps?

hollow spots?

walls precisely vertical?

missing foam?

all dimensions match plans?

9-1. Potential problem areas in ICF walls.

foam. They just cover over the hole with something like plywood, so the concrete comes all the way out to the wall surface. This leaves an uninsulated patch of concrete. That's something you definitely do not want.

You have to be careful when you inspect for this, though. On many houses there are a few spots where some patches of concrete are intentionally left exposed. The crew cuts out neat squares or circles of foam and covers the holes over so the concrete flows up to the surface. The purpose of these is to provide a solid backing for a floor or other heavy assembly that will be connected to the walls there.

Tell me about straight, vertical walls.

The importance of having walls that are straight and vertical should be obvious (Fig. 9-3). If they lean in or out significantly, they can throw off other things in the house. At the extreme, they might cause structural problems down the road. If they are wavy, the wall may look poor even after it is covered.

If the ICF crew braces the wall well before pouring concrete and adjusts the bracing properly during the

pour, the walls should be nice and straight. If they don't, some of this unevenness can occur. But note that minor unevenness is unimportant. There will always be a few slightly uneven points on any wall made with any material. These are rarely of any

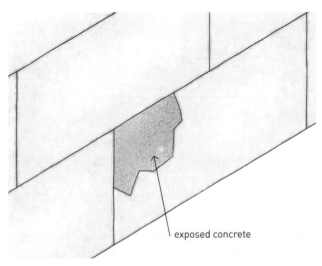

exposed concrete

9-2. Spot on the wall with foam accidentally missing.

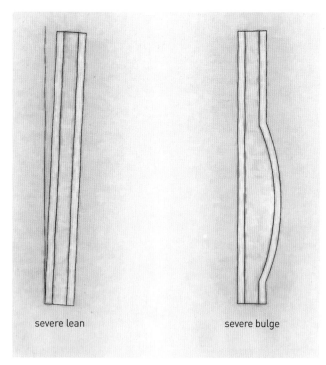

severe lean   severe bulge

9-3. Tilted walls and bulging walls.

structural importance. Visually, they hardly ever show once they are covered with finishes. Anywhere they might show, the finish crews can shave the foam down slightly to even out the surface before they cover it over.

What's the concern about hollow spots in the wall?
Hollow spots occur when the concrete fails to fill parts of the wall completely. Technically, these spots are called **voids**. You can think of them as large air bubbles in the concrete.

The truth is that a concrete wall can have some voids without becoming weak enough to cause structural danger. But why risk it? Large voids are certainly a potential problem, depending on where they occur. Furthermore, if you are missing concrete somewhere, that is one spot that lacks the benefits you were looking for in the first place—thermal mass, sound deadening, and so on. Voids generally occur because the crew that placed the concrete did not consolidate it thoroughly (Fig. 9-4). We'll go over consolidation later, but, in brief, it refers to vibrating

the concrete to get the air pockets out of it. If you simply verify these four things, you will have covered the most critical factors for a quality ICF installation.

How do I inspect for these things in my ICF walls?
Let's start with a simple overview of the things to inspect at each phase, given in the ICF Inspection Checklist, by Construction Phase.

ICF Inspection Checklist, by Construction Phase

PHASE 1: Footing, slab, or pier-and-beam complete:
- Outline matches where the walls go
- Dowels sticking up where walls go

PHASE 2: Forms for basement/first story in position:
- Walls are in the right place
- All openings in the right place
- Horizontal rebar around walls on top
- Horizontal rebar around walls below
- Vertical rebar every 1 to 4 feet
- Vertical rebar along each side of openings
- 1+ horizontal rebar over each opening

PHASE 3: Basement/first-story walls filled and hard:
- No bare patches of concrete showing
- Walls appear flat on both sides
- A level shows walls to be plumb
- No significant voids (hollow sound)

PHASE 4: About to set forms for upper-story walls:
- Dowels sticking up from lower-story walls

PHASE 5: Forms for upper-story walls in position:
- Same as for basement/first story

PHASE 6: Upper-story walls filled and hard:
- Same as for basement/first story

9-4. A void in an ICF wall made visible by removing the foam. (Portland Cement Association)

What does each of these inspections mean?

To explain that, I have to explain the typical sequence of construction for an ICF house. But, first, bear in mind that **you must never put yourself in danger to inspect the house.** A construction site can be a dangerous place. There can be spots with bad footing and long falls, exposed nails and splintered lumber. **If at any time inspecting the job site would put you in danger, don't do it.** Wait for a better time or get professional help instead.

What is the construction sequence for an ICF house, and how do my inspections fit into it?

Every house is a little different, but commonly the construction goes something like this. Heavy earth-moving machinery comes out to excavate the site (Fig. 9-5). If you will have a basement or stem wall foundation, it digs a hole for this. If your house will have a floor slab foundation, the machinery levels off the spot where the house will go. This may take anywhere from a couple of days to a couple of weeks depending on the size of the job and the weather.

For a house with a basement or stem wall foundation, workers next build a strip of concrete about a foot wide around the perimeter of the basement

9-5. Excavation under way. (New Holland Construction)

that will go under the exterior walls (Fig. 9-6). This is called a **footing.**

To guide you, we've included a detailed checklist of what to look for at each inspection phase, as we come to it.

INSPECTION 1: After the footing is complete, before the forms for the basement/foundation walls go up:

- Check the concrete footing to make sure it matches the locations where the walls are supposed to go. The walls will have to rest on top of the footing.
- Look for **dowels.** These are pieces of steel-reinforcing bar that stick up 2 to 3 feet from the footing. Their bottom ends should be embedded in the concrete footing. Their top ends will extend into the formwork in the walls above, so

they can be embedded into the concrete in the walls. These steel dowels tie the footing and the walls together. If you don't see them, ask. There should be one sticking up every few feet along the line where the walls will go.

After the footing hardens, the ICF crew builds up the forms for the basement/foundation walls. This usually takes 2 to 4 days, unless the design is very large or complicated. Then it's time for Inspection 2.

INSPECTION 2: **After the basement/foundation forms are up but before concrete is poured:**

- Walk around outside and inside the basement with the plans. Do the walls appear to be in the right position? If there are any windows or doors in the basement, are they in the right place? Go ahead and take out a tape measure to check some dimensions. Ask about any significant discrepancies.
- Look inside the forms if you can do it safely. There should be more steel-reinforcing bar inside the forms. It is impossible to tell you exactly what the pattern of rebar inside the wall should be because it is different for every project. Depending on such structural factors as the size of the house, the condition of the soil, and the local wind speeds and earthquake risks, more or less rebar may be required. But generally speaking, you should see the following (Figs. 9-7 and 9-8):
  - ▸ A horizontal line of rebar running all the way around the perimeter near the top of the wall.
  - ▸ At least one other horizontal line of rebar farther down inside the wall.
  - ▸ Bars standing up vertically inside the wall, extending up to or past the top of the form-work. These may be anywhere from 1 to 4 feet apart, but they should be all around the wall and at the corners.
  - ▸ At least one vertical bar standing up on each side of each window and door opening.

9-6. Footing with dowels sticking out of it and guides on top. (Reward Wall Systems, Inc.)

  - ▸ At least one horizontal bar directly over each window and door opening. These bars should extend past the opening about a foot or two on each side.

Next the crew fills the walls with concrete. This usually takes less than one day. The concrete cures to the point that it is pretty solid after a few days. Then it's time for Inspection 3.

INSPECTION 3: **After the basement/foundation walls are cured and before the crew starts work on the house again:**

- Look over the surface of all the walls on both sides. Do you see any spots where there is a patch of concrete without foam covering it? If so, ask about these. If they are spots where foam was intentionally cut away to connect something like a floor, that's okay. If they are unintentional, you have lost your insulation in that spot.
- Stand at each corner and sight down the surface of each wall. Does it appear to be nice and straight, or does it have a bow or some

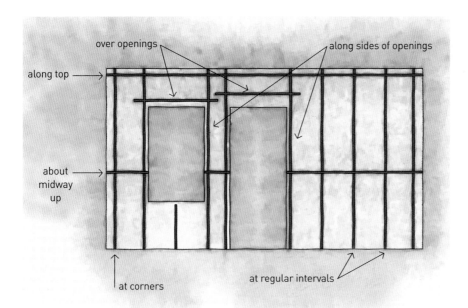

9-7. Typical locations for rebar.

over openings

along sides of openings

along top

about
midway
up

at corners

at regular intervals

9-8. Rebar visible inside the forms.
(Portland Cement Association)

waves? Small deviations are not a problem, so if you have to hunt for a while to tell whether the wall is flat, it's probably fine. But if it's immediately obvious and extreme, you should complain and make sure there's no problem before construction resumes.

■ Make sure the walls are **plumb**. This means straight up and down, not leaning in or out. The best way to do this is with a carpenter's level. This looks something like a fat yardstick, but it has bubble chambers set in it. A level at least 3 feet long is best for checking a wall. If you set the side of the level up against the wall and hold it vertical, the bubble should be in the center of the horizontal chamber. That indicates that the wall is straight up and down. If it is very slightly off, you probably don't need to be concerned. The carpenter's level is a very sensitive instrument, and a wall that leans in or out less than an inch is probably not a problem. Check each wall every few feet.

■ Besides helping you check for plumb, the level will also show whether the wall is flat. If the level does not contact the surface of the foam up its entire side, the wall is bowing in or out a little. Again, if this is very slight (leaving, say, a quarter-inch gap or less), this is hardly worth worrying about. Much beyond that and you should call it to your general contractor's attention.

■ Check for voids. You can do this simply by rapping on the walls and listening for a hollow sound. You can use a small piece of wood to spare your knuckles. Start on one side at a spot you will remember. Rap up and down the wall. Then move over a foot and do it again. Work your way around the perimeter to get back where you started.

■ If you hear a hollow sound, mark it with a permanent marking pen. Then rap around it and see how far it extends until you find its outer limits. Mark this outline, as best as you can determine it, with the pen. If you end up with very few very small hollow spots, you probably have little reason for concern. If you have some large hollows, I advise you to bring them to the attention of the GC and ask to have them corrected.

- After the basement/foundation wall cures, the workers usually build the first floor next, on top of the basement walls. Then they start putting up the forms for the first-story walls.

INSPECTION 4: After the basement/foundation walls are cured and before the crew starts work on the house again:

- Look at the top of the walls that have already been completed. The ends of rebar should be protruding from the top of these walls. The walls of the next story above will be built to encase the ends of these bars. That is important because they tie the lower-story and upper-story walls together. If you don't see at least one bar every 4 feet along the wall, ask the GC why not.

INSPECTIONS 5 AND 6: For upper story walls:

- To inspect the walls of upper stories, you follow the same procedure you would for basement walls, as listed in Inspections 2 and 3. Inspect once after the forms are up (but no concrete is put in them yet) and once after the concrete is in and hard. Do this for each story.

IN WARM CLIMATES

What if I live in a place where we don't have basements?

In warm climates the construction often begins differently. Many houses in warm climates are set on a concrete slab that is poured on the ground instead of a basement or stem walls. The excavators first level off the ground. Separate workers put up boards around where the slab will go and place concrete into it.

9-9. A slab with steel dowels. (ECO-BLOCK, LLC.)

They level the concrete off while it's still wet and let it cure. The construction of the slab usually takes a couple of days. When your house has a slab, your first inspection comes when the slab is in place. You can inspect it much as you do a footing.

INSPECTION 1: After the slab is complete and before the workers start setting forms on top of it:

- Check that the slab dimensions match the dimensions of the house floor on the floor plan.
- Check that there are dowels extending out of the slab along the lines where the exterior walls will go (Fig. 9-9).

9-10. Forms stacked for a stem wall foundation. (Arxx Building Products)

What if I live in an area where some other kind of foundation is most common?

Most of them you inspect in about the same way. Stem walls are usually about 3 to 4 feet tall and extend down into the ground only a couple of feet. Inspect those just as you would a basement (Fig. 9-10).

In some areas with unstable soils, a **pier-and-beam** system is used. Crews dig cylindrical holes deep into the ground and fill them with concrete. These are the **piers**. On top of these piers they cast heavy concrete crosspieces. These are the **beams**. The walls rest on the beams. You can inspect a pier-and-beam foundation the same way you inspect a footing.

What about the construction of the first story above ground? What do I look for then?

The first story is always essentially the same, whether it goes on top of a basement, a slab, stem walls, or a pier-and-beam foundation. There should be steel reinforcing bars extending out of the foundation about 2 to 3 feet. Like the dowels extending out of a footing, they will extend into the forms for the story above and be embedded in the concrete there. This connects the first story securely to the foundation below. The walls of the first story are constructed much the same way basement walls are constructed, and you should inspect them the same way before and after the pour.

What about stories above the first one?

If there is a second story, it is constructed after the floor is built at the top of the first story. Inspect the second story as you did the first. Continue the inspections for each story of the house. They should be the same each time: one inspection before the forms go up, one after they are up (just before the pour), and one after the pour.

What about the rest of the house? Can I inspect things other than the ICF walls?

Certainly you can, but the other parts of the house are beyond the scope of this book. The other materials are usually conventional, and you can get books on conventional construction that covers them.

9-11. Inserting rebar in holes in the footing with adhesive. (Simpson Strong-Tie Co., Inc.)

FIXING PROBLEMS

What if I do find problems? For example, what if there aren't dowels coming out of the footing or the slab?

Almost anything can be corrected without too much trouble if it's caught in time. No dowels would be an unusual error, but it's not overly hard to correct. The usual way to do it is to use a rotohammer (basically, a concrete drill) to make holes where the dowels need to go. Then pieces of rebar of the proper length are set into the holes with a high-strength adhesive to hold them securely in place (Fig. 9-11).

What if the shape and size of the footing or slab don't match where the walls are supposed to go?

The footing or slab is supposed to be a bit oversized, so don't jump to conclusions. But if it is truly not in all the right places for the walls above, this can also usually be corrected without too much trouble. Typically the crew will come out and place additional concrete anywhere it's needed. This may require tearing apart some of the original concrete to create a place for the new concrete to tie into the old.

What if I notice before the pour that the foam walls are not all in the right places, have the wrong dimensions, or have window or door openings that are the wrong size or in the wrong place?

Foam is quite easy to work with. If anything needs to be corrected in the form walls, the crews can disassemble the incorrect parts and put the forms back the right way. If necessary, they can cut pieces apart and glue them back together. This can be a bit messy, but it is relatively quick and easy, as construction errors go. The key is to *tell the contractor about it right away*. The more other things get put in place, the more work will be required to correct the errors. Once the concrete is poured, the cost of changes skyrockets, because then you're not working with soft foam anymore—you're working with concrete and steel.

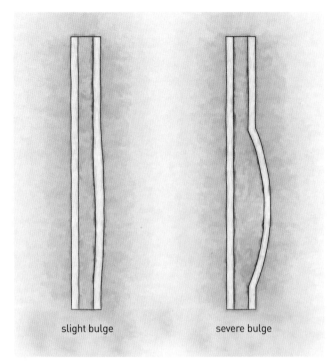

slight bulge   severe bulge

9-12. Walls with reasonable (left) and unreasonable (right) bulges.

What if the steel reinforcing bars are not all in, or are not all in the right place?

This is also easy to correct before the pour. There are various easy tricks for sliding in any missing rebar. But again, you have to call this to the contractors' attention before they pour concrete, not after.

What about after the pour? What if there are patches of concrete on the surface of the wall?

First of all, someone needs to make sure that these are really a mistake. As discussed before, the crew often has to cut out some sections of foam and put a cover over the hole to allow concrete to flow up to the surface of the wall. This creates so-called **pads**. Pads provide a spot where heavy structural items like floors can be securely attached to the walls. Obviously, no one should try to get rid of a pad.

In addition, sometimes concrete splatters onto the surface of the foam. Depending on what finishes will go over the foam, it might be a good idea for someone to scrape off this material. It is usually thin, brittle, and

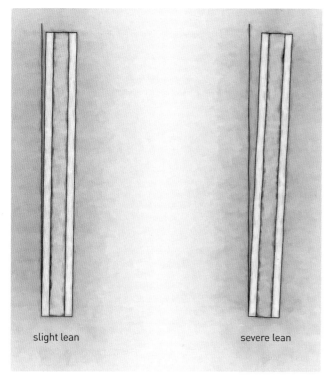

slight lean   severe lean

9-13. Walls with reasonable (left) and unreasonable (right) lean.

easy to remove. But it is not particularly harmful. If there is truly a patch of concrete that is not a pad, and it extends from inside the forms to the surface of the wall, it is probably the result of a blowout that was not repaired properly. This creates a leak in the insulation. The usual way to fix it is to chisel down the concrete back to where it was supposed to end—that is, at the *inside* surface of the forms. Then a patch of foam is glued over the hole to replace the missing insulation.

What if the wall surface is uneven in places?
That depends on how uneven it is. If there are some minor high and low spots on the surface, in most cases there is little reason to do anything. The foam will be covered by finishes that will tend to even out surface imperfections.

If there are high spots that stick out, say, an inch from the rest of the wall, they are usually more a cosmetic problem than a structural one. They are what we call **bulges** (Fig. 9-12). A bulge is a spot where

the pressure of the wet concrete has bowed the forms out. Where there is a bulge, the wall is likely to be no weaker. It is easy enough to get the surface of the wall flat again by shaving off some of the excess foam. There are a few different tools used to do this. You will lose a little insulation in that one spot of the wall, but this usually has too small an effect to worry about.

But always check the other side of the wall from where you see a high spot. If the opposite side is sunken in, then you do not have a simple bulge. The wall has a **wave** in it. In other words, the wall is not thicker at that point; it is curved like a bowl. This is rare, but more serious. Particularly if it has a depth of over an inch or two, it could create a structural problem that does not go away when you shave away some foam. There is no simple way to fix this. You have to bring it to the GC's attention and make fixing it his responsibility.

What if the walls lean in or out?
If the top of the wall is in or out less than about an inch, I usually don't consider this dangerous. Again, it can be covered cosmetically by shaving foam, and even that may be unnecessary. But a much more severe lean is an error and can be dangerous (Fig. 9-13). If any lean concerns you, you should show it to the GC for an

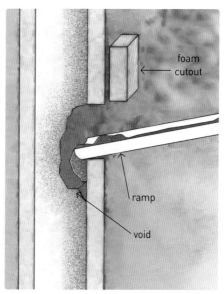

foam cutout

ramp

void

9-14. Using a ramp to place concrete in a void.

explanation and possible correction. Fortunately, this kind of error is also rare.

What if I find hollow spots?

The occasional void is easy to correct. Most contractors cut a hole in the foam at the top of the void. Then they cut a pipe in half the long way to create a ramp (Fig. 9-14). One end of the ramp goes in the hole, and the contractor shoves concrete down it until the void fills up. Then the cutout goes back into the hole with a little glue to hold it in place.

ATTACHING THINGS TO WALLS

Aren't there other things I should be looking for? What about all the things that attach to the ICF walls? How can I be sure they're being attached correctly?

That's a fair question. Attaching things to ICF walls is a bit new and different, just as the construction of ICF walls itself is. Therefore, it may require a little extra attention.

Attachment of other structural parts of the house (like the floors and the roof) is complex and differs from one part of the country to another and from one type of house to the next. It is almost impossible for me to give you any set rules for what to look for. Anyway, these structural connections are among the things that the building inspector is supposed to know about and look for. You can and should count on him to check these things. Attachment of interior walls to the ICF walls is almost a matter of personal preference, so that is difficult to generalize about, too.

But the structural connections sound important. Is there anything I can do to help ensure that they are done correctly?

They *are* important, and there *is* something you can do if you would like. At some point after you have selected your general contractor and before construction starts, you should have a meeting or two with the GC to go over the house design.

9-15. Roof truss attached to a concrete wall with a hurricane plate. (Simpson Strong-Tie Co., Inc.)

At these design meetings, simply *ask* the GC how the floors and the roof will be attached to the ICF walls. Let your general contractor educate you about how it will be done and why. Write this down somewhere, or draw a picture. Then, when you are looking at your house, study how these connections are being made. If they are different from what you were told earlier, call the GC's attention to this and ask for an explanation.

What about using hurricane straps on the roof for wind resistance? You mentioned the importance of that before.

Yes, that is one specific thing you might want to inspect yourself, especially if you have requested hurricane straps or plates and you are in an area where they are not common (Fig. 9-15). In an area that does not have very high wind-resistance requirements, the inspector might not be familiar with them. Or the inspector might know that they are not required in the area, and so will not consider it a concern if they are not used. It is a good idea for you to double-check to make sure you're getting what you requested.

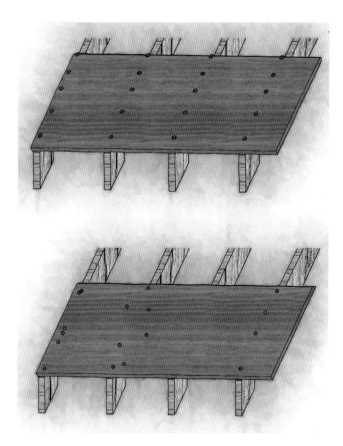

9-16. Correctly attached (top) and incorrectly attached (bottom) sheathing on a roof.

Is there anything else I should be checking to ensure that my house will have good wind resistance?
If you have ICF exterior walls, the roof is the biggest weak point. If the roof is held down securely with hurricane straps, that should help a great deal. As I mentioned before, the other weak points are the connection of the roof framing members to each other and the connection of the sheathing to the roof framing. You can certainly check these things as well.

The roof sheathing is supposed to have nails through it into the roof members at close, regular intervals (Fig. 9-16). Full round-head nails are better than the clipped-head nails used in some nail guns. And staples should not be used at all on roof sheathing in high-wind areas. Also, sometimes workers get careless and their spacing starts to get irregular. Worse, with the use of power nail guns, the worker often

cannot "feel" when a nail has missed the roof member completely. That's when you'll see the ends of nails sticking out inside the attic. They've come through the sheathing but are alongside the roof member, not in it.

If you want to check for these things, get a pair of binoculars and look at the spacing of the nail heads on the roof. Make sure there are nails all over each sheet of sheathing. Then walk through the attic, if possible, and see if there are stray nail ends sticking in. If so, that's a problem. If anything is amiss, the contractor can easily correct it by adding nails. But this really needs to be done before the roof covering goes on.

What did you mean when you said that attaching the interior walls is a matter of personal preference?
There is no written requirement that the interior walls be attached to the ICF walls at all. About 98% of the time, the interior walls are frame. They are attached to the floor below and the floor or to the roof above. If the walls are built correctly, you will be able to lean against them and they will not flex noticeably. But where an interior wall butts up to an ICF wall, some people like to attach the end of it to the ICFs (Fig. 9-17).

9-17. A frame wall butted to an ICF wall without connection.

9-18. End stud screwed to a steel strap that is screwed to the ICF ties.

It makes some sense to attach the interior wall to the ICF walls in places where the interior wall might be subject to a lot of vibration or pressure. An example might be in a laundry room, where the washer and dryer will cause vibration. Another example might be an interior wall where a door is located right near the end that butts up to the ICFs. The idea here is that the forces on the wall might eventually move the wall so much that the wallboard finish starts to show cracks at the joint. I am not aware of wallboard cracks showing up frequently, but this is the type of worry that leads some people to attach the interior walls to the ICFs.

Even on walls that won't be subject to great stresses or vibration, some people still prefer to attach the two walls to each other as a general quality consideration. They feel that things will be more solid.

You can specifically ask your contractor to make this connection if you would like. But you should

expect to pay a little more for it. Connecting each interior wall takes time and money. It's a little like asking a framing contractor to build his wooden walls with 50% more studs just to make sure everything is strong. You can do it, but it takes more work and the benefits are not really clear.

When they do attach the end of an interior wall to an ICF wall, how is it done?
Contractors use different methods. One of the most common is simply to put a screw through the end stud of the interior wall into the ties of the ICF forms. The second most common method is to attach steel straps to the ties, and screw the end stud to the straps (Fig. 9-18).

ATTACHING FINISHES

Tell me about attaching the interior finish to the ICFs.
This is easy, because 95% of the time the interior finish is gypsum wallboard. The wallboard crew simply runs screws through the wallboard and into the ties. This is very much like how it's done in frame construction, where the crew screws into the studs.

Is the attachment of exterior finishes also simple?
Well, it's more involved because there are more possible finishes.

What are the exterior finishes that can go on ICFs?
Different finishes go on the foundation walls and the walls of the main house above. By the foundation, I mean a basement or stem walls. The parts of the foundation walls that are exposed above the ground need to be covered by something with high impact strength—something that can take a hit from a lawn mower or trimmer without getting damaged. Most contractors use wire mesh covered by a layer of stucco. However, there are some innovative new coatings that look like stucco and are put on with a trowel like stucco, but don't require the mesh.

9-19. Attaching siding to ties. (Reward Wall Systems, Inc.)

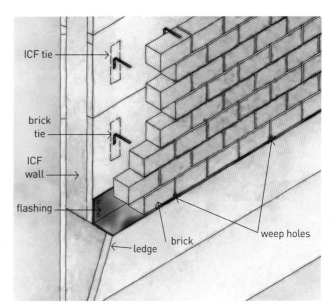

9-20. Brick veneer over ICF walls.

This is one of those details that you might want to ask your contractor about upfront. What does he intend to cover the exterior of the foundation walls with above grade? How can he be confident that it will be strong enough to protect the foam? Then, when the work is being done, you can check to see that it is done the way he told you it would be. Of course, this is not an issue with a house resting on a slab because it has no foundation walls.

By the walls of the main house above, I mean the first-story walls, the second-story walls, and so on. For these walls you can put virtually anything onto the ICFs that you put onto conventional houses. The most widely used exterior finishes in all of home construction are:

Most Widely Used Exterior Finishes

- Vinyl siding
- Brick
- Stucco
- Textured acrylic finish (TAF)
- Beveled wood siding
- Fiber-cement siding
- Hardboard
- Wood shakes and shingles

So how does vinyl siding go onto ICFs?
The same way it goes on a wood-frame wall. The crew nails or screws the sections of siding to the wall. The only difference is that the fasteners go into the ICF ties or metal attachment strips instead of into the wood studs or plywood sheathing (Fig. 9-19). If the attachment strips are metal, the siding must be installed with screws rather than the nails that are typically used.

What about brick? How is it attached to an ICF wall?
This is also similar to conventional construction. The masons lay bricks outside the ICF wall. At the bottom, the brick rests on a horizontal ridge along the base of the wall called a **brick ledge**. This ridge is where the basement wall flares out to create a sort of shelf or ledge just for this purpose (Fig. 9-20).

The masons position the brick wall a bit out from the ICFs to leave a gap between them. Attached to the ICF wall are **brick ties**, which are metal strips that stick out from the wall. As they work their way up, the masons embed the free ends of the brick ties in the mortar between the bricks. This connection helps hold the brick wall plumb and steady.

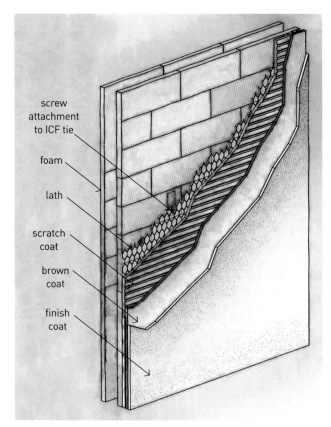

9-21. Layers of stucco over an ICF wall.

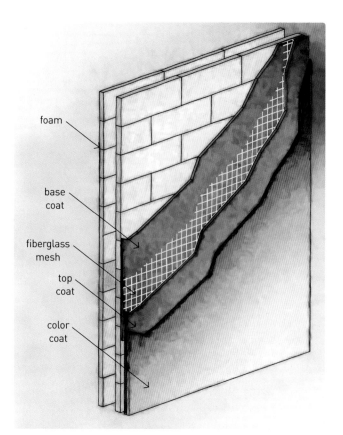

9-22. Layers of a textured acrylic finish (TAF) over an ICF wall.

At the bottom of the brick wall are small holes called **weep holes**. These are extremely important in any house. If any water gets past the brick and into the gap between the brick and the main wall, it drains out from these holes before it has much chance of getting into the house. This is all about the same as it is when the structural wall is wood frame.

How is stucco attached to the wall?

On an ICF wall, crew members screw **wire lath** to the ties. Lath is often called *chicken wire* because that's what it looks like. It is a sort of screen made of steel wire or sheet steel full of holes. It gets attached in a layer all over the walls. Then the workers put a layer of stucco on and smooth it with trowels, usually in two or three coats (Fig. 9-21).

This is about the same procedure as it is with wood frame. But one difference on a frame house is that

before the lath goes on crew members cover the house with a layer of special water-resistant paper. This keeps the wet stucco from making contact with the wood wall. That's not needed on an ICF wall because there is no wood to get wet.

If you want to inspect stucco work, one thing to check for is that the crew attaching the lath is hitting the ICF ties. If they have not worked with ICFs before, they might sometimes miss the ties and run their screws into the foam instead. Obviously, that will not attach it securely.

What is a textured acrylic finish?

A lot of people confuse this with ordinary stucco, but it is different, its installation is different, and the differences are important. So let's get it straight.

Traditional stucco is a mixture of portland cement, fine sand, and often some other minerals. Technically, it is a form of concrete, just one without any large stones. Mixed with water, it becomes a paste that workers can trowel over a wall. Like any concrete, it hardens, and it creates a tough shell over the wall. The metal lath acts as a reinforcement to help it resist cracking or breaking.

A **textured acrylic finish (TAF)** is also applied over foam in layers. Workers trowel on a layer of a stuccolike material, push a sheet of fiberglass mesh into the wet material, and trowel on one or two more layers of material. The mesh acts as reinforcement to help create a hard shell over the foam (Fig. 9-22).

The troweled-on material of a TAF differs from traditional stucco because it has a lot of acrylic plastic material in it. The top layer of material usually also has coloring in it, and it is possible to give it some very bright colors.

TAF is an outgrowth of a finish that has been around for decades, called an **exterior insulation and finish system (EIFS)**. But with a traditional EIFS, the workers start by installing a layer of foam over the wall. Then the other layers go on. This made sense when applying the EIFS over a wood-frame wall. The layer of foam was needed to give the wall a surface that the material could adhere to correctly.

But when the system goes over an ICF wall, it is not necessary to add a layer of foam because the wall already has one. So the crews can skip right to adding the finish layers, and the system is technically no longer an EIFS but a textured acrylic finish. Because this type of finish goes onto ICFs without a layer of foam first, it is less expensive than it would be to attach it to a standard frame wall. Usually you end up paying about a dollar a square foot less, compared with putting it on frame.

How do I make sure my textured acrylic finish is installed correctly?

This is mostly a matter of dealing with good contractors. There have been some concerns about EIFS in the past because some wood-frame homes had problems. Apparently, water got into the wall somehow, and the EIFS helped hold it in. Some of the wood

studs and sheathing rotted, requiring repairs that were sometimes expensive.

But this is hardly a concern for ICF buildings. Once the walls are filled with concrete, there is little place for water to accumulate or penetrate. Even if water does get in, it cannot rot the concrete. But this does point out the need for quality installation.

How does beveled wood siding, or clapboard, get attached?

Pretty much the same way it does on wood frame. Beveled siding, or clapboard, consists of long, slender boards of wood with a beveled edge. High-quality clapboard is usually made of red cedar. The installers set them against the wall horizontally, lapping each one over the one below it, and nail them to the wall. The only difference is that on an ICF wall they are nailed to the plastic ties, rather than to wooden studs or sheathing.

As an option, it is also possible to install furring strips on the wall before you put up the siding.

What are furring strips and why should I want to put them on before the siding?

Furring strips are wooden strips about ¾ inch thick that are installed on the surface of the wall. Usually you put one vertical strip about every 16 inches, plus around openings. After they're up, you attach the siding to the strips instead of directly to the ICF. The advantage to installing furring strips is that they create a small cavity behind the siding. If any water penetrates the siding, it drains out through the cavity. Also, air can circulate. This stops water that might otherwise get into the house, and keeps the siding dry so it lasts longer.

Attaching furring strips adds some cost to the project. The amount varies a lot, but you might expect to pay somewhere around a dollar extra per square foot of wall area. You also need to have a siding contractor who knows what he's doing. There are some important details with the strips that need to be done right at places like around openings and at the top and bottom of the wall, to keep insects out of the cavity and to make sure the drainage and air flow work properly.

What is fiber-cement siding?

This is a new material that is growing rapidly in popularity. It looks like clapboard, but it is actually made of a mixture of wood fibers and cement that is pressed into the shape of boards. Often it is imprinted with a grain pattern to resemble real wood even more closely. It can be more durable than wood and is often a little less expensive, so its use is spreading (Fig. 9-23).

How is fiber-cement siding attached to an ICF wall?

Almost exactly the same way clapboard is. Although it is typically nailed in place on wood-frame homes, fiber-cement siding can also be screwed directly into the vinyl ties or light-gauge steel strips.

What about hardboard? What is it and how is it attached?

Hardboard is a wood product made by pressing wood fibers together with adhesives. It is usually shaped to look like clapboard or some similar type of wood siding. But it generally comes in larger panels, so it is faster to put up. Workers fasten it to the ICF ties just as they do conventional wood or vinyl siding.

What about shingles? How are they attached to an ICF wall?

To attach shingles, the crew has to attach furring strips, or **straps**, to the ties. The straps go horizontally around the building. They have to be placed at the heights where the shingles will be attached. This means there will be a line of them about every 8 inches up the wall (Fig. 9-24). Then the workers nail the shingles to the straps. The straps are necessary because a lot of the shingles will land between ties, so you need something all the way around to nail to.

This is a bit more involved on ICFs than it is on wood frame. On wood, the shingles are nailed directly to the wood sheathing. Because of this, you will probably pay about a dollar more per square foot to put shingles onto an ICF wall, compared with frame.

9-23. Installing fiber-cement siding. (CertanTeed Corporation)

What about electrical cables? How are they attached to an ICF wall?

It's actually quite simple. Electricians who have never done it before may complain, but once someone shows them how to do it, they see that it's no harder than it is in a wood-frame house.

There are various tools they can use to cut grooves, called chases, in the surface of the foam. They cut a chase for each cable and push it in. Wherever a switch or outlet goes, it is necessary to install a rectangular **electrical box**. The workers cut a rectangle out of the foam and push the box in. There are several ways to attach the box to the ICF wall to secure it in place. This all gets covered over later with wallboard, just as in conventional houses (Fig. 9-25).

9-24. Attachment of shingles to an ICF wall with furring strips.

What about plumbing? How is it installed in an ICF wall?

There is very little plumbing that runs through the exterior walls these days. However, if desired, pipes can be put in the ICF walls the same way electrical cable is: The plumber cuts a chase in the foam and pushes the pipe in. If he needs to secure it to the wall, there are special clamps that can be set over the pipe and screwed into the concrete of the wall.

What else do I need to know about construction?

Those are the critical points. The rest you can learn as you go. Remember to speak regularly with your general contractor. Don't be shy about asking questions, and don't hesitate to keep close track of the ICF work. You don't have to be a pest to take an interest and to point out whenever something doesn't look quite right.

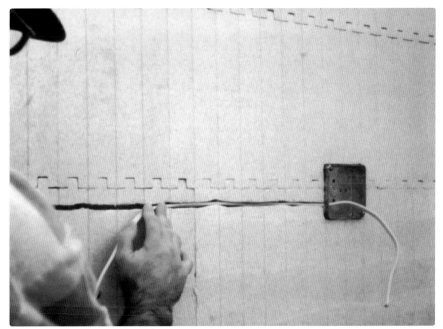

9-25. Inserting electrical cable into a chase in an ICF wall. (Portland Cement Association)

10

So You Want to Do It Yourself

BY NOW IT SHOULD be no secret that I do not think it is a good idea for most people to act as their own general contractors. In my experience, even though they do not have to pay a general contractor, the house usually ends up

An owner-builder getting started.

costing as much or more, the quality of the work can be lower, the project almost always takes longer, and the owner has to devote many hours each week for many months to supervising things. But I know that, despite my pleas, some people will choose to go this route anyway. And for those of you who do, it is better to do it with some advice than without.

BASIC CONCEPTS

How is running an ICF construction project different than running the construction of a regular wood-frame house?

Your key tasks will all be the same. The main difference is that you may need to spend more time lining up your ICF subcontractor than you would need to spend getting a conventional wood-framing subcontractor. The same goes for some of the subcontractors who install things that are attached or related to the ICF walls—the electrician, the interior and exterior finish crews, and the HVAC subcontractor (Fig. 10-1). You will also need more knowledge about their work and will need to spend more time supervising them.

10-1. Be prepared to supervise many different subcontractors.

Why will I need to spend more time to line up the crews?

There are still fewer contractors who have experience with ICFs, so you may have to do some more looking.

How can I find the crews?

To find an ICF subcontractor, refer back to Chapter 6 and use the same methods recommended for finding a general contractor who has ICF experience. They're listed in the same places. While you are digging up names of ICF subcontractors, you can also ask about people in the other trades who have experience with ICFs. Once you find the ICF subcontractor you want to use, you can also ask who the subcontractor recommends for the other tasks. The ICF subcontractor may have experience working with various electricians, finish crews, and heating and cooling subcontractors on past projects.

In every case you should be checking references, just as you would for a general contractor. This is one of the tasks that will be a bit harder for you than it would be for most professional general contractors. Most GCs have a network of people they can call to find out who is available to do specific kinds of work and to check how good these people are. You probably do not have a network of people to call.

Why do I need to know more about what the subcontractors do?

Because you will be the one supervising them. You need to understand enough to recognize when they are doing a good job. When they are not doing things well, you need to tell them what to do differently.

How do I learn to recognize and correct poor work?

You can start with the information in Chapter 9. Another good source of information will be the distributor from the company that is supplying the ICF forms to the job. Most distributors have trained and supervised a lot of different subcontractors working with ICFs. Distributors are also willing to help, since they want projects with their product to go well.

If you leave the purchase of the ICF forms to your ICF subcontractor, ask who the distributor is that sold them to him. Then you can contact the distributor for advice and information. You should mention to the subcontractor that you are doing this so it doesn't appear as if you don't trust your workers. Everyone should understand that you, as the GC, need to learn all you can about how this product connects to and relates to the other ones that will go into the building.

Your ICF subcontractor is also a possible source of information. It is very likely that the ICF sub has had to educate other subcontractors about ICFs on previous projects. The ICF subcontractor may even have had to train or supervise a few of them, and so he may have advice for you about how to do these things.

Personally, I would also recommend that you get formal ICF training and read the supplier's manual thoroughly before you start work on your house.

GETTING TRAINING

Where do I get formal ICF training and a manual?
From the company that is supplying your forms. The major companies offer training courses. Also, almost every ICF company has an installation manual that it provides free of charge.

How do I get into the ICF course?
Contact the ICF company's headquarters and ask for their course schedule. Pick a class session and sign up. Most courses carry a fee of $100 to $300 and run about two days. The one major obstacle is availability. Most companies offer classes in only a handful of cities around North America, and only once every several months in each city. You will have to pick your best option from the schedule. Be prepared to wait up to a

10-2. Townhouses built with ICFs. (Arxx Building Products)

few months for the next convenient class, and be prepared to travel.

What's involved in an ICF training course?
Most of them have a mix of lectures and hands-on work with some actual forms. You'll learn all the basics of recommended construction methods. You'll probably also get advice on how the other key subcontracted tasks—electrical, finishes, and HVAC—should be performed.

Can I just read the ICF manual, or should I read it in addition to taking the course?
In my opinion, you should do both. They will cover a lot of the same material, but you learn different things from each one. At a course you usually get a fuller understanding because you see the product in action and you can ask questions. It can also be difficult to keep your attention on a manual. But with a manual, you can spend as much time as you like on any topic, study it when you don't understand something right away, and reflect on things more than in a course. You will learn the most if you use both. If you cannot take the course, you can try to learn by studying the manual and talking with the distributor and the ICF subcontractor.

OTHER THINGS TO KNOW ABOUT

What do I need to know about supervising the construction of the other parts of the house?
That question goes way beyond the scope of this book. There are plenty of other books about serving as the general contractor on your own home. Many of them refer to it as "building" your own home, although in most cases you don't personally do a lot of the actual construction work. The books vary in quality, but the good ones cover all the important tasks you have to carry out. I suggest that you pick up a couple of these,

read them, and follow them as best you can. For the parts of the work where you are substituting ICFs for wood, use the information in this book and the supplier's materials instead. In fact, there is a lot more to learn about than just the physical parts of the house and how to construct them.

What do I need to know other than how to construct the house?
These books will cover many other topics. A typical list is given below.

Other Things You Need to Know About

- Legal contracts
- Getting financing
- Land acquisition
- Evaluating lots
- Design
- Cost estimation
- Soliciting bids
- Selecting subcontractors
- Building department submissions and permitting
- Arranging utility connections
- Buying materials
- Project scheduling
- Project management
- Disbursements
- Inspections
- All trades and phases of construction

Under the different phases of construction, you will likely find the things shown in the list on the next page.

Different Phases of Construction

- Excavation
- Foundation
- Framing
- Roofing
- Plumbing
- Heating, ventilating, and air-conditioning
- Electrical
- Windows and doors
- Insulation
- Exterior finishes
- Wallboard
- Interior trim
- Painting and wall coverings
- Cabinets, counters, and fixtures
- Flooring
- Exterior flatwork
- Landscaping

I understand that I need to learn a lot of specific things to be my own general contractor. Do you have any general advice?

You have touched on my first piece of advice yourself. You have a lot of details to learn, so do a lot of listening and ask a lot of questions. Studying ahead with books and courses is important, but keep on asking and listening when the project is under way.

When you look for your subcontractors, try to talk to at least two from each trade. You fare much better if you choose the best plumber or electrician from a group than if you just take the first one you hear about.

Try to meet all the people you will be working with early on, introduce yourself, and ask them for their advice. Talk to the local building department when you are just beginning to plan the house and meet the person who will inspect it. Try to talk to the inspector at length. Ask what you should be doing and whether there appear to be any obstacles to the project.

10-3. Walls going up in a snowy climate.

When you have your subcontractors lined up, invite them to the building site some day after work *before* construction starts. Promise them a cold beer and food to get them to come out. Bring the plans and have a preconstruction meeting. Let them look over the plans and discuss how the pieces will come together.

Draw up a realistic schedule and give everyone a copy. More than likely you'll fall behind, but either way keep the crews informed.

Since the schedule is unpredictable, make sure you are living in a place where you have the flexibility to stay for an indefinite period. Good options are to live with relatives that you can get along with, or in an apartment you rent month to month.

If a subcontracting crew stops showing up and doesn't return your calls, they may be busy with another job. Keep calling every couple of days and eventually they will probably return and finish. You have to remember that you are a low priority for them because you are not likely to give them another job. The general contractor down the street hires them to work on several houses each year, so when that GC says, "Jump," they jump. If things are looking desperate, contact your second-choice subcontractor for the job or track down another crew until you find one that will pick up the task and get the work moving again.

Resist the temptation to pay any subcontractor the final installment of his fee until his work is entirely done, and that means when the final nail goes in or the last drop of paint has been applied. It is not uncommon for subcontractors to finish their main tasks but leave a few minor details undone, intending to take care of them when they have a free moment from their other jobs later on. But in the press of work, they may let the return trip slide for weeks, even months. Reminding them that they get a couple thousand dollars when they finish helps motivate them to send someone down for a few hours to take care of the last few details.

Is that it?

Isn't that enough? All I have left to say is, Good luck!

11

Living in a Different Kind of House

IT SURPRISES MOST PEOPLE that a completed ICF house looks just like any other house on the block. It can be a ranch house with vinyl siding, a mansion faced with brick or stone, a colonial sided with clapboard, or a Mediterranean covered

An ICF house after completion.

11-1. A view of a window from inside an ICF house under construction. (ConForm Pacific, Inc.)

with stucco and a red tile roof. Any floor plan, style, and finishes common in frame construction are also possible with ICFs. But although you cannot easily tell the difference between an ICF house and a frame house simply by looking at it, the ICF house behaves much differently. In fact, this is why you built with ICFs in the first place. The ICF house has distinct advantages for living.

Is there really no way I can see the difference between an ICF house and a frame house?
One thing you might notice is that the walls are thicker. This is apparent at the windows and doors, where you actually get a view of the edge of a wall. It is covered with the finishes so you can't see what it's made of, but you can see that a window is mounted in a wall that is maybe 8 to 12 inches thick, rather than one that is 4 to 6 inches thick (Fig. 11-1). In fact, many people consider the deeper windowsills a distinct advantage. The sills inside act like shelves. They are deep enough for a vase of flowers, candles, or photos.

Isn't there anywhere I can see the guts of the wall?
Not easily. The top of the wall might be exposed in the attic, but probably only a small bit of it would be visible. If your basement is not finished, you may see a wall of foam. You should not be able to see the concrete, except maybe for a drip or splatter here or there.

DIFFERENCES

How does the ICF house behave differently?
Your fuel bills should be much lower than those of neighboring houses of the same size.

Comfort will be higher. The temperature will remain relatively even throughout the day and night, even as the outdoor temperature shoots up and down. The heating or air-conditioning unit will come on less often. You should feel fewer drafts. You shouldn't feel cold spots or hot spots near the walls.

Unless you open windows, it should be quieter inside. Traffic and lawn mower noise will be muffled. When storms pass through at night, they will be less likely to wake you or the kids. The house will have a more solid "feel." When you slam doors, there will be little vibration.

Hope that you are never in a tornado or hurricane, but if you are, the house is much less likely to get twisted or demolished. Also, projectiles and wind-blown debris are much less likely to break through the walls. The structure of the house will be very durable. You should not have to worry about it rotting, warping, or sagging over the years.

Can just the walls really do all this? Doesn't it depend on what the rest of the house is built of?
Yes, it does. If the windows and doors are flimsy, a lot of energy and sound will get through them and take away some of your benefits of low bills, comfort, and quiet. If your roof is poorly constructed, you'll have these same problems, plus a much greater chance of damage in a windstorm. If your floors are constructed

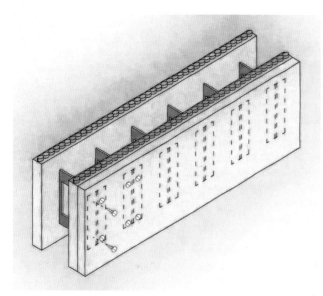

11-2. A screw going through wallboard and into the ICF ties.

with the bare minimum of material, you'll still get lots of vibration in them. But I'm expecting that you are a quality-conscious homebuyer, so you will see to it that decent materials are used in these other parts as well.

This is the point where I like to remind people of the advantages of adding a concrete roof and floors. This will be beyond many people's budget, but if you can afford it, you will find that you get even *more* of the benefits you get with ICFs. A concrete floor will help cut vibration in the house sharply and enhance the solid "feel." It will also cut sound transmission between the stories of the house. A concrete roof does the same things concrete walls do because it, too, separates the inside from the outdoors. Adding the proper concrete roof produces another sharp jump up in comfort, quiet, solidity, resistance to disasters, and durability. But if you go this route, remember that it is doubly important to include the proper ventilation or filtration in your heating and cooling system. The house will be very tight, so moving fresh air through at a measured pace becomes key.

MODIFICATIONS

How do I hang a picture in an ICF house?
In about the same way you do in an ordinary house. Most pictures go on hooks that are designed to be fastened to the wallboard in one way or another. ICF houses have wallboard just like any other house, so you can install the hooks the same way.

As a second option, remember that in most ICF forms there are **ties**—pieces of plastic that have a narrow strip (called a **tie end**) running vertically in the form. These tie ends are spaced every 6, 8, or 12 inches along the wall. They are very handy places to attach things to (Fig. 11-2). If you have a picture that is too heavy for wallboard-mounted fasteners, you can find a tie and put a screw into it the same way you would find a stud in a conventional house. Most ordinary stud finders you get from the hardware store will find an ICF tie the same way they find a wooden stud. It's best to use a screw to go into the tie. A nail will work, but a screw will resist pulling out much better.

What if the picture is very heavy?
Something that screws into the tie should still work. The ties from the different manufacturers vary, but it's a pretty safe bet that yours will be able to hold up to at least 25 pounds. If you have a picture that weighs more than that, it is probably very large, so you can put up two screws in two different ties that are side by side and still cover them with the picture.

What about other things that I want to attach, like towel bars and shelves?
The same methods apply. The product will probably come with fasteners made to go into wallboard or studs. Put them into the wallboard or ties of the ICF wall. Items supporting a lot of weight, such as bookshelves, should be secured to ties.

What about window treatments?

Around windows and doors you have these same two options, plus a third. Running all the way around a window or door is a rigid frame called a **buck** (Fig. 11-3). It is made of wood or high-strength plastic. You can't see it because the finishes are covering it. But if you sink a screw into the wall within about an inch and a half of the opening, you will hit it and it will hold the screw securely.

How do I attach something that is too heavy for the wallboard, but that has to go in a spot that is in between two ties?

This is like the problem of attaching something heavy on a frame wall that has to go between two studs. If you plan ahead, someone can install something

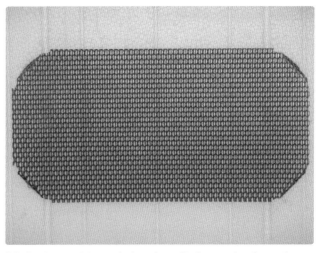

11-4. A special steel plate installed over the foam for attaching items after the wallboard goes on. (Wind-Lock Corporation)

11-3. Cutaway of a window buck behind wallboard.

between the ties that you can attach to. For example, some contractors install thin steel plates on the wall that are covered when the wallboard goes on. When you run a screw into that section of the wall, it catches the steel and is held securely (Fig. 11-4). There are some other similar "fastening" plates that can be preinstalled. The trick is to determine in advance the locations where the medium-weight attachments will have to go and notify your contractors that some sort of attachment surface needs to be installed there.

What if I want to install something really heavy after the house is done, like extra kitchen cabinets, or suspended bookshelves?

You may be able to hang them by putting enough screws into enough ties. If you followed this plan, you would attach the item with a lot of screws, and preferably each screw would go into a different tie. However, there is some risk involved in this, so consider everything carefully.

So what is the big risk of attaching heavy fixtures to the ties?

The ties from different brands of ICF have different strengths and different holding powers. So your connection could be plenty secure with some products, but more questionable with some others. Obviously, it would be disappointing to install something heavy like a set of kitchen cabinets and have them start shifting. If you really want to take this risk, I suggest you contact your ICF subcontractor or the manufacturer of the ICFs for their recommendations. Many products are being made stronger and stronger, so yours may now be deemed strong enough for hanging heavy things like cabinets.

What if I don't want to take the risk or I can't get enough screws in the ties for something very heavy?
Usually these kinds of heavy objects are planned in advance, and special heavy attachment points are built into the wall. You should be alerting your GC of the need to install very heavy fixtures on the wall from the beginning of construction, and the GC will work with the ICF subcontractor to install something strong that you can attach them to. A typical arrangement is to notch out the foam to make room for pieces of heavy lumber that will be connected to the concrete with **concrete fasteners**. These are essentially screws, bolts, or other fasteners that install in small holes the contractor makes in the concrete itself. This may involve such things as cutting away the foam and using a concrete drill. The wood gets covered over when the wallboard is installed. Later the fixtures are attached by running screws through the wallboard and into the wood.

There is always the rare occasion when we discover the need for suspended bookshelves or a wall-mounted sink after construction is done. In these situations, someone can use various types of concrete fasteners that go through the foam. Rather than try to do these things yourself, it's usually best to get a contractor. You can ask the general contractor who built your house what he recommends, because that's the person who will be most familiar with your situation. Or the ICF installer on your house might be able to handle it.

There is a good chance that either one of them has done this kind of thing before.

What if I have to make changes to my house later on? Isn't it hard to change the concrete walls?
It really isn't. Some kinds of changes might be more expensive than they would have been in a wood-frame house. But the most common ones are straightforward. It should be no harder to find a contractor than it was to find the ones who built your house originally, and the time involved won't be much different from doing the same remodeling job on a frame house.

What if I want to put on an addition?
For most additions, you put a new section on one side of your existing house. Usually the new section contains a room or two. It generally goes where there is a door to the outside, and that door becomes the doorway to the new part of the house.

When you want to do something like this, you find a qualified contractor, just as you found the contractors who built your house in the first place. Essentially, they will build a little "house" alongside your existing one, connecting the walls between new and old as they go.

If your addition will also be built out of ICFs, probably they will cut away the foam on the old wall where the new ones will attach. They will probably then drill holes into the exposed concrete, and adhere or attach the ends of pieces of steel rebar in the holes with a high-strength adhesive (Fig. 11-5). This will leave these pieces of rebar sticking out of the original walls. They will assemble the forms for the new walls so they butt up to the old walls. The free ends of the rebar will extend into the center of the new forms. When they fill the new forms with concrete, the rebar will connect the old walls to the new ones securely.

If your addition will be built out of frame, the contractors will probably cut away the foam, drill holes into the concrete, and adhere or attach heavy bolts in the concrete. Then they will connect the frame walls to the ICF walls with the bolts.

11-5. An ICF house with foam cut away and rebar installed for an addition.

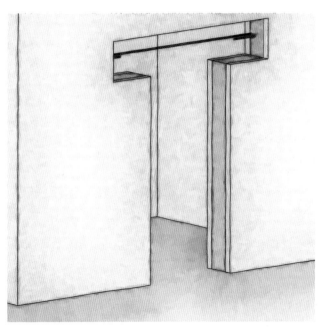

11-6. A new doorway cutout has a place for a beam over the doorway, reinforced with rebar.

What if there is no door, or we want to enlarge the door to create a more open passageway between the house and the addition?

Then your contractors will call out a special cutting crew. They have saws to cut an opening of any size in concrete. They will probably also have to cut out an extra horizontal section above the new opening. This will allow the ICF crew to build a new concrete "beam" that will span over the opening (Fig. 11-6). They will do this simply by putting some rebar in position, putting up some forms, and filling them with concrete. This is necessary because the old narrow opening may not have enough rebar to hold the wall up over a wider opening. If there was no opening there to start with, there will almost certainly not be enough rebar over the opening, and this step will be necessary.

The cutting and construction of a new "beam" (if any) may cost anywhere from a few hundred to a couple thousand dollars. This is not so different from the same job in a frame house. To create an opening in an exterior frame wall, contractors normally remove

the finishes from the part of the wall involved, cut out the framing in that location, and cut out a space at the top that is wider to install some form of wooden beam over the new opening.

What if I just want to add a window or door?

You go through the same procedure for cutting an opening as described above. And again, it's similar to the way this is done on a frame wall, except that the crew works with concrete and rebar instead of studs and plywood.

I thought it was harder to make changes in concrete.

It takes slightly more time and somewhat more money, but usually not as much as people imagine. Because concrete is such a durable material, they imagine that it's impossible to change. But there is so much concrete construction in the world—all the large and small commercial buildings, bridges, sidewalks, culverts, dams, and such—that people have devised plenty of tools for making all the changes that are commonly asked for.

What about finishing my basement or my attic?
You can still do this in an ICF house. In fact, finishing an ICF basement may be cheaper and easier than finishing a conventional basement. With a conventional concrete basement, the crew usually finishes it by building frame walls inside the concrete basement walls. Other workers fill the frame walls with insulation, install wiring, then cover it all with wallboard. With ICF walls, they get to skip the first two steps. They just install the wiring and put the wallboard up. The ICF walls are already insulated and they already have something (ties) to attach the wallboard to. Finishing an attic involves more or less the same process with ICFs as it does with wood frame.

What about wiring? What if I want to add power outlets or cable or telephone wires in my house later on?
You do it pretty much the same way you do it now. Most electricians avoid running any new wiring in exterior walls because these walls, including frame ones, are filled with insulation. So they first try to find a route that takes them only through interior walls and floors. In this case it doesn't matter what the exterior walls are made of.

But what if they really have to go through the exterior walls? What if I really want a new outlet on the exterior wall, for instance?
Then they find a way to get through the insulation, just as they do with a frame wall. Here's one trick I've heard of some electricians using. They slide a steel tape behind the wallboard where they want to run the new cable. They attach a short piece of steel pipe to the end of the tape and heat the pipe up. They then pull the pipe through with the tape. The pipe melts the foam along the way, creating a neat chase to hold the cable. They fish the tape through again and use it to pull the cable through. Other electricians might remove a baseboard and cut a chase in the foam. There are dozens of tricks. Most of these are just variations on things that are already done in frame walls.

You make it sound as if it's no harder to make any kinds of changes or additions to an ICF house than to a frame one.
For the most part, it isn't. A few things are harder, but they're not a lot harder. As far as I'm concerned, the story that you can't make changes to an ICF house is either the misstatement of someone who doesn't know much about ICFs, or a scare tactic from people who sell frame houses and don't want to lose your business. The fact is that ICF houses have been standing since the 1970s, and as best I can tell, no one has been blocked from making the kinds of changes on them that we commonly make in frame houses.

You make it sound as if living in an ICF house isn't that much different from living in a frame house.
Oh, but it is. It's noticeably better in a number of ways. It just isn't harder, which is what most people worry about. In fact, the surprises are mostly pleasant surprises. Things are more solid, more comfortable, quieter, you save money on your fuel bills every month, and you have greater peace of mind. So build the house, relax, and enjoy!

A Final Word

WATCHING YOUR OWN NEW HOUSE go up is exciting. As the house takes shape, it suddenly hits you that you will soon live in something entirely new, something designed to fit your tastes and needs.

It adds to the excitement to know that you helped in the building process. In decades past, builders and homeowners took pride in the quality of their construction. You can still see it today if you go house hunting. You walk through houses that are fifty, sixty, seventy, and eighty years old and find many that are as solid as a rock. The plates in the china cabinet don't rattle when you walk across the floor, you barely feel a ripple when you slam the front door, and exposed in the basement you see wooden beams the size of a steel girder. But many of these old gems are giving way to the ravages of time. Settling and humidity are warping the lumber, leaving walls that lean, and leaving floors with a slope that will roll a marble briskly across the room. A thorough renovation might bring these homes back to glory, but straightening everything out could cost more than a completely new house.

The older builders I chat with tend to agree that somewhere around the 1960s the quality of wood-frame home construction began to decline. The wood itself became poorer, and contractors were putting less and less effort into each house. The framing crews I worked on in my youth routinely received shipments of wood studs with 30% of the pieces warped or bowed. In earlier times we would have thrown the bad studs out, but it would be too expensive to throw away that many. Instead, the crews put them in the walls, using them as best as they could. In the meantime, some builders have "optimized" wood framing. This is another way to say that they have taken out nearly every single piece of wood from the structure that is not absolutely required or necessary. Of course, that saves cost, but it also results in buildings that shake, bounce, and rattle more than they used to.

The mentality of minimizing cost now appears to be deeply ingrained (pardon the pun) in wood-frame construction. Builders stayed competitive by taking a little bit more out of the structure each year so they could keep their prices lower than the other guy down the street. Now this is routine in the industry. I have worked with contractors who tried to offer a stouter wall and stiffer floors, and went to great lengths to explain to customers why it was better. In the end they couldn't attract enough buyers who were willing to pay more for a little better house structure, so they gave up.

But now you have the opportunity to pay a little more for a *much* better house structure. Not only will it not flex, it will be as hard as a rock. Not only will it start out straight and square and plumb, it will stay that way. It will not warp, twist, or sag. It will resist high winds and other disasters. It will be significantly quieter, more comfortable, and more energy efficient, yet it will have all the beauty and appeal of any other new home. You can choose virtually any of the styles, colors, and finishes available on the other houses around the block or across the country.

In addition to costing a little more money, getting an ICF house is a little more work. But if you do it right, it's only a *little* more. The key is to find qualified people to build it, and learn enough about the process yourself to direct them along the way. When you boil it down, that's really all this book covers. I've included considerable advice about how to find and select qualified contractors and designers. Then there is a lot of description of ICF homes and construction that enables you to communicate with these people, understand the things they tell you, evaluate their work, and give them good instructions. So in a sense, there are only two really important topics in the whole book.

Having said that, do not minimize the importance of either of these topics. There is no way to compensate for having substandard workers building your house. So take the time to find the best general contractor or architect you can get. This should take you several weeks of steady effort. *Do not force a decision faster.* Take the time to get a few names—not just one or two. Talk to all of them, get their references, and call as many former customers as you can. Consider everything you learn carefully to pick the best person and the best business you can. Good work done by conscientious people will save you hundreds or thousands of dollars and possibly months of time down the road. It will also give you a quality, long-lasting product, which is the point of going with ICFs in the first place. Making sure you get this kind of work is easily worth a few weeks' effort upfront.

Learning as much as you can about ICF construction will only help you guide and evaluate your construction team along the way. If you are a bit of a technology nut, that's great. Odds are you will enjoy the learning experience and be more thorough. If you are not technical-minded, try to take an interest as best you can.

Do *not* expect that you will know more about ICFs than your contractor and will be correcting him or hunting for mistakes. If you have an adversarial relationship, either you have selected the wrong contractor or you have gotten off on the wrong foot.

Very possibly you will find things that should be corrected here and there, and it is proper and important that you point these things out to make sure they are dealt with. But the purpose of learning about ICFs is to serve as an intelligent guide and a quality control inspector for a well-intentioned group of professionals. You can be detail-oriented. As long as you are not picky, unreasonable, or hostile, a good general contractor should view you as a help, not a hindrance.

If you're like most ICF homeowners, once you're in your house you will truly appreciate all the benefits. Some—like quiet and comfort—most people cannot fully imagine. They have to live with them to understand just how great they are. All the benefits are impressive and gratifying.

Don't be surprised if you find yourself comparing your fuel bill with your neighbor's, taking guests to the basement during parties to show off the wall system, and bragging to the patient next to you at the doctor's office. It's fun to revel in the quality of a well-constructed ICF house. This is part of the reason you had one built in the first place.

I hope this book has given you the information on ICFs that you were looking for. I believe it will prepare you to get your house built well with a minimum of aggravation. I am confident that you will be extremely pleased with the house once you are in it. Enjoy.

Metric Equivalents Table

[to the nearest mm, 0.1cm, or 0.01m]

inches	mm	cm	inches	mm	cm
1/4	6	0.6	20	508	50.8
3/8	10	1.0	21	533	53.3
1/2	13	1.3	22	559	55.9
5/8	16	1.6	23	584	58.4
3/4	19	1.9	24	610	61.0
7/8	22	2.2	25	635	63.5
1	25	2.5	26	660	66.0
1 1/4	32	3.2	27	686	68.6
1 1/2	38	3.8	28	711	71.1
1 3/4	44	4.4	29	737	73.7
2	51	5.1	30	762	76.2
2 1/2	64	6.4	31	787	78.7
3	76	7.6	32	813	81.3
3 1/2	89	8.9	33	838	83.8
4	102	10.2	34	864	86.4
4 1/2	114	11.4	35	889	88.9
5	127	12.7	36	914	91.4
6	152	15.2	37	940	94.0
7	178	17.8	38	965	96.5
8	203	20.3	39	991	99.1
9	229	22.9	40	1016	101.6
10	254	25.4	41	1041	104.1
11	279	27.9	42	1067	106.7
12	305	30.5	43	1092	109.2
13	330	33.0	44	1118	111.8
14	356	35.6	45	1143	114.3
15	381	38.1	46	1168	116.8
16	406	40.6	47	1194	119.4
17	432	43.2	48	1219	121.9
18	457	45.7	49	1245	124.5
19	483	48.3	50	1270	127.0

Index

National Association of Home Builders (NAHB), 12
noise (sound) reduction, 2, 29, 42, 45–46, 49, 55, 159, 159–160

oriented strand board (OSB), 54

patches, 142–143
pier-and-beam system, 141
piers, 24
plank system, 9
plans and planning, 99–113
  beefing up roof, 106–109
  case study of two GCs, 127–132
  chart for, 112–113
  contract details and allowances, 104–105
  crew availability and, 102
  energy-efficiency features, 109
  ICF design flexibility, 31–34
  level of detail, 100, 104
  making and adjusting plans, 100–104
  sources and types of plans, 100, 103
  strength/wind resistance issues, 106–109
  types of, 100
  ventilation system, 110
plumbing system, 3, 84, 151
portland cement. See concrete
Portland Cement Association (PCA), 12, 97
professional workers. See architects; contractors; general contractor (GC)

radiation, 61
rebar (reinforcing bars), in walls, 7, 138, 139, 142, 163
Residential Energy Savings Network (RESNET), 58, 118–119, 123, 124, 125
resources
  energy efficiency/credits, 58, 116–117, 118–119, 124, 125
  finding contractors, 92, 97
  ICF Web sites, vi, 12, 92, 97
  mortgage assistance, 123
roof members, 107–108
roofs, 17–18, 48–53
  advantages of, 49
  beefed up, 51, 52, 106–109, 144–145
  concrete other than ICF, 52
  contractors, 50
  covering, 50–51
  disadvantages of ICF, 50
  durability, 49
  energy efficiency and R-value, 72
  frame, on ICF walls, 17, 106–109
  inspecting, 145
  lower design flexibility of ICF, 49–50

safe (disaster-resistant) ceilings, 51, 52, 106–109
  SIP, 54–55, 72, 106–107, 109
  slope limitations, 48–50
  trusses, 107–108
  wood-frame compared to ICF, 49–50
R2000 program (Canada), 125
R-value, 15, 62–64, 66–68, 72

safe (disaster-resistant) ceilings, 51, 52, 106–109
safe rooms, 42–43
SEER (seasonal energy efficiency ratio), 70
semi-custom home construction, 84
shapes of ICFs, 9–10
sheathing, defined, 3
siding, installing, 11, 149–150. See also finishes
SIPs. See structural insulated panels (SIPs)
solar energy, 61
sound. See noise (sound) reduction
spec (speculative) homes, 84–85
steel framing, 53–54
stem walls, 6, 39, 40, 109, 137, 141
storm surges, 22, 23, 24
strapping, for roofing, 50–51
strength and durability, 29, 159–160, 166
structural engineers, 96
structural insulated panels (SIPs), 54–55, 72, 107, 109
structural strength, 24, 25, 85, 109
stucco, 32, 36, 146, 147, 148
stucco, synthetic. See textured acrylic finish (TAF)
subcontractors. See contractors

tax credits, 124–125
temperature inside house, 26–27
tensile strength, 22
termites, 29–30, 31
textured acrylic finish (TAF), 32, 148–149
tie ends (ties), 8, 9, 10, 32, 160–162. See also finishes, attaching
tornadoes, ICFs and, 15–18, 42–43. See also flood resistance; wind resistance
training, ICF, 154–155
two-story houses, 32–34, 38
types/shapes, of ICFs, 8–11

unreinforced concrete, 22

ventilation system, 52–53. See also HVAC
  air changes per hour (ACH), 76
  energy efficiency and, 77
  mechanical systems, 76–77
  planning, 110

voids in walls, 136–137, 139–140, 143, 144
wallboard, 3, 7–8, 19–21, 63, 64, 44, 110, 146, 160–162
walls. See also wallboard
  above grade, 2–3
  attaching things to, 7–8, 144–146
  bulges in, 136, 142, 143
  checking for plumb, 139
  conventional above-grade, 2–3
  crooked, 36
  dowels for, 137–138
  exterior, 40–42
  fixing problems, 142–144
  footings for, 38–39
  in garage, 43
  hanging things on, 160–162
  inspecting. See inspections
  interior, attaching to ICF walls, 145–146
  interior, of ICF, 42–43
  leaning, 143
  mixed ICF and wood, 42
  patches in, 142–143
  second-story, misaligned, 32–34
  shapes of, 32, 33
  steel framing, 53–54
  stem, 6, 39, 40, 109, 137, 141
  straight, vertical vs. leaning, bulging, 135–136, 139, 143–144
  support for, 43
  supporting ICF floors, 44–45
  voids in, 136–137, 139–140, 143, 144
Web sites, vi, 12, 92, 97
weep holes, 147, 148
wind-blown debris, 18, 19
windows
  adding or moving, 11, 163
  case study comparing two projects, 129–130
  differences in ICF houses, 7, 31, 159
  energy efficiency, 14–15, 29, 60, 62, 71–72, 73, 159
  inspecting, 138
  low-E coatings, 71
  odd-shaped openings, 32, 42
  storm-resistant, 109
window treatments, 161
wind resistance
  design considerations, 106–109
  hurricanes, tornadoes and, 15–18, 42–43
  inspections for, 145–146
  other factors affecting, 159–160
  roof integrity and, 17–18, 51, 52, 106–109